ALSO BY HERBERT RAPPAPORT
Personality (with J. Lamberth and M. M. Rappaport)

MARKING TIME

Herbert Rappaport, Ph.D.

SIMON AND SCHUSTER

NEW YORK ■ LONDON ■ TORONTO ■ SYDNEY ■ TOKYO ■ SINGAPORE

Simon and Schuster
Simon & Schuster Building
Rockefeller Center
1230 Avenue of the Americas
New York, New York 10020

Designed by Nina D'Amario/Levavi & Levavi
Manufactured in the United States of America

1 3 5 7 9 10 8 6 4 2

Library of Congress Cataloging in Publication Data

Rappaport, Herbert.
Marking time / Herbert Rappaport. p. cm.
Includes bibliographical references.
1. Time—Psychological aspects. 2. Conduct of life.
3. Psychotherapy—Case studies. I. Title.
BF468.R36 1990
155.9—dc20   90-33679
                                    CIP

ISBN: 978-1-4391-9379-2

To Amanda and Alexander, who without their knowledge taught me all about time.

ACKNOWLEDGMENTS

By the time this book was finished, a great debt was owed to many people who helped me shape it in diverse ways.

Some of these debts are owed to individuals who had a special impact on my perspectives early in my career. The late Professor Walter Cohen introduced me to the pivotal work of Eugene Minkowski at a time when I was searching for an alternate way to approach psychological inquiry. Adelaide Dollin's early clinical supervision helped formulate my perception of the therapeutic relationship as an adventure in the most human terms; this structure continues to provide a highly energizing framework. James Marcia gave me the sense that meaningful and complex problems could be translated into productive research paradigms.

I am grateful for having had the opportunity to collaborate with three very important people in the psychotherapy field. Jerome Frank helped me integrate my work with traditional healers in East Africa into a "metatheoretical" outlook. Rollo May, in a few brief conversations, helped me find a unifying thread which allowed me to come to terms with difficult questions. The late Frederick Melges was instrumental in the development of the psychotherapy model presented in this book. Our fruitful dialogues about his work on future-oriented psychotherapy helped provide the validation of ideas in an area without broad representation.

I would like to thank the many students whose research and clinical work I have supervised. They were invaluable in helping formulate my ideas over many years. In particular I would like to acknowledge Michelle Berdy, Katherine Enrich, Arnold Wilson, Martha Fried-Cassorla, Donna Gilden, Michael Penn, Robert Fossler, and Mary Ann Koenig for their direct involvement in my temporality research.

A great deal of credit goes to John Brockman for encouraging me to undertake the task of writing this book. A special debt is owed to Robert Asahina, senior editor at Simon & Schuster, for his invaluable help with the development and organization of my ideas. I am also grateful to Belinda Loh, whose patience, skill and attention to detail were of immeasurable support, and to Laura Bross for being "on the spot" to provide help whenever it was needed. I want to thank Elizabeth Emery for her effort in the preparation of this book, especially her "evenness" in the face of frequent deadline pressure. I am also very appreciative to Guenter Wesch for offering me, as a summer workplace, a beautiful room that overlooks Nantucket Sound.

On a different note, I would like to thank my tennis partners, Tom Culp, Bert Keller, Ken Wallace, Thomas Butler, Pat McGarvey, and Jim Ledyard for their weekly interest and friendly teasing. It was not irrelevant that they let me win a few games at just the right time in an arduous work schedule.

I would like to extend my appreciation to the many clients who entrusted me with the intimacies of their lives. It was these interactions which originally opened my eyes to the critical role of "lived time." These people, from many parts of the country, were clearly partners in the development of my theories.

Finally, I would like to extend my deepest appreciation to my wife, Margaret, for her intellectual and emotional support. The foundations of my ideas are deeply embedded in our wide-ranging dialogues on theory, practice and the nature of life. I would especially like to thank her for shouldering a greater share of family responsibility while I wrote *Marking Time*.

CONTENTS

Time present and time past
Are both perhaps present in time future,
And time future contained in time past.
If all time is eternally present
All time is unredeemable.

—T. S. Eliot

INTRODUCTION: ROUND ABOUT MIDNIGHT

Almost everyone has gone to a New Year's Eve party at least once. We are all familiar with the rite of hailing the New Year: the popping of champagne corks, the crowds and cheers in television specials, the making of resolutions for the coming months.

Yet beneath the extravagance and gaiety there is a weighty quality to the evening as well. Adults wonder who should be part of the evening, or whether they should even celebrate. Single people are particularly concerned that they have a date and, more important, that their date be significant. Somehow, New Year's Eve is not just like any other holiday—the passing of the old year and the birth of the new one carry enormous meaning and bring forth a whole array of emotions. Some people are happy, while others sink into intoxicated melancholy. Some revel at having accomplished what they set out to do for the year, while others are depressed about failing yet again to live up to expectations and resolutions. As the calendar changes, everyone experiences the anxiety inherent in examining one's life and asking difficult questions. What have I done with my life? Why isn't my life happy? Where is my life going? Each of these questions addresses a different element of time—the past, the present, and the future. It's no wonder that we associate New Year's Eve with an elaborate consumption of alcohol. Coping with the reality of time passing is an arduous affair. Looking at New Year's Eve we can see how people feel about the momentum of their lives, and how modern society struggles with the concept of time passing.

One reaction to the New Year is that of the sentimentalist. Often, but not exclusively, female, this person approaches the occasion with trepidation, and everyone expects an emotional upheaval near the stroke of midnight. She does not anticipate the future but only laments what has passed, and her mourning is similar to an "anniversary reaction" to a tragic event. New Year's Eve becomes an anniversary for belittling present and future life by longing for lost people and past experiences. In her nostalgia, she dismisses the future. This response to time is closely related to what psychologists and psychiatrists call depression.

For others, New Year's Eve signals that the "clock is ticking." These people feel annoyed, tyrannized, and frightened that life is "happening" so rapidly, and they react angrily to the turbulence of another year. They can't seem to adjust to the passing of the seasons. They live wishing that time had a static quality, as though life ought to be unchanging. They refuse to accept a fundamental aspect of the human situation: that life involves transience and change. At New Year's Eve parties, they cynically refuse to participate in the festivities. Often, they will simply not attend, because the occasion is "not worthy" of their attention. Despite their struggle to deny the inevitable, these individuals usually remain anxious about time.

Some people simply lose themselves in the festive party spirit of "here and now," seeking to be oblivious to the changing of the year. Yet these people may feel as uncomfortable as the sentimentalist or the denying individual. They are unwilling to face the future or acknowledge that the year is indeed gone. This struggle to stay immersed in the present is common among many young adults today. This particular method for coping with time leads to motivational difficulty and an inability to set meaningful goals.

The most common reaction to the New Year is making resolutions. Acutely aware that time is passing, many of us take inventory of our lives. With an eye on the future, we proclaim a set of goals. In my clinical practice, I often use this opportunity to see how my clients perceive themselves. Most adults focus on what does *not* please them about past behavior. Over and over, they talk about the yearning to be thinner, in better physical health, and rid of certain bad habits. They swear to stop overeating, to quit smoking, to cut down on drinking. And yet they are instinctively skeptical of their own ability to change. New Year's resolutions, more than almost any other decisions, suggest that we are not always honest with ourselves and that we frequently engage in self-deception to avoid certain feelings.

New Year's resolutions are also rarely long-term, and seldom deal with substantive issues. Though resolutions sometimes touch on such weighty subjects as improving marriages, changing jobs, or becoming more involved in the community, more often they merely address immediate concerns with appearance and appetite.

American society in general does not foster long-term goals. Our resolutions target immediate and superficial concerns. Our younger generations are growing up with a strong emphasis on instant gratification. When pressed about the future, people of all ages proclaim that they prefer to live one day at a time. We are a society preoccupied with timesavers and shortcuts. We have frozen foods, instant coffee, and microwave cuisine. We communicate by telephone and fax, and "access" information onto computer screens. Yet in spite of our laudable successes at saving time, we are also a culture that constantly complains about not having enough of it. The days run together, and then suddenly another year is gone. We feel disorganized, have trouble setting priorities, and often wonder "if it's all worth it." My European and Latin American friends frequently comment that Americans race from sunup to sundown with little capacity to appreciate the day. So we travel to faraway places and become enchanted with the slower and "more civilized" pace of life, only to return to ten-minute lunches and drive-in windows.

We have a lot of theories about social behavior, and they encompass everything from dependency and introversion to aggression and the need for control. Yet we find no mention of time or temporal organization in most of these theories. Most current psychotherapies cannot tackle "lived time," the psychological awareness of time that we all experience. Time perception has traditionally been relegated to the periphery of psychological disorders.

Time, in fact, is *central* to all modes of behavior. From early childhood through all stages of adulthood, we must respond to the passage of time. Feeling positive about time passing generally indicates psychological well-being—having an attitude described as fulfilled, meaningful, authentic, centered. When one's life has consistency and coherence, when one can draw upon the past and manage the present, it's easier to cope with the future's uncertainties. How one lives life is intrinsically and inseparably linked to how one marks time. The New Year's Eve example is revealing because even though the celebrators have distinctive reactions, the single common thread in their behavior is how they manage time. Whether they are sentimental, angry, or detached, we find, after sifting through layers of circumstance and attitudes, that the underlying reasons have to do with handling—or not handling—the past, present, and future.

In trying to manage one's life, one must find a kind of *temporal balance,* a way of handling the three zones of time in a meaningful and fulfilling manner. More significant, one must learn how to deal with the future as an extension of one's present life.

In the past ten years of research, I have devised an instrument called the Rappaport Time Line (RTL). Borrowing from contemporary research, this approach helps subjects map out their lives and assess their temporal orientation. Though still in their early stages of development, time-line studies have illuminated a wide range of psychological problems from a temporal perspective. We will see in what follows that often practitioners are too busy treating symptoms to identify their underlying causes. The threads of existing theories about personality and behavior are woven into a more comprehensive approach which I have labeled Temporally Oriented Psychotherapy (TOP).

This is not a self-help book. It does not promise to take away the pain or anguish of life, nor does it suggest a simple formula to find the good life. But it does examine some of the fundamental issues involved in planning and living, with the hope that the right idea at the opportune moment may help launch an inward journey to some novel and valuable places. Time is, after all, our most precious resource.

I

LIFE LINES

In looking at the ways individuals struggle with the "motion" of time in the context of New Year's Eve (as I described in the Introduction), we are faced with a vexing question. Have we simply noted that "Father Time" is an unfriendly metaphor and that some individuals do not successfully deal with "lived time?" Can we say that some individuals simply have trouble dealing with time passing while others have achieved a sense of "balanced temporality?" How important is temporality to the overall functioning of the individual?

The questions began to plague me almost as soon as I started working with clinical patients, while I was being trained as a psychologist. One of my first memorable cases was an eighteen-year-old girl to whom I was assigned during my internship. In that period of the late sixties, private hospitals were still treating individuals diagnosed as schizophrenic with long-term hospitalization. When I began working with Megin she had already been an inpatient for more than six months and had shown little improvement. I remember thinking she did not live up to my stereotype of an inpatient schizophrenic patient. She didn't hallucinate, nor was she delusional. Before hospitalization she had shown a pattern of marked withdrawal, social isolation and panic attacks.

Because she was confined to the hospital, I was able to see her three times a week. At first, it was very difficult to establish rapport. She was very agitated and had a hard time sitting through our sessions, answering me with blunt, short phrases. After several weeks of getting nowhere, I obtained my supervisor's approval to change the arrangement between Megin and me. I informed her that since I seemed to be "imposing" on her time, we should operate by appointments, which she would initiate through her ward nurse. After a nerve-wracking week in which we began to doubt our plan, she finally called and insisted on an appointment.

The shift in format was extremely helpful in that I could now ask how I could help her. The first few sessions were marked by anger and ambivalence about relating to me. Within a week or two, however, she began to talk freely about her experience in the hospital, particularly about her relationship to ward staff and other patients. After several weeks on what could be called day-to-day matters, I tried to shift to a dialogue about her life before the hospitalization. She wouldn't or couldn't relate to what had happened during her "breakdown." I also found she was unable to relate to the question of life beyond the hospital. Typical subjects such as her vacation plans, school concerns and goals were similarly off-limits, as she seemed totally immersed in a narrow slice of present-centered time. This difficulty in projecting herself into the future seemed deeply connected to her overall inability to function adequately.

I began a dialogue about this phenomenon with my supervisor, who was a psychoanalyst. His position exemplified mainstream thinking of a broad segment of the clinical field. His view of my temporal observation was that time disorientation was a symptom of schizophrenia. He felt strongly that pushing her out of the present would make her anxious and cause a setback. He added that my predecessor had tried to get her to deal with the past and that Megin had essentially closed up shortly before I began working with her.

Unconvinced by his position, I feverishly began to read what I could find about temporality in the literature. To my surprise, there was very little work done in the United States that treated temporal "imbalance" as a serious part of mental disorders. I did, however, discover that there was a fairly extensive European literature that had sprung from the work of the German philosopher Martin Heidegger. Using this "existential" line of thought as a framework, I was able to persuade my supervisor to allow me to gently steer this young woman into her psychological future.

Applying what I had read, instead of trying to get her to talk about her future, I worked with Megin to deal with the future as an entity in itself. As one might expect, early results were mixed and I was frequently tempted to heed the consensual advice and drift back to the experiential present. Our persistence paid off, however, as she eventually began to relate to her feelings of living in a world *without* a past or future. She began to ask me how I thought about the future. Again, I had to deviate from standard protocol, which generally discouraged psychotherapist disclosure. I began to speak of my short-term plans and interests and my own apprehension about the future.

During this process, we had an unusually dramatic breakthrough. She spoke of feeling as if she had undergone a psychological death of sorts, wherein her sense of herself had vanished. She began to feel reconnected to the "person she was before" as she reestablished a sense of life's continuity. Ironically, as she began to speak of the "tomorrows" in her life, so did the "yesterdays" begin to reemerge. Over a period of about four months, she became able to extend herself into the future and began to attend hospital-based classes, and she was able to leave the hospital shortly before I finished my internship.

Certainly this case was very dramatic and some would raise questions about cause and effect. It was certainly not a controlled study, and it is important to add that Megin was on medication throughout my work with her. Nevertheless, psychotherapy had *not* had impact on her before while she had been on the same medication. I received a considerable amount of attention at this hospital for my achievement with Megin, though I suspect that my teachers were reluctant to heap too much praise on such a green clinician. I also think that their withholding of accolades was objectively valid, since I did not repeat anything like the clear-cut results of this case.

Although therapeutic results were not so readily achievable, I continued to find that temporal dynamics were at the core of my patients' difficulties. The sense of deep temporal disturbance that was evident in the hospitalized young woman was also there, with qualitative and quantitative differences, in other patients. As I found myself attempting to apply the plethora of models available to the developing clinical psychologist, I found myself continually directed back to what seemed to be an emerging central concept: *temporal imbalance*. It was the patients themselves who began to inadvertently teach me the significance of time experience as we attempted to address their symptoms. Moreover, the individuals who were manifesting temporal imbalance problems were not drawn only from my experience in hospital settings. On the contrary, most of my work over the past ten years has been with what could be termed "high functioning" individuals whom I have seen on an outpatient basis. The clients with whom I have worked over these years are representative of a wide cross section of contemporary society. As such, they are not dissimilar to the stereotypes that were identified around New Year's Eve.

Depression, a common problem in contemporary life, typifies a difficulty that revolves around temporality. Depressed patients speak of time dragging and of a "break" in the continuity of their lives. A thirty-eight-year-old male physicist whom I saw several years ago came to see me because of a relationship with a woman that had ended and left him very depressed. He could not sleep consistently and found himself without the energy to maintain his usual demanding schedule. As we began to talk, he shifted from the sadness associated with the break-up to a general feeling that his life had gone badly. As is typical of depressed individuals, his focus was on the past, as if the "bridge" to the present and future had been ruptured. When the future ceases to be part of experience, the result is a sense of hopelessness that we call depression.

Months went by with this young man lamenting this relationship and feeling hopeless about the rest of his life. Simply letting him "get the sadness out," which is the approach in many of our psychotherapies, did not help him reorient himself to the future. He had to be tugged or pulled out of his melancholy the way an individual who has slipped into quicksand needs a sharp jerk to bring him to new solid ground. If a therapist only helps the person relive the problematic past, it is, in a sense, like jumping into the quicksand and trying to push the person to safety. The new and solid ground is the psychological future, which has become detached and obscure. When therapeutic efforts focus on the sense of possibility that is linked to the individual's past and present, the feeling of hopelessness eventually lifts.

The task of breaking into this man's future was not easy. As is often the case, he resisted projecting himself forward, claiming that he needed to understand what had happened. In addition, he repeatedly claimed that he was never able to think about himself very far ahead. After many sessions and much mutual frustration, we were able to use his comfort with the scientific concept of "linearity" to help him see that he could develop "predictions" about the future based on what was known: his past. After about eighteen months of psychotherapy, he was much less depressed and was clearly more comfortable shifting between past, present and future aspects of his experience.

The case of a woman whom I saw professionally last year shows how similar events can disturb temporal harmony in distinctly dissimilar ways. A forty-one-year-old art dealer came to see me when her second marriage broke up after eight years. Like the physicist, she came to the therapy anxious and unable to sleep. She was not depressed but rather was highly energized, to the point of appearing what is often called manic. She expressed great trepidation over her future, feeling that in order to maintain her life she would have to replace the lost relationship as rapidly as possible. She suddenly felt time was moving too fast and that the future had actually constricted to the point where she was racing against the clock. The result was a state of continuous frenzy in which she was literally plunging ahead in her life rather than fluidly moving forward. Interacting with this woman was, like her internal experience, somewhat hectic. She expressed her thoughts in a scattered way, did not complete sentences and often interrupted me. Though aware of her tendency not to listen, she nevertheless continued in this vein as though her thoughts were one step ahead of herself and me. To her, the present was a series of disconnected images that all seemed to run into one another.

As with the other individuals we have been discussing, her temporal flow had been disturbed so that she experienced herself as cut off from her past. The trauma of a relationship ending had disturbed her sense of certainty about how her life would evolve. Her image of herself and of the hopes, plans and values that sprang from a viable sense of personal identity were disrupted. For all practical purposes, she was cut off from the accumulated resources of her past experience. Her frantic quality stemmed from the feeling that she was on a journey without the benefit of navigational aids. Our task became to reestablish continuity with her prior life and sense of self. We geared therapeutic efforts toward reestablishing a more integrated flow of experience, which was not so out of synchronization with external events.

Regardless of the complaints that clients brought to psychotherapy, temporal imbalance seemed to be at the center. The nature of temporal experience seems best conveyed by the metaphor of a "thread." When the thread is "stretched taut," there seems to be a flow of experience that reflects a harmony among past, present and future. However, certain life events and subjective experiences can bring about a dramatic change in this thread or sense of linearity.

This notion of a unifying thread to our experience is extremely important for a number of reasons. Around the turn of the century, when there were novel efforts to describe the nature of human experience, great pioneers in psychology such as William James concluded that subjective experience is akin to a "stream of consciousness." James (1980, p. 270) says: "Consciousness, then, does not appear in itself chopped up in bits. Such words as 'chain' or 'train' do not describe it fitly. . . . It is nothing jointed; it flows. A 'river' or a 'stream' are the metaphors by which it is most naturally described." Henri Bergson, the great French philosopher, had a tremendous impact on James and on many others concerned with the nature of experience. Bergson (1971) had persuasively concluded that "time is the heart of human existence." In other words, the sense of flow James mentioned in his "stream of consciousness" metaphor can only be understood if we consider the relationship between motion and time. To express this more basically, we sense our life's happening in the context of our perception of time passing. Henri Ellenberger referred to the "flowing of life" as synonymous with the energy of life itself.

Humans, like all living organisms, live with a biologically based "time sense." Sleep cycles, eating cycles, reproductive cycles and migratory cycles all occur in timed patterns. Since the beginning of documented human history, man has also used a variety of external means of measuring the passage of time. The sun, moon, stars, tides and seasons were the most universally used means of anticipating and remembering events. Different cultures and civilizations approached the task differently and had different notions of how events were linked to one another. Nevertheless, all cultures developed some standard for recording important occasions and planning the continuance of useful routines.

After centuries of ingenious inventions for measuring time, perhaps the most significant was the mechanical clock, which is said to have been invented in the thirteenth century A.D. This development was reflected in Newton's classical physics, in which he expressed time as a function of distance and velocity (t = d/v). Frederick Melges (1982) has pointed out that the mechanical clock is "a spatialized notion of time, based on comparing relative motions in terms of distance traveled" (p. 6). The mechanical clock was thus predicated on the notion that we could use a standard unit of time (minute), based on the clock's gears traveling at a constant velocity over a fixed distance. This convention gives us essentially modern-day "clock time," which presumes that time flows in a linear fashion from past to present to future. Today, the twenty-four-hour clock and the 365-day calendar are standards all over the world.

Embedded in the concept of time is the notion of flowing or passing. That is, the concept of time would have little meaning if it were not linked to a sense of change. Fraser (1975) points out that time can be considered as a construct that refers to the perception or attribution of changes against some background that is taken to be permanent. Melges (1982, p. 7), in his enlightening book on time, sums up elusive concepts by stating, "For a change to be perceived or imputed there has to be both *succession* and *duration*. That is, when two successive events are separated by an interval, the interval between them is called *duration*." In other words, our sense of time moving is triggered by a sense of change in perception, thought or feeling with the awareness that an interval has elapsed.

In addition to succession and duration, the concept of time includes *perspective*. The elements of temporal perspective are *past, present,* and *future*. Perspective is, in a sense, the easiest component of time to address. Westerners, using a linear approach to how their life flows, tend to experience events emerging from the future, becoming present and then becoming past. One looks forward to eating lunch in a few minutes (future), enjoys the taste and experience of the sandwich (present) and remembers the pleasure when ordering lunch another day (past).

One of the key assumptions of temporal theorists and of this book is that temporal perspective has to be integrated for an individual to function in an effective and satisfying way. The past, present and future must be of comparable valence so that the three zones of temporal experience operate fluidly. Of course, it should be apparent from your experience and from what we have already said that temporal perspective is not always integrated for every individual and that the balance we achieve one moment can be disturbed by dramatic changes in life or by a simple but disturbing thought process. Temporal integration, as we will see, is a solid indicator of mental health and can easily be upended. For example, a young woman who was in the closing months of a long-term successful therapeutic relationship with me had achieved a solid sense of temporal balance and was working on "tying up loose ends in therapy." Coincidentally, a good friend of hers who was on the faculty of a major university was shocked when he was denied tenure after five years of productive work. My young client was initially outraged at the "injustice" and felt very bad for her friend, who was suffering and having a difficult time figuring out the next step in his life. Gradually, my client's concern and anxiety began to shift from the plight of her good friend to herself. She became preoccupied with issues of personal security, the "arbitrariness of life" and all kinds of uncertainties concerning her personal future.

You may be thinking that a "healthy" person is not deeply upended by such events, especially when they happen to someone else. In a sense, that is correct, and my client was able to reestablish a sense of balance after a short period of turbulence. On the other hand, "neurotic symptoms" are usually precipitated by outside circumstance, often an event not totally pertinent to one's well-being. The point, which has been developed more fully by Swiss existential psychiatrist Ludwig Binswanger, is that seemingly innocuous events can trigger frightening and destabilizing reactions. Binswanger spoke of one client who became gripped with anxiety after losing a heel from her shoe. She was reminded of the fragility of life and "how easily things can be undone." Perhaps a more familiar situation is the disturbing sequence of feelings and thoughts that often follow one's attendance at a funeral. One is left with a powerful sense of vulnerability as the awareness of mortality sets in. Often it takes weeks or longer to shake off its effects, and frequently professional help is sought when the mourning process (for oneself) persists too long. During this period, one's temporal perspective is markedly disturbed. Future and past are thrown out of balance.

Needless to say, life is filled with "minefields" that directly affect our temporal perspective. We lose jobs, develop unexpected physical problems, lose loved ones and find that political conditions can suddenly change our entire sense of futurity. Though we in the United States are not often touched by arbitrary and dramatic changes, the world is filled with victims of drought, poverty, civil war and devastating economic misfortune. Consider the impact on her outlook when an educated professional from a country like Iran is forced into long-term exile and must accept an unskilled job in a new culture that cannot make use of her professional training. I have met many "orderlies" in hospitals from countries like Cuba, Vietnam and Russia who were forced to change their expectations and outlook in accordance with shrunken economic and social possibilities. Only the heartiest of individuals withstand such dramatic insult to their life's momentum. Others lose their faith in the future and succumb to various levels of despair. In such cases, temporal balance becomes disturbed and the individual may no longer be able to project him- or herself into the future. The person will become past-focused, developing symptoms such as depression.

We do not need, however, to look only at the extreme cases triggered by calamitous circumstances. A normal life's disappointments, successes and plateaus are sufficient to produce convulsions in the ever-shifting pulse that represents our temporal balance. Discovering that one is not *really* the favorite child, not getting into the school that is one's first choice, not making a team or not being asked out by the right person can all trigger processes that alter temporal balance. Apparent success can also have positive or sometimes negative impact on past, present and future relations. Perceiving that one's life is changeless can also put strain on our delicate temporal balance.

In addition to integration of temporal perspective, we can speak of *orientation*. On New Year's Eve, different individuals responded to the task of marking time differently. Although there is a predictable way in which we all respond to certain situations, we tend to deal with contingencies in terms of our prior experience. Temporal research on "lived time" strongly suggests that temporal orientation may well be considered a somewhat stable personality variable. Though longitudinal research is not yet available, clinical data suggest that a present-oriented person tends to function that way over an extended period of his life. By the same token, we see chronically depressed clients who are past-oriented over many years.

I have already indicated that temporal orientations can be geared toward past, present or future. As with other personality characteristics, orientations are not pure and will involve features of the other kinds of orientation. While it is not entirely clear how temporal orientation endures over the course of a lifetime, clinical experience suggests that orientation is part of the personality structure. In other words, orientation tends to be similar over a definite period of time. As with other familiar parts of oneself, when orientation is the target of therapeutic change, the process is slow and requires much repetition and reworking.

Finally, in looking at the dimensions of subjective temporality, we must consider *rhythm*. As the pendulum clock has a perpetual and repetitious rhythm, so do we experience subjective time in a personal rhythm. The temporal elements—duration, succession, perspective—all interact to produce a tempo. As with music, the tempo of our lives can vary, and as with music, that tempo can feel in synchrony with our experience or somehow at odds with it. In fact, the external tempo embedded in music can correspond or conflict with an internal standard. All of us in the United States can testify to the predictable shifts in musical tastes that seem to cut across generations. We watch the simple melodic taste of childhood give way to the more turbulent, driven tastes of adolescence, which in turn eventually succumbs to the "easier" sounds of eclectic popular music. It is always entertaining to watch young people make the transition to softer music after vowing never to lose their taste for something like hard rock. It should be evident that the rhythms of music reflect the tempo of our internal states and that this inner "beat" is subject to the same variability as other temporal dimensions. When the internal rhythm of temporality is right, one feels as though all is well with the world. When the rhythm is disturbed, one often feels harassed, as if there isn't sufficient time to live one's life.

In the converse situation, one's life tempo can feel flat and slow as though time is passing dreadfully slowly. There are cases that roughly correspond to what psychiatry has labeled "cyclical mood disorders" (manic-depressive syndromes), in which the internal tempo and corresponding behavior vary in extremes. There is even the suggestion that young children can have temporal rhythm problems that might be associated with the ubiquitous hyperactive syndrome. These children, who are constantly out of synchronization with others in their surroundings, may have a distinctly different need to be "in motion" in order to feel as if time is flowing.

Based on my clinical observations and on temporal theory embodied in the work of some of the European pioneers, I became interested in developing a tool that would help illustrate and assess temporal dynamics. However, the task of developing a psychological instrument that would effectively measure the elusive and highly subjective construct of temporality would be extremely difficult. The great pioneers writing in this area, especially Martin Heidegger, worked within a philosophical rather than a psychological framework. Their ideas were deductively constructed and did not easily lend themselves to scientific study. In addition, the phenomena they were attempting to delineate were, by definition, elusive and almost too deeply subjective for adequate description. Many of us remember reading those esoteric existential philosophers in our college days and shrinking in the face of arcane hyphenated terms like "being-in-the-world." I recall trying to read Jean-Paul Sartre as an undergraduate and wondering why my philosophy professor was so excited. Sartre seemed pessimistic, and his most psychological work, *Being and Nothingness,* was nearly impossible to grasp.

Although these mostly European writers were attempting to deal with human experience on the most fundamental level, their work has not been extensively incorporated into the mainstream of scientific psychology. Concepts like temporality, meaning-in-life, and authenticity, for example, are imprecise and do not lend themselves to measurement by the methodology of science adopted by the academic psychology community. A philosophy professor of mine, in attempting to describe the narrowness of psychology's epistemology, came up with the "five p's." He pointed out that our approach to research has been limited by "pragmatic, positivistic, probabilistic, paradigmatic and parsimonious" methodologies. Rather than try to define these terms, let it suffice to say that together they represent a research strategy adopted from the modern physical sciences. Due to the success of disciplines like physics in the late eighteenth and early nineteenth centuries, psychology became enamored of experimentation, laboratory method, instrumentation, the mathematical depiction of reality, interobserver objectivity and reductionism. If we add the application of statistical models to what could be called the infatuation with the brass instrument approach, we roughly have modern psychology.

For the last twenty-five years the body of knowledge in psychology has largely been derived from experiments using college sophomores.

Just about every facet of psychological theory has been tested on these captive twenty-year-olds. Learning, motivation, cognition, phobias, depression, sensory deprivation and a host of other things have been tested using groups whose size is based on statistical models. The typical experiment involves more than thirty undergraduates whose responses to tests or psychological manipulations are summarized through the statistical analysis of the group's data. The aim of this research approach has been to study a few variables that can be measured with a fair amount of objectivity (usually defined by what researchers call reliability). When results are evaluated, they are usually called "statistically significant" based on the assumptions inherent in the particular inductive statistics used.

There are many problems in the experimental method as practiced by the social sciences. First, the use of the "mean" or average certainly obscures individual behavior. The learning curve that is so universally cited has often been referred to as an artifact of group averaging. Put in a more lighthearted vein by an accounting colleague, "When you average a group of telephone numbers, the resultant number belongs to no one." Second, college students have been a convenient and fairly homogeneous group to work with. Frequently, in an attempt to control extraneous variables, groups are further refined by focusing on a particular sex. The result is that while researchers often pay lip service to the limitations of such studies, these limitations tend to be forgotten or ignored when a study is cited in other work or summarized in abstract form. In all fairness to the field of psychology, fields such as developmental and geriatric psychology have concentrated on age-appropriate research samples in recent years. There are also some studies in which college students are appropriate subjects.

Thus, the spirit of measurement in psychology that I was exposed to in my training and that young doctoral candidates are still exposed to is not conducive to grappling with complex subjective variables. Nevertheless, I discovered that in the work of both Eugene Minkowski and Martin Heidegger there was a reference to the way temporality was experienced that seemed to have great promise. Minkowski and Heidegger both thought that temporality was best expressed as a "linear spatial metaphor." Minkowski, working mostly with depressed patients in the 1920s, and Heidegger, in his philosophical work, had concluded that the experience of "lived time" was probably best represented by a horizontal line. When thinking about the flow of time, most individuals would organize their experience of past, present and future in a linear configuration with experiences placed on successive points from left to right.

Early case findings were exciting, as it was clear that this "lines" approach supported the notion that there was indeed a relationship between the problems an individual presented and his orientation to temporality. Around this time, several doctoral graduate students began to express strong interest in temporality both in clinical assessment and as a research tool. We began to refine the lines approach, trying lines of different format, with varying degrees of size, structure, and supervision. After months of informal experimentation, we devised a procedure that, at first glance, seems almost absurdly simple.

Subjects were given a blank strip of adding machine tape twenty-four inches long, which, they were told, was meant to represent "the span of time which makes up your whole life." Subjects were asked to think of the tape as a condensation of the most significant experiences that *had* happened, *were* happening and *would* happen. They were asked to mark these experiences with a vertical line and indicate their age or expected age at the time of the event. When the subjects finished noting their experiences, they were asked to make a large dot that was to be labeled "now." In addition, in keeping with the subjective spirit of such measurement, we asked them to put brackets around the dot to represent "your present life." This designation of the psychological present marked an area of uncertainty.

In a sense, the strip of paper is like the *tabula rasa* with which we are born. Just as our lives become "filled up" by the process of living, so does the time line get filled up. We end up with a series of indicators that the individual has projected onto the line. As there are no boundaries, we find that subjects begin at different points in their past and end at different points in their future. The distribution of experiences along the line gives us an opportunity to observe several parameters of temporality while the individual is engaging in a task that simulates the way we ordinarily deal with our lives in the context of time.

Perhaps owing to our lack of creativity, the instrument, the scoring and the interpretation of the findings has come to be called the Rappaport Time Line (RTL). We have continued to develop the RTL along two paths. Several research projects have been done and are being planned to ascertain the most useful information available from the RTL. In addition, whenever a new psychological tool is developed, it is essential to see whether the concepts the instrument purports to measure are predictably related to more established theoretical constructs. This is the method by which we "validate" a psychological test. So far, studies have been done or planned to connect temporal factors to identity formation, future defensiveness, death anxiety, purpose in life and sex differences.

The research results have been encouraging so far. We have found the RTL to be a useful tool that is slowly breaking down some of the barriers against using "mainstream" approaches to study phenomenological concepts such as temporality. Nevertheless, the RTL must still be considered to be in its developmental stages. The network of research that is required for a new tool is continuing to emerge. We have been finding a fair amount of editorial resistance in our efforts to publish some of the early studies. For reasons that will become clear later, the statistical analyses that are possible do not completely conform to the standards typical of much psychological research. For one thing, temporal organization is, by definition, very fluid and can be expected to vary over time. It is difficult to demonstrate what psychometricians have called "test reliability" since we are dealing with shifting temporal states. Nevertheless, the studies are beginning to find their way into some of the more established journals, indicating that psychology could be moving toward a new receptivity toward the exploration of subjectivity.

The RTL has also been used in the clinical context. I have been administering the time line to patients for many years at different points in their treatment. The first exposure to this task is often accompanied by reticence and, not infrequently, a polite refusal to do it. Though the RTL is a relatively simple procedure, it arouses some very complex emotions. As the individuals begin the task of conceptualizing their lives "over time," they can become anxious, since one or more

4	6	9	11	18	21	28
moved to Illinois	twin sisters born	rheu-matic fever	father dies	away to college	met Phil	first child

Time line of thirty-seven-year-old married woman in early stages of therapy

of the zones may be a source of difficulty. The job of selecting the "significant" experiences raises an immediate awareness of values and the meanings one attaches to different "pieces of life's puzzle." Complex defenses come into play, as people vary in the degree to which they block out segments of the past or the future. Later, I will explore a new concept in the psychological defense of the future that we call "telepression." It is the counterpart to repression, a way of avoiding the future with its disturbing uncertainties.

As the RTL is administered later in the psychotherapy process, one is able to see shifts in temporal organization in the selection of experiences.

The time line of a thirty-seven-year-old married woman with three children is illustrated below. The RTL was administered in the early stages of therapy when she sought help for a moderate depression coupled with a feeling of having little personal direction beyond marriage and parenting.

Her time line provides a clear image of how she experiences her life. The most notable feature of her line is the heavy emphasis on past experience. She has listed ten experiences in the past, but only three in the future (temporal density). She experiences the past as much larger in space while the future occupies a position of much less prominence (duration). While she is able to project backward (thirty-three years) and forward (twenty-three years) in a somewhat more symmetrical way (extension), the future is clearly a sparse part of her experience. Most depressed individuals are living heavily in the past, with little future outlook. She has no clear image of herself in the distant future, and her present life is figuratively and literally empty of experiences. It is also quite evident that her chosen experiences have little to do with herself. Except for a vague plan to return to school when she is forty, she experiences the future totally in terms of "endings" for others. She

30	31	[37	o]	40	53	60
second child	third child	started therapy	NOW	back to school	Edward goes to college	Phil retires

29

sees her youngest child going off to school and her husband ending his career. As she put it, "I do not feel like a person except for what I do for my family."

An examination of this woman's time line provides an immediate sense that this "linear representation of her life" provides a definite sense of the fluidity of her life experience. As therapy proceeded, a later RTL indicated that her future had opened up considerably. She moved her "now point" closer to the middle of the line, indicating that she had achieved a better sense of temporal balance. However, despite this apparent validity to the RTL, it is still a relatively new device. A great deal more must be done to establish its validity over the course of many studies. In addition, the concepts that underlie the interpretation of the time line must be elaborated and more fully connected to existing psychological theory.

Each person who is given the RTL responds in a unique way. Individuals place varying degrees of emphasis on different parts of their life and are "oriented" to time differently. In order to develop this theory more fully, I must first address the developmental aspects of temporality. In the next chapter, I will look at early childhood experience and explore how differences in orientation to the future might develop based on the child's interactions with parents and culture.

II

IN THE BEGINNING

When we begin the monumental task of trying to explain individual differences in "lived time," there are three typical places to begin. First, we can speak of inherited traits or genetic influences on behavior. Second, we can speak of acquired behavior that suggests some form of learning. Finally, though this is not a widespread approach to psychology in the United States, we can think in terms of the individual "freely" choosing approaches to living. While different branches of psychology tend to approach individual differences differently, I think it is fair to say that most meta-theoreticians give credence to the nature-nurture/free-will basis for understanding human behavior. In other words, when we tackle the challenge of trying to understand complex dimensions of behavior, we must tolerate complex bases for understanding them.

Owing to the pioneering work of Sigmund Freud in the clinical realm and Jean Piaget in the developmental realm of psychology, we tend to look for the origins of behavior in early childhood. We in the field of psychology have a belief that the basis for adult adaptive and mal-

31

adaptive behavior can be found in various stages of childhood. Schools within psychology do not differ significantly on this subject; both behavioral and dynamic theorists, for example, see childhood as the learning crucible in which later patterns develop. Though inherited tendencies or temperamental factors have not usually been emphasized in understanding behavior, developmental psychologists in the past decade have returned to examining dispositional factors. In formulating his theory of neurosis Freud placed heavy emphasis on "constitutional" factors. Over the years, however, the biological basis has been paid lip service and the main focus of investigative efforts has been acquired behavior.

The free-will approach to understanding behavior is more problematic than the constitutional. First, most social scientists see the concept of human choosing as philosophical rather than psychological. Second, since the ethos of scientific psychology rests on a branch of the philosophy of science called logical positivism, there is little room for a premise that is not oriented toward the prediction and control of behavior. This philosophical orientation has led to what theoreticians such as W. F. Overton (1984) have called the mechanistic approach, which does not leave room for understanding behavior in anything but a cause-effect framework. It has been difficult for mainstream psychology to accept that it is possible to study human behavior from what Overton has termed an "organismic" perspective, which does not simply reduce behavior to a set of antecedent causes.

To be sure, we have not always studied adults as thinking, feeling, conscious organisms with will and spirit. Freud and his followers tended to regard conscious phenomena as the "tip of the iceberg," while the behaviorists have only recently conceded that awareness in the form of thought has a place in the new "cognitive psychology." It is no wonder, then, that children have been studied almost entirely in terms of observable behavior with little attention paid to thought processes except, perhaps, to problem solving. Developmentalists have recently, however, begun to shed the yoke of behavioral psychology and probe the experiential basis for children's behavior.

Very little work has been done on the subject of the temporal dimension of the experience of adults, and virtually no such work has been done with children. We do know something about how children relate to clocks and calendars, particularly as we adapt Piaget's findings with respect to the development of abstract thinking ability. We have studied how and when children learn the days of the week, the months of the year and how to tell time. However, we have spent less time understanding how children deal with the passage of time. Rather, by default, we have assumed that children live in the narrow band of the present and are unaware of the complexities of marking time or incapable of perceiving time passing in a linear manner across three zones. We tend to assume that children have little memory and cannot extend their thinking into the future. As I begin to address the manner in which children relate to "lived time," I will thus not be drawing on any significant body of empirical research. Rather, I will draw on what has been labeled "anecdotal" data or the more informal observations we make in everyday and clinical situations. Such observations are not less pertinent than those that are formally derived. They are part of the deductive process of creating theories rather than the more customary inductive process with which the scientific community is more familiar. Assembling diverse observations aids in developing more formal pathways for research. Thus, as I outline some ideas on childhood experience, bear in mind that the effort represents an early step in creating the foundation from which to proceed more extensively.

I was once invited to my son's first-grade class to generate a discussion about time. The teacher was very enthusiastic about the idea of having the children extend backward and forward. Before I attended the class, she asked the customary questions about whether little children can really remember early experiences and whether they are capable of projecting into the future. My answer was and is that it is a question of human subjectivity and verbal expression rather than a question of the experience not being present. In a sense, we have the same problem with adults. Ask an adult to recall early childhood experiences and you find that initially there is little success. With some guidance, however, either in the form of psychotherapy or through other encouragement, the unfolding process occurs. I find that at the beginning of psychotherapy my patients are not able to go forward or backward very easily. Some of the images are consciously censored while others have been subject to defensive processes elicited by anxiety.

Children have the same early reticence. However, if the inquirer does not quit quickly, assuming that children are totally present-centered, they do indeed begin to relate to the past and future. Ironically, young children between three and six are sometimes more in touch with the past than adults. They recall names, activities and other aspects of their experiences. In my son's first-grade class, several boys (it was a boys' school) recalled experiences in nursery school dating back two to four years. When I inquired about teachers' and friends' names, they had little trouble remembering. Similarly, when they spoke of positive memories, several had no trouble recalling momentous occasions like the first fish they ever caught, including the kind of bait they used and what body of water the fish was caught in.

Naive interviewers of children are often misled by the preschoolers' reluctance to relate to the question. It is not different from asking the ritual parent question, "How was school today?" That usually elicits defensiveness, the result being an apparent amnesia, which seems prevalent all the way through adolescence. If, on the other hand, a parent or interviewer is able and willing to tolerate a more free-form dialogue, lo and behold, a plethora of rich material suddenly surfaces. Unfortunately, research situations frequently inhibit children (and adults), with similarly lean results. Children are further limited by their only partially developed ability to express memories through language. There is also the problem of recollecting preverbal experiences. We certainly know that learning begins to take place in the womb and continues postnatally at a rapid pace. Though there is no language in the first year of life, we can presume that the associations that are formed provide the basis for learning.

One of the cornerstones of Freud's theory of child development addressed the relationship between emotion and memory in early childhood. Freud and other psychoanalytic investigators assumed it was axiomatic that very early, preverbal memories influenced the development of personality, psychological defenses and adult behavior. One of the intriguing debates in Freud's inner circle had to do with the sequence and content of early memories. There was fairly general agreement that experiences associated with distress or trauma tended to be cut off from the consciousness or repressed. Thus, our first-grade children would tend to report such positive memories as fishing trips rather than scoldings from parents. Some of Freud's followers, such as Margaret Mahler and Melanie Klein, formulated what have come to called "object relations theories," which assert that the memories of infantile trauma are repressed and form the basis for later relationships with children and adults. Freud himself saw childhood before his well-known Oedipal/Electra stage as being fairly open, with a close correspondence between children's day-to-day fears and the eventual repressed material of nightmares. For Freud, children had open access to early memories dating back to infancy. Otto Rank (1929) became famous for his theory that it was the trauma of birth that provided the foundation for all later anxiety, a theory which many see as farfetched, but which a well-respected theoretician considered feasible in terms of children's recall process.

One of the most compelling arguments that Freud made to support his theory of development had to do with the child's movement in what he called the "latency" period, the time in childhood when children develop a certain sense of durability and resourcefulness. This is the period in which early childhood ends and the child begins to achieve at a rapid pace. Teachers seem to adore this age group (from about eight to twelve), as it appears relatively conflict-free, with a great openness to learning. Freud argued that this serenity is achieved as the final turbulence of the phallic stage is put to rest through a process of major repression. He claimed that as the child's psychosexual development reaches maximum intensity at around age seven, it is resolved by "burying" the associated conflicts in the unconscious. Along with the conflicts, however, other memories from earlier childhood are also buried. Whether one is an adamant Freudian or not, it is interesting to note that the earliest memories of most adults begin around age seven!

Children are clearly different from adults with respect to their ability to extend into the future. Nevertheless, our first-graders were able to grasp the task and made a surprising effort to deal with their personal future. Children tend to live in a narrow temporal band related to present needs. They do, however, begin the process of marking time at an early age, even if crudely and imprecisely. Asking them to project forward aroused anxiety, but adults are also uncomfortable with the task. The children became noticeably unsettled when confronted with the uncharted waters of their lives. Yet what was significant was the wide latitude of responses. Some children could not relate to more than the remote present, with responses such as "I'm going to the park with my brother," or "When I get home from school I'll probably fight with my brother." Other first-graders, however, produced some clear future-related responses. One or two boys referred to occupational choice and marriage. One said he was going to be a "tree cutter and a father." Another said that he would be a NASA astronaut but "would *not* be killed in a crash." Still another said that there would be "a war." One visibly distressed little boy ended the task by simply stating, "I will be dead."

There are parallels in the time experience of nonscientific cultures and of very young children. The consensus is that infants have little if any conception of temporality. Freud (1933) described the infant as dominated by "id processes." In his characteristically melodramatic way he describes id as "a chaos, a cauldron of seething excitement. . . . There is nothing corresponding to the idea of time. . . . The ID knows no values, no good and evil, no morality" (p. 65). Freud says that the infant, who begins life connected to the umbilical cord and residing in 98.6 degrees Fahrenheit amniotic fluid, is essentially dominated by biological urges in the first phase of extra-uterine life. The difference, however, is that irritations or cravings that were once relieved instantly in the womb now are not dealt with automatically. It is out of these early experiences of frustration, when the infant has to delay gratification, that the first sense of time develops.

Thus the newborn's earliest experience with life has some inherent frustrations. Freud does not see these frustrations as negative, since postponing satisfaction allows the infant to develop "reality-oriented" functions, which eventually include a rudimentary sense of self and an early sense of temporality. In fact, this concept of child development suggests that some level of frustration is essential to the development of the child's early ego. The infant begins to become aware that there are objects (people) who minister to his needs but are not always accessible. It is the anticipation of these remembered objects that produces the first sense of future time. P. Hartocollis (1972) says that the interval between the cup and the lip during periods of hunger provides the first sense of time duration the newborn experiences.

During the first year of life, then, because of having to cope with the realities of the environment, the infant begins to sense a separateness from the environment. Otto Fenichel, an elaborator of Freud's theories, points out that the child begins to tell a primitive sort of time with only the heartbeat and respiration as a frame of reference. If the world is relatively predictable, temporal consciousness develops in a comfortable way and the child learns what Erik Erikson (1963) calls "basic trust." The infant's images of being fed get activated when he is hungry, and soon afterward the image is approximated by the mother's appearance. When, however, early experiences of nurturance are not reliable, basic trust is not developed and the most early sense of anticipation is fraught with peril. Some theorists, such as Melges, strongly indicate that inadequate mothering produces a clearly impaired sense of time.

When we consider inadequate nurturance for infants, there is a tendency to assume we are speaking about that indefinite group of individuals who are abusive parents. By the same token, we often link overwhelming neglect to the more serious psychological disorders such as schizophrenia. The fact is, however, that new parents respond to infants with a wide range of variability and with a surprising amount of confusion. One of the most common sources of conflict for new parents is how to respond to the needs of their newborn child. Both in clinical practice and in other contexts, they always ask what to do with a baby who is not easily made comfortable. After attempting to feed the baby and checking the diapers, they wonder, "Should we simply let the baby cry itself to sleep?" There is a fear present in our "psychologized" society that little babies begin to "manipulate" parents very early on and that a failure to set limits early will lead to spoiling. This view is often reinforced by a call to the pediatrician, who usually agrees that there is no harm in letting the baby cry "so that he learns you won't jump every time he wants you."

Many young women whom I have taught or worked with in a therapeutic relationship have also wondered about breast feeding after giving birth. They were convinced, often from what they read, that breast feeding provides the best nurturance from nutritional and psychological viewpoints. They also learned that breast feeding was beneficial to the mother. However, several of these women found the experience more difficult than they had imagined. They reported that their breast-fed children were not as "robust" as their friends' bottle-fed children. They meant that their children seemed to "waste time" at the breast rather than "getting down to the business of eating." The breast-fed babies tended not to sleep through the night and were perceived as more demanding. Some of the young women quickly became disillusioned with breast-feeding and began to abandon what had seemed like a wonderful opportunity.

Perhaps because of the invention of the infant bottle and because of novel demands on young women, who must meet both parental and economic pressures, there is great conflict about how much to gratify or please young children. After many years of research and theoretical developments, we know that infants require more than food. They are very social and require both psychological and physical handling. Breast-fed babies definitely appear more active and more socially oriented, and they tend to find eating inseparable from interaction with the mother. Many women, even those who feel prepared for the task of breast feeding, find the confinement and constant demands for nurturance to be incompatible with their needs for mobility outside the home. I have found that without support and encouragement, there is a tendency to supplement breast feeding with the "less troublesome" bottle. In addition, the bottle can be provided by either mother or father, which appears more consistent with the expected role blurring of contemporary marriages.

The main point here is that the quality and consistency of early nurturance has a powerful impact on the emotional and temporal development of the infant. In a society in which the extended family has all but disappeared, early childhood nurturance has, I suspect, become complicated by new notions of what is proper. The ideal of a close breast-feeding relationship is becoming harder to achieve and there seem to be considerable differences concerning optimal child-rearing behaviors. As a result, I find husbands and wives arguing at 2:00 A.M. about whether "to leave it cry." Some parents cannot decide how long to let it cry, and others are confused about whether to let a child wander into the conjugal bed. My own view is that there is little danger in meeting a child's needs whenever you possibly can. There will be sufficient opportunities for benevolent levels of frustration to develop the reality functions of which Freud spoke. When there is confusion and conflict, however, the results may be catastrophic.

Consider how prolonged periods of frustration involving feeding might affect temporality. The primitive anticipation of the infant becomes associated with discomfort and fear when gratification is very long in coming. The framework for fear extending into the future in later life may be established. The impact of erratic and conflictual handling of early infant needs may be far more damaging to many aspects of development, including temporality. When examining the relationship between family patterns and the presence of symptoms in a given child, it always seems clear that inconsistency is far more damaging than erring in one direction or another. Moreover, the earlier in life one is confronted with inconsistencies in nurturance, the more fundamental are the disturbances.

Piaget, like Freud, saw time awareness as beginning in the first two years of what he termed the sensorimotor period of childhood. Piaget, more concerned with normal development than Freud, saw the process as largely determined by the development of appropriate psychophysiological structures. As the child develops an increasing ability to move about, his action facilitates the development of such cognitive structures as causality. As soon as a child is able to anticipate how his action will cause a given result, there is an associated component of temporal duration. For example, when a child presses the button on a Jack-in-the-box, he learns that after a certain interval, a surprise doll will pop up. This elementary sense of causality or temporality continues to develop and is expanded to more abstract levels as language develops. Language grows alongside the child's ability to postpone needs so that the capacity for anticipation and planning form a foundation for more complex temporal tasks. By the time a child is about eight years old, language and symbolic thought should have progressed sufficiently to encompass an understanding of past, present and future. Unlike the earlier sensorimotor period, when time was perceived in only a personal way, in this later stage of childhood, temporality is perceived as a phenomenon in itself. The experience is that "time passes whether I am doing something or not."

We can actually see the transition to a more abstract sense of time in a very common experience. Those of us who are parents most certainly remember the tyranny of those interminable car rides with a young child or children. If you have not experienced this treat as a parent, you have undoubtedly taken a car ride as a young child and should have recollections from the child's perspective. No sooner does the trip begin than the child begins the universal litany, "Are we there yet?" It is astonishing that toddlers or even four-year-olds can ask that question moments after departure and have so little capacity to estimate distance and duration. They remain impatient and can make the less robust parents of the world vow never to embark on an automobile trip with a young child again. To everyone's astonishment, after having sworn off those "suicide missions," parents one day notice that the car trip has taken on a new serenity. Their "sensorimotor" youngster, around age six or seven, passes into another stage of cognitive development in which he begins to sense that time is passing even when he is not in action. This profound realization represents the achievement of temporal abstractness and creates new possibilities for family life.

There is a tendency when looking at the development of young children to examine "cognitive" or intellectual development on the one hand, and "emotional" development on the other. We tend to view the two domains of human functioning as if there is little crossover. The fact is, however, that thinking capacities cannot develop without reference to emotional factors. When children are referred to psychologists, there is often a notable deficiency in school performance. The use of psychologists suggests an implicit recognition that the problems with academic productivity are related to something other than the learning process. Assuming we are not dealing with a neurological condition, the question often takes the form, "Are emotional factors interfering with school learning?"

This common situation dramatically illustrates a widespread awareness that children sometimes fail to learn because they are emotionally disturbed. When psychological evaluation supports the hypothesis, we find that the child may be distracted by unconscious or conscious conflicts related to anger, competition, neglect and so forth. Emotional overloading in early childhood appears to interfere with both emotional and cognitive development. Freud developed the concept of fixation as a means to explain how adults get "stuck" in a certain stage of childhood. We are all familiar with terms borrowed from Freud, such as "anal personality," which connotes a certain pattern of rigidity and stinginess. In attempting to diagnose and understand such patterns, we make use of the verbal and written products on psychological tests. In other words, we frequently use thought processes to illuminate emotional conflicts.

The development of temporality as a cognitive structure is particularly connected to emotional development. In fact, it must be considered as inseparable and *dialectical* rather than occurring *along with* emotional progress. The child's first experience of duration has to do with the anticipation of nurturance. The expectant child is certainly in an aroused state and quickly learns to attach emotional value to processes like extending into the future. Delays in being relieved of hunger or cravings for contact will begin to create fear of anticipation. By the same token, as memory develops, the past will be recalled in connection with real or perceived emotional states. It can be deduced from the tremendous latitude of adult memory that the past is selectively inaccessible, depending on how it was experienced. Defenses against remembering seem to develop in direct proportion to how much trauma is associated with early experiences. In clinical situations, individuals who recall that they were abused during childhood have uneven memories, which usually begin at a later age than those of others with less extreme histories.

Whether or not there are negative experiences that affect remembering or anticipating, all humans must begin to deal with their awareness of death. Irvin Yalom, one of a rare group of psychologists, argues persuasively that children are dealing with death as early as age two. Melanie Klein (1948), a disciple of Freud's, extends the process further and suggests that infants in the first year of life show signs of struggling with fears of nonbeing. Klein makes the observation that primal anxiety or the most fundamental human fear is based on the fear of death. Ironically, other theorists, such as Freud, have focused on fundamental concerns such as separation from parents and fears of sexual expression. It is rather astonishing to find how few theorists see the awareness and fear of nonbeing as playing a role in the development of children. Yalom suggests that the subject of dying is generally missing from psychology as a whole. He notes that there is a profound bias in our literature that is perpetuated by the defensive views of death that are taught to us as children.

The importance of Yalom's position cannot be overemphasized. The concept of futurity is obviously connected to the ominous distant and inescapable event of death. Writers like Sören Kierkegaard have written about those terrible moments when we really experience the possibility that we will cease to exist. He referred to such experiences as "night terrors," a perfect description of those chilling moments we try to push out of consciousness. It is not possible to keep the anticipation and fear of death out of consciousness for long, especially as we approach the developmental age for worrying. Yet as we examine the institutions of psychotherapy and psychopathology, we find that "death anxiety" is treated as a very specific disorder rather than as a central determinant in many human problems. Yalom underscores the folly of considering that humans will become distraught over matters of aggression, success or sexual expression while basically ignoring the overwhelming fact of our temporary position in life. Yalom explains the lack of attention to death anxiety in terms of what could be termed the philosophical "subject-object" problem. In other words, when man is the object of study, we are limited in our objectivity because of our subjective errors. In the case of death, we tend to minimize the impact of the human capacity to project ourselves to our end because to "study death is to experience it on some level." Even trained psychotherapists, Yalom suggests, "put on blinders" when the appropriate issue to be handled is the patient's fear of dealing with death and its various concomitants.

In a way, we have a collective cultural phobia concerning the acceptance of death. For many decades, the thought of dying at home was terrifying to both victim and family. It has been commonplace to assume that a hospital is where one dies—"They have the necessary equipment for it." This rather preposterous idea is deeply ingrained in our industrialized society. I was reminded of how hospitals might be perceived by an objective observer when speaking to some American Indians in Montana. They all agreed that one should not seek treatment at a hospital. The feeling was clearly that "hospitals are places were people go to die and one would not find a good spirit for healing in such a place." Only recently, with the rise of the hospice movement, have we begun to recognize that dying does not require "treatment." Implied in the hospice approach is that dying is a part of living and should not be treated as an anomaly. However, going to hospitals "spares" the living from witnessing death. In a sense, we operate on the premise that if we never see anyone die, we can live our lives as if death is not a personal affair.

When I was working with traditional healers in East Africa, I was struck by the importance of ancestors and ancestral spirits in the understanding of how the shaman explained misfortune. It was only after talking to a great many healers that I became aware of a profound difference in the way our cultures view dying and the state of being dead. It is not difficult to imagine how ancestral influence has such a strong impact when one considers two factors. First, in rural Africa most individuals have an opportunity to interact with dying loved ones. Since they are not usually drugged in their last stage of existence, there is frequently an opportunity to have a dialogue in the final hours. This final conversation is usually well remembered and seems to serve as a basis for long-term connectedness to the lost person. In addition, people are usually buried close to town, so that one encounters the marker of a dead relative often. Proximal burial is not alien to our culture—the church cemetery began to vanish less than a century ago.

Nowadays, however, cemeteries are centralized, with most individuals paying their respects to the dead once a year or less.

Children, on the other hand, are curious and rather direct about death. They show early signs of concern about existence and nonexistence with their "all gone" response to swallowing food. By the same token, the "peek-a-boo" games they play also deal with issues of permanence, or "conservation" in Piaget's system of thought. By the time they approach two, they express many fears, especially at bedtime. Apparently, they have not developed confidence in the sleep-wake cycle, so they are reluctant to go to sleep at night. They frequently ask for all sorts of reassurance that there are no snakes, crabs, monsters or other dangerous things lurking around their beds. Perhaps as testimony to the death fears of young children, universal prayers such as "Now I lay me down to sleep . . ." have evolved to help provide security for the innocent child's concern about reawakening.

Children can be candid and upsetting to adults in their direct approach to death. It always sends chills up our spines when a child visits a sick grandparent and asks, "When are you going to die?" They are often rebuked for what Anna Freud called their matter-of-fact approach to death. At times they show emotional response when they attend such rituals as funerals. At other times, they do not accept the gravity of the situation and are scolded for not showing proper decorum. One of my fondest and most mortifying recollections involves a funeral chapel and my four-year-old son. We were attending the viewing of a close family friend. These occasions are somewhat protracted for the average four-year-old, and my son decided to wander around the chapel a bit. After some time, during which I had not focused on his whereabouts, he appeared, enthusiastically wanting to show me "something neat." He proceeded to drag me into another wing of the chapel, point to a group of mourners and say, at the top of his lungs, "Hey, Dad, look at that old dead guy over there. Is he sleeping or something?" Needless to say, the group looked up astonished, without the usual look of approval customarily given to precocious four-year-old boys.

Children are trying to come to terms with the life cycle in the games they play and in the rhymes they love to repeat. The well-known game "Ring Around the Rosey," which is played in most of the Anglicized world, ends with the foreboding "Ashes, ashes, we all fall down!" I have come to understand (though I cannot trace the source) that this game had its origin during the European bubonic plague and was apparently a means for young children to work out apprehensions about being striken with the deadly disease. The ever-favorite nursery rhyme "Humpty Dumpty" ends with the somber line, "All the king's horses and all the king's men couldn't put Humpty together again." Again, this little rhyme, which has entertained very young children, has to do with the fragility of life.

Many parents who read my interpretation of these "innocent" little ditties will take offense at the meaning I suggest. They probably take more offense than would the young children to whom such rhymes are read, if the children were cognizant of their "real meaning." Our culture begins to place very soft lenses over the child's more direct conception of life and death very early. Yalom points out that the young child's candor seems to threaten the defenses of the adult. As a result, adults begin to impose rather extreme fantasies about the phenomenon of death very early on. G. Rochlin (1967) puts it succinctly: "What is remarkable is not that children arrive at adult views of the cessation of life, but rather how tenaciously throughout life adults hold to the child's beliefs and how readily they revert to them" (p. 63). Rochlin is saying that adults provide children with their own childhood defenses against the fear of death and that the myths are especially compelling.

Yalom elaborates on this viewpoint and actually provides us with some names for the basic defenses against death fears. The *personal uniqueness* fantasy is learned early on and takes a highly individualized form. Many of my patients have recalled this feeling of specialness that protects them from everyone else's vulnerability. It would appear that our fascination with "superheroes" bears testimony to this fantasy. Superman, for example, has a few close calls with death when his one weakness is discovered. Many adults stricken with near-fatal illnesses such as heart attacks talk as if their sense of personal uniqueness is shattered. Other patients simply remember maintaining this "specialness" fantasy well into adult life and could understand making certain poor life choices because of the premise.

Parents, even those with equivocal religious feelings, quickly introduce religious conceptions of death to allay children's apprehensions. Yalom refers to the "ultimate rescuer" fantasy in which most individuals see divine intervention in the everyday world. I, personally, am not comfortable reducing our many theological convictions to psychological defenses. It is important to understand, however, that there are tendencies to anthropomorphize our God's motivations when it comes to assuaging the fears of our children. Thus, children are often told things like "God watches over children," or "Little children can't die." While there are contradictions to these beliefs that children hear about or see on television news, they tend to combine the personal uniqueness idea with religious faith to fend off notions that they could be in danger. Idyllic images of heaven are also introduced in early childhood to help children deal with the images of lost adults or pets and perhaps to extrapolate to themselves privately when overcome with reservations about other beliefs.

By the time children have passed into childhood, they have read a fair number of books and seen a great deal of television. They have learned the term "happily ever after" from whatever fairy tales have filtered into contemporary life and have seen countless cartoons. Cartoons deal with fears of death and mutilation in a rather direct way. Both villains and heroes in cartoons are frequently flattened, stretched, dissected or dismembered in some way. Very soon, as if by magic, the character is restored to natural form with no change in appearance or vigor. The continued resurrection of animated heroes such as Wile E. Coyote or Popeye, juxtaposed with the happily-ever-after themes in children's literature, offers a solution to death fears that children find appealing. These art forms taunt death with the unstated belief that life is indestructible. The sheer reversibility of death and injury which we see in the cartoon is modified for the school-aged child in the "near misses" of favorite heroes. The cowboys of a previous generation have given way to such heroes as Indiana Jones (Harrison Ford in *Raiders of the Lost Ark*) who has an only slightly more realistic interaction with the finality of death.

It should be pretty clear from children's rhymes, cartoons, movies and books that death is a focal concern that is handled in a veiled, protective fashion. Some children, depending on the intensity of their fears and the "answers" they get to their questions, will adopt the provided solutions more totally than others. No matter how much they are shielded from adult anxieties about the life cycle, they will be exposed to experiences that strain their defenses. They continue to witness the death of loved ones, they see plants die and begin to understand that when you step on a bug, it remains motionless. They also encounter places like children's hospitals or hear of friends' siblings who are born with life-threatening physical conditions or of a child in the neighborhood who is hit by a car and killed.

Thus, death for children, as for adults, remains a constant source of disquietude. Our capacity and need to extend ourselves into the distant future is always set against our ability to include death as part of life. If Yalom is correct and the methods we provide our children do not facilitate handling concerns of death and dying, then our children grow to be adults for whom the future is foreboding. If there aren't appropriate and effective psychological resources to include the end of life in the equation of existence, then the whole equation is thrown off. If we are frightened of a certain place, such as a high mountaintop, we will not be able to experience the joy of climbing the mountain or the view from the top. Similarly, if the future is associated with dread, we will struggle as it unfolds and will do little to extend ourselves forward.

This is a good point to establish that everyone will, indeed, have some measure of trouble with their experience of life unfolding. It is very much like talking about going to the dentist. Almost no one looks forward to this experience, but some do it gracefully while others totally avoid it. It is unlikely that anyone approaches the "dental chair" without apprehension. Similarly, the perception of time's passage will generate a full range of reactions. The question for the moment is: What constitutes a wholesome reaction?

There are individuals who manage to move forward into their lives in a fluid, purposeful way. There seem to be as many, however, who are ambivalent and defensive. Realistically speaking, however, we all think about time every day, all day. We start the day with a rush to meet schedules. Most people I know carry a wide assortment of calendars, reminders, organizers and planners, all of which promise to help one deal with life on a daily, weekly, monthly and annual basis. While some simply make notations on their calendars, others are considering more the complex relationships between what they are doing in the short run and how it affects longer-range behavior.

Even without the assistance of diaries, people of all ages and all walks of life think about the "time of their lives" or how to use the ultimate resource of life: time. Children think about when school will be finished or the presents they will get on birthdays or holidays. Teenagers are in a decided hurry to reach certain milestones that give them access to certain age-based opportunities. We all recall and see younger relations eagerly awaiting the chance to partake of driving, employment, legal alcohol consumption and sexual expression. Adolescents begin to think about their future in high school as they take standardized tests and consider higher eduction and career possibilities. We see many young people who are damaged by sociocultural and family factors already struggling with planning. Much of the trouble associated with teenagers is a direct product of disturbances in their ability to feel certain about the relationship between current and future life. Children who have come to be termed "disadvantaged" live in a vicious cycle of present-centered life not because they do not *have* a future perspective, but rather because they have learned *not* to consider the future.

Even when one feels good about the last year and about the direction one is pointed in, there is still a sense of mourning. Each opportunity we use to mark off the time of our life, we feel that we have lost our most fundamental life asset: time. We do not simply mourn what we have not achieved. There is a sense in which we even mourn what we have accomplished. This begins early in life. I recently attended my daughter's graduation from middle to upper school. Parents behaved much as people did at the New Year's Eve party. They smiled with pride and became teary with the sense that their daughters were forever beyond a certain stage. Parents, however, were not alone in their mixed emotions. The girls were excited about the new adventures before them. They were embarking on a journey that would take them to the beachhead of adulthood. However, they, too, showed signs of mourning. While not terribly articulate, they said things that showed that an aspect of their life had been lost forever. They also expressed fear about the unknown circumstances of their next school experience. Can I handle the pressures of upper school? Will my teachers be decent? What will I be like when I'm seventeen years old?

We expect the normal fourteen-year-old to brush aside the grief and get lost in the pleasures of summer and the anticipation of middle and late adolescence. Often this happens, as life for the fourteen-year-old stretches out with few boundaries and great possibilities. Teenagers also have the ability to be drawn deeply into their current life. Some, however, do not manage to get beyond the terror of the past or the future. We have become more aware of a state of mind in our children that resembles the feelings of an older depressed person. "Hopelessness" has become a term associated with a growing proportion of teens as well as younger children. For the first time in our history we have begun to consider the possibility that preteen children as well as teenagers may be suicidal, directly and indirectly. While it has been traditionally considered unlikely for children to feel or act suicidal, that perception is changing, apparently, as the "love/hate" relationship with time has shifted.

By adulthood, the time-based decisions and imagery of one's life intensify. Career planning, family planning, financial planning and the achieving of life goals become the order of the day. As life proceeds, the decisions and goals become more individualized as we find it necessary to deal with specific physical, psychological and cultural conditions. Some have to cope with great native talent with or without opportunities for expressing their gifts. Others find themselves with great ambitions but without the resources or abilities to achieve their goals. Still others find themselves in extraordinary situations such as war or economic crisis, or with inherited or acquired physical handicaps.

As we leave childhood and pass through the various stages of early adulthood, the concern about time becomes deeper. The sense of "infinite" time gives way to a sense of "finite" time. No matter how one tries, whether using normal patterns of avoidance or the more precarious psychological mechanisms that distort reality, the indicators are too strong not to see. Even if we try to totally shut out the signs that we are "using up" our lives, the evidence is not very far from view. From the teenage years on, when things like skin blemishes, body hair, changing facial structure and new biological urges are perceived, life becomes a process of reacting to physical, biological and psychological changes in ourselves. When middle adulthood is reached, as one of my patients remarked, "Every day is an adventure in bodily changes." Sleep patterns, eating patterns, hair color and sexual drive all undergo transformation. One senses that certain achievements will not be possible. I recall a thirty-nine-year-old male patient who said he woke up depressed one morning, realizing that he would never be able to play major league baseball at his age. It is not that he was actively pursuing a sports career, but that he suddenly felt a shift in the "possibilities" of his life.

As one approaches later stages of adulthood, the concerns become more dramatic. Serious health problems begin to develop. In a way, one gets a sense by the time one approaches fifty of what a likely cause of death might be. As one sees relatives become ill and die, one's genetic legacy is unveiled. Often grandparents, parents and even siblings are dead by the time one reaches this age. In addition to the weight of biological consciousness, other concerns begin to emerge during this period. Job security, economic security, geographical preferences and future possibilities all assault one's psyche with constant reinforcement from the environment. Friends die premature deaths, acquaintances are summarily dismissed from long-held positions and comments are made by teenagers who refer to that "old person" who turns out to be you!

It should be clear, then, that from the beginning to the end of the life cycle, we are dealing with the passage of time. The infant has little or no sense of the past as he deals with present needs and begins to develop a primitive orientation to the future. Very early in childhood, however, temporality begins to be a factor, as anticipation and memory begin to work in concert to produce the temporal dimension of experience. By the time adolescence approaches, great differences begin to appear in the way individuals are oriented to the past, present and future.

It is important to understand that temporal organization is a complex and dynamic process. Depending on what has happened today and what we expect to occur next month, we will think about time in very different ways. One day the future is perfectly clear, only to be totally obscured a day later. At a given time in one's life, one's childhood may seem very bleak. Yet a new perspective or an unexpected success can alter the meaning we give to the past. Despite the fluidity of our time experience, research has indicated that by late adolescence, we begin to demonstrate a nuclear temporal pattern that is somewhat stable. In other words, people begin to have a temporal perspective that becomes part of their personality structure.

As I will show in subsequent chapters, this characteristic way of handling time functions for many of us. However, for others, temporal "traits" become part of disturbed ways of handling their experience and lead to major problems.

Using the parameters associated with the time line (RTL), I will look at some psychological problems that seem endemic to our society. I will include an analysis of typical clinical problems such as depression and substance abuse. However, I will also try to apply some of our temporal concepts to areas that have been less thoroughly explored by the clinical sciences. I will be looking at workaholism, aging, and recently evolved groups we generally call "yuppies." All these individuals have a common problem. They have difficulties with time.

III

TIME ON MY HANDS

Depression has been called the "common cold" of psychological problems in the United States. According to the American Psychiatric Association (1988), it is estimated that approximately 19 million "diagnosable" cases will be recorded in a given year. In addition, it has been estimated that about ten persons in a hundred, or more than 25 million Americans, are likely to experience a depressive episode in their lifetime (Brown, 1974). These statistics are particularly dramatic when you consider that we are speaking about "diagnosable" depression, which has some fairly severe accompanying symptoms. According to the *Diagnostic and Statistical Manual* of the American Psychiatric Association (*DSM-III*), at least four of the following complaints must be present for a major depression to be diagnosed. The individual must have distressed mood, sleep or appetite disturbance, loss of energy, physical retardation or agitation, loss of interest, self-reproach, concentration difficulties or thoughts of death and suicide for at least two weeks. A cluster of these psychological complaints certainly points to someone with a serious break in the continuity of typical functioning. The problem is so pervasive that it has been estimated that the cost of treatment for depressed individuals is more than 2 billion dollars per year in the United States (Stoudemire et al., 1986).

Obviously, many more individuals experience what we might refer to as a lesser or minor depression. Almost everyone who decides to seek professional help is suffering from some degree of depression. While the dramatic symptoms of major depression may not be present, the individual nevertheless feels sad, unenthusiastic, unenergetic and pessimistic. Very often, despite a life that appears full or adequate, the individual perceives things to be "gray" with little chance of revision. Jerome Frank, in his classic book *Persuasion and Healing* (1961), noted that the common denominator among those who enter psychological treatment is their sense of "demoralization." Frank points out that when an individual seeks the services of a therapist, he has acknowledged that he cannot by himself come to terms with the business of living. This feeling of not being "the master of oneself" for Frank is suggestive of depression.

Feelings of sadness and pessimism occur in most individuals' lives in some intermittent way. Most people, on some days, will wake up without their usual level of energy and interest in their everyday affairs. On these days, they dislike work or colleagues or spouses or school. On these days, most individuals tell themselves that they're "a bit under the weather," or that their "battery needs recharging," or that they "have the blues." These common expressions are a way of saying that periodic depressive feelings are part of life and that they come and go. These low states often trigger different approaches to uplifting the spirit, which range from sleeping in, to eating more, to exercising and, in some cases, turning to drugs or alcohol. Women are more aware than men of mood changing fairly regularly as a function of monthly hormonal variability. It is not that men do not experience mood variability but, rather, that they are less apt to expect such regular changes in outlook.

This "normal" occurrence of depressed mood seems universal and has been documented by psychiatrists as existing in all societies. Each society, like each individual, copes with this intermittent shift in mood in different ways. In a highly religious culture, for example, a sad individual might turn to familiar prayer or ritual to break through the heaviness of a depressed period. The use of mood-altering substances, especially alcohol, is prevalent in every society. However, the incidence of alcohol abuse is particularly high in industrialized cultures that have a substantial rate of depression. Europe, along with five countries that have been influenced by European cultures (Argentina, Canada, Chile, Japan and the United States), consume 80 percent of the world's alcohol, despite making up only 20 percent of the world's population (Barry, 1982). One explanation for the fact that women in the United States are twice as likely as men to be diagnosed as depressed is that men drink more heavily and may "mask" the symptoms of depression (Page, 1975).

As I indicated in earlier chapters, almost immediately on beginning my work with depressed patients, I noticed that there were two prevalent experiences they reported concerning time.

The first was a sense that time moved too slowly or that there was too much time to be filled. This sense of disturbed rhythm seemed to produce an accompanying fear that "relief would come only when the day was over." I commonly heard these patients say that the first thought they had on awakening was that they couldn't wait for the day to end so they could go back to bed. In addition to the rhythm problem, I discovered that these depressed individuals were almost exclusively oriented toward the past. They appeared to be totally fixed on what had happened as if there were a profound sense of unfinished business. They resisted any attempts to focus on the present and future.

With respect to the Rappaport Time Line (RTL), I have repeatedly found that depressed patients show two consistent patterns. First, they produce fewer life experiences than other individuals. Second, there is pronounced imbalance, with a dramatic loading of experiences in the past. The more depression is evident, the more I have seen the present and future unrepresented in the spatial representation of temporal experience.

Several years ago I treated a forty-four-year-old married man, with two teenage children, who came to see me at his wife's urging. Though unsure about seeing a psychologist, Ed said that his wife was adamant that he seek help. According to her, he conveyed, he had become solemn, moody, lazy and unresponsive. He was a fairly well-paid engineer/designer who had been given a sizable severance package when his company was bought by a European corporation. He was told that they were "going in another direction" and did not need his skills any longer. At first, he said, he was thrilled, as he had become increasingly tired of his job and dreaded being there anyway. When they offered a year's salary plus the benefit of outplacement counseling, he said he was delighted and felt "lucky."

Shortly after he began his outplacement work, however, he began to "lose interest" in the task of repositioning himself in the workplace. He began to sleep later and became less particular about his appearance. His wife complained that he had become "isolated," unresponsive to her and the children and very sloppy at home. She also said that he was talking continually about "the good old days." He started to watch television incessantly, lost interest in his friends and began to gain a great deal of weight. He said that what convinced him to see me was a suicidal feeling that had come out of nowhere. He said he began to think about dying often and, at times, actually became fascinated by thinking of his funeral arrangements. On one occasion, while he was shaving, he cut himself with his safety razor and, on seeing the blood drip into his sink, became panicky and ran out of the room.

In our first session, Ed was very suspicious, looking at me intermittently as if he didn't want me to know something. He also acted skeptical about the value of seeing a psychologist, and tended to answer in short, direct phrases. He maintained this bearing until near the end of our session. When I suggested that he seemed to have a solid grasp of his problems and that he might *not* need my help, he began to tell me about his concern about death, and his eyes filled up quickly. He tried to suppress his tears and I did little to let him know I was aware of his imminent sobbing. In short, Ed was quite depressed.

If you look at Ed's RTL on the following pages, you will note that he included only six life milestones (not counting death, which is not dated). Only one notation was in the future. This is a very sparse time line indicating a constriction of experience and an inability to extend himself forward. Apparently, when Ed thinks of the future, death plays an indefinite but prominent role, since he had experienced some suicidal feelings. The other noteworthy aspect of this line has to do with the "unidimensional" nature of his experiences. Apart from his marriage when he was twenty-five, the experiences are related to his work life. This singularity revolves around the "negative historical" event, in this case his job.

Ed's experience with psychotherapy was neither easy nor continuous. He stayed in treatment for about six months which concluded when he began a new job of marginal interest. When he found he was be-

18		24	25
army		got degree	married

Time line of depressed forty-four-year-old male engineer

coming increasingly depressed again, he resumed treatment. This time he worked harder and made greater strides in overcoming his depression. Though I would have preferred him to continue his therapy, he left after one year. Another client who is a friend of Ed's has let me know that Ed is, for the most part, doing much better.

Ed's temporal experience is not foreign to the mental health professions. There have even been a few definitive studies that demonstrate how depressed patients exhibit temporal problems. In a typical study of this type, Wyrick and Wyrick (1977) had hospitalized patients write stories and complete standardized sentences. They found that these depressed patients referred almost exclusively to past events, while "normal" control subjects' temporal referents were distributed among past, present and future. In addition, they discovered that their patients had trouble estimating the passage of time. They found that when their patients were placed in a room without a clock for thirty minutes, they reported that about forty minutes had gone by. In other words, time seemed to be passing too slowly. (This is consistent with my clinical observations.)

The distortions of time experience that characterize depression are well known to the experienced diagnostician. Time disorientation, however, has historically been treated as simply another symptom of a depressed state rather than as being the center of the disturbance. It is fascinating to note that while these temporal symptoms are omnipresent, they do not really appear in the *DSM-III*, the "bible" of American psychiatry. This "oversight" is just another example of how our theoretical formulations of human experience do not fully correspond to the nature of human experience. Typically, it has been reasoned that the patient cannot relate to the future *because* he is depressed.

One of the earliest attempts to explain depression was made by Freud in his classical paper "Mourning and Melancholia," in which he attempted to explain two prevalent features of depression: bereavement

39		[43	o	45]	
job contract		lost job	NOW	new job	death

and self-recrimination. Freud noted that depressed patients acted like people who were grieving over lost loved ones:

> In grief the world becomes poor and empty; in melancholia it is the ego itself. The patient represents his ego to us as worthless, incapable of any effort and morally despicable; he reproaches himself, vilifies himself and expects to be cast out and chastised. He abases himself before everyone and commiserates with his own relatives for being connected with someone so unworthy. He does not realize that any change has taken place in him but extends his self criticism back over the past and declares that he was never any better. (Freud, 1956, p. 155)

While this quotation from Freud's seminal paper is a bit arcane, it has served as a major point of departure for modern psychiatry's view of the depressed patient. Freud contended that the depressed individual was responding to the unconscious memory of a lost love object from early childhood. Depressives, according to Freud, feel the same mixture of emotions as the mourner: vulnerability, despair, worthlessness and anger. The anger, through a complex sequence of psychoanalytic processes, is seen as eventually directed inward with the individuals becoming oriented toward their past, blaming themselves for vague transgressions.

The concept of anger turned inward became the essential feature for the Freudian school. The therapeutic task was to direct the patient's consciousness to the *distant past* so this anger could be redirected away from the self. Later, however, in the 1950s, modern analytical theorists such as Edward Bibring (1961) began to shift the focus of depression from unexpressed anger to learned helplessness. Ironically, it was Bibring's observation that paved the way for behavioral psychology's adaptation of the term "learned helplessness."

Martin Seligman (1975) developed the concept of learned helplessness in the 1970s based on his work with dogs. He noted that dogs who were given electrical shocks and prevented from escaping would behave "helplessly" in other shock situations in which they could escape. Like Seligman's concept, Aaron Beck's "cognitive" theory of depression is based on the premise that individuals who are depressed believe they will suffer no matter what happens. Beck's theory is based on the depressed person's "faulty logic" which leads them to conclude that they are worthless, unlovable or incompetent. In describing the depressed person's reaction to a painful past, Beck states: "These traumatic experiences predispose the person to overreact to analogous conditions in later life. He has a tendency to make extreme, absolute judgements when such situations occur" (1976, p. 107).

Beck's and Seligman's "cognitive behavioral" view of depression has become the mainstream in contemporay psychology. Like the learning theories of human behavior that have dominated psychology, this approach is appealing in that it reduces the complex omnipresent phenomenon of depression to manageable terms. From the standpoint of causation, it suggests that the search for precipitating factors lies in identifying the negative stimuli in this new version of the old $S \rightarrow R$ equation. In addition, the treatment has an equal appeal in its "common sense." When we are confronted with a person who feels worthless, unlovable, incompetent and hopeless about his life, we tend to try to talk him out of these beliefs. We encourage, support and try to persuade him that he is *not* to blame for what has happened and can make future events more positive by approaching them differently. This cognitive approach has offered a technology and justification for doing the obvious: talking depressed people out of their negative system of cognition.

My cynicism about the new cognitive behavioral therapies is based on two factors. First, it always seemed somewhat preposterous that psychological debate for many years centered on whether the science of man could accommodate the thinking and feeling faculties at all. In the heyday of Skinner's behaviorism, it was argued that the subjective aspects of behavior (thinking and feeling) were not observable and should not be included in the formulae of prediction. Only now, with the advent of these new approaches to depression, are we finally and somewhat belatedly arriving at this new intersection when we accept that beliefs can affect mood. It has been astounding to note how the behavioral school of psychology has embraced this new perspective. Journals have been dedicated to this formulation, and a whole generation of psychologists currently in training are being educated as "cognitive behaviorists." When I review the personal statements of aspiring candidates to doctoral training, it is clear that they think that we regard their acceptance of this new model as a basis for accepting them.

Second, there are some important substantive problems. Just as Freud's approach to depression implied an early trauma, so do the "cognitive" theorists suggest that we learn to become depressed from upsetting events. While some individuals clearly become depressed in response to problems such as divorce, death, job loss and natural calamities, there are also individuals who seem to be depressed without a clear precipitating cause. Moreover, there are those who drift into this common cold on the heels of success. This issue of whether depression can be traced to a particular event in someone's past has been connected to the question of whether there is a biological basis for certain conditions. Up to about ten years ago, the mental health professions distinguished between "psychotic" and "neurotic" depression along two lines. Psychotic depression was thought to be obviously more severe and without clear cause. Neurotic depression (the common cold) was considered less severe, shorter in duration and connected to particular circumstances.

Current diagnostic practices distinguish between "major" and "minor" depressions in terms of the severity of the person's symptoms. The other dimension, however, has to do with the cause of the depression. The term "endogenous" depression has been used for some time to explain the depressive episode with little connection to life events. An endogenous depression is said to be present when the depression seems to "come out of nowhere" with a certain pattern of regularity. On occasion an individual of this type is seen to have what has been termed a "bipolar" disorder, when mania is also cyclically present. Because the endogenous disorder is not easily connected to trauma, it has been inferred that it is best explained in terms of aberrant biochemical processes. It is now widely accepted, particularly in psychiatric circles, that most major depression is caused by a disturbance in brain chemistry. Serotonin, a neurotransmitter in the brain, is thought to be present in insufficient levels in cases of nonreactive (endogenous) depression. It follows, from this perspective, that with neurotransmission blocked, mood and related behavior will be considerably slowed.

The rise of drug treatment for depression has also lent support to the biochemical explanation for depression. In the last fifteen years there has been a tremendous rise in the use of such drugs as lithium carbonate, the "tricyclics" (imipramine, amitriptyline, protriptyline), and the "monoamine oxidase inhibitors" (phenelzine and tranylcypromine). Without going too far into the chemical actions of these drugs, it can safely be said that they alter the levels of serotonin and other neurotransmitters, with subsequent changes in mood. Lithium is thought to lower serotonin levels and is thus used in cases of mania. The other two classes of drugs are routinely prescribed by psychiatrists for major depression.

The relative success of these drugs has sparked debate about both the causes and treatment of depression. The biochemical camp has argued that if the drugs are effective, it must mean that brain chemistry is involved and that depression should be treated as a medical illness. The medical establishment has been waging a major campaign of late that suggests that depressed individuals should primarily seek the help of physicians, specifically psychiatrists. This much-publicized viewpoint has found its way both to medical journals and to newspapers' Sunday magazines. The idea that mood disturbances should be the exclusive domain of medicine is worrisome. First, it has that distinct feeling of "guildsmanship" that Perry London (1964) discussed in the 1960s. It would appear that American psychiatry has become more protective of its "turf" as other professionals, notably psychologists, have made strong inroads in the treatment of mental disorders. That psychologists have achieved parity with respect to insurance reimbursement has certainly created an atmosphere of greater competition.

Besides professional rivalry, there are other serious problems with the psychopharmaceutical approach to depression. The most obvious problem is that these powerful medicines have serious side effects. One has only to examine the *Physicians' Desk Reference* to become aware of the many risks of prolonged drug use. A thirty-five-year-old female was recently referred to me for a long history of depression. Soon after I began to see her, I discovered that a physician who was not a psychiatrist had been prescribing lithium for her for over five years. Some time after therapy began, she began to develop weight problems and a serious swelling in her neck. An examination by a psychiatrist with whom I collaborate indicated that extended lithium use had caused pronounced thyroid difficulties, which required independent treatment.

Another major problem with the biochemical approach to depression, and perhaps to all disorders, is the fallacy of causation. While there are certainly profound depressions that require the assistance of chemotherapy, most depressions are inevitably connected to the vagaries of being human and living in a complex world. It seems capricious and downright dangerous to medicate on the assumption that all depressed moods stem from a chemical deficiency. That abnormal levels of substances like neurotransmitters are found in depressed patients does not necessarily imply a cause-and-effect relationship exists. It is equally plausible that psychological experience alters biochemical states. In a very important article in *Science*, J. D. Barchos and his associates state:

It may well be that effects of early experience on subsequent behavior—an important idea in behavioral sciences—might be reflected in biochemical changes that alter communication patterns between neuronal units later in life.... In susceptible individuals certain psychological states may lead to changes in neuroregulatory activity. (1978, pp. 968–969)

A good example of how mind and body interact to produce surprising results might be the case of a woman who erroneously believes that her husband is having an affair. The assumption and the network of apparent data that support it make this individual very anxious and depressed. The panic that ensues most certainly causes physiological changes, which may even produce symptoms like colitis, backache or skin rashes. Yet it would certainly be fallacious to presume that these symptoms were the cause of the anxiety and depression.

If Ed, our case illustration, had seen a psychiatrist when his depression became pronounced, there is a strong chance he would have received medication. Even though his depression was a "reactive" type, the severity of his mood might have concerned his psychiatrist enough to prescribe an antidepressant. In this case, Ed would deal with neither his past nor his future. The medication would attempt to "elevate" his mood in the present so that he could resume his normal functioning as soon as possible.

Since psychotherapy is often suggested in conjunction with chemotherapy, Ed would undoubtedly have become involved with psychoanalytic or behavioral treatment. In psychoanalysis, he would have explored his past and in behavioral therapy he would have attempted to reshape his negative self-image in the present. In both cases, it would be assumed that he could not relate to the future *because* he was depressed.

Eugene Minkowski (1970), in his profound treatise on temporality and depression, suggested the opposite. "Could we not, on the contrary, suppose the basic disorder is the distorted attitude toward the future" (p. 127). Minkowski was suggesting that depression needs to be understood as a *manifestation* of a disturbance in temporality rather than the other way around. His definition of depression centers on the "phenomenology" of time experience. The future and its possibilities are for Minkowski and a host of other existential theoreticians the force that energizes us and carries us forward in our lives.

Our very sense of self, according to this view, is connected to the creation of our personal future. Minkowski refers to this flow toward the future as the "élan vitale," which "creates a future before us. . . . In life everything that has a direction in time has *élan*, pushes forward, progresses toward a future. . . . I tend spontaneously with all my power, with all my being toward a future" (1970, p. 38).

Minkowski's élan vitale is a difficult concept to describe, as it is both abstract and concrete. On the abstract level, it is the unifying force that energizes us, moves us forward and gives life a sense of coherence. On the concrete level, it represents a feeling of momentum of internal force that flows forward.

In the case of depression, he argues that time is no longer experienced as "propulsive energy." The stream of time flows back as if a dam had been erected. Attention flows backward and the present becomes stagnant and devoid of meaning. The sadness, apathy and lack of energy that we see in depression are symptoms that evolve when the person feels that the future holds no possibilities. Minkowski elaborates on how a serious depression differs from the normal ebb and flow of mood: "With most of us these are only transient episodes. Life forces, our personal impetus lift us and carry us over such a parade of miserable days toward a future which reopens its doors widely to us" (1970, p. 133).

Thus, depression is part of being human. All of us experience a loss of momentum from time to time and begin to fret that we won't get it back. Minkowski eloquently points out that for the depressed person, the gateway to the future remains blocked. Of course, a critical question is what happens that causes the future (our life) to become blocked. I have already reviewed mainstream psychology's approach to this complex question. In gross terms, our preoccupation with causality has guided our attention to the ever-present antecedent conditions. Usually this has meant the search for the historical trauma or the abnormal blood index.

Psychology, as a social science, continues to ignore major ideas that emerge from other fields of inquiry. For at least fifty years, major theoreticians have been addressing the relationship between personal memory and current behavior. Alfred Adler, a disciple of Freud, pointed out that memory was:

> a creative process. That we remember what has significance for our "style of life" and that the whole form of memory is therefore a mirror of the individual's style of life. What an individual seeks *to become* determines what he remembers of his *has been*. In this sense, the future determines the past. (May et al., 1958, p. 69)

The last sentence of Rollo May's quotation from Adler is extremely profound, in that it directly attacks the naive determinism that has plagued psychology's view of behavior in general, and depression in particular. May integrates the thinking of the existential writers of the last one hundred years in order to make the continually forgotten point that the past as we remember it is in constant flux.

According to May, the problem for the depressed patient is not that historical trauma caused him to be sad. Rather it is the feeling of being controlled by the past. As May puts it, "The deterministic events of the past take their significance from the present and the future" (p. 69). When Minkowski's "doors to the future" close or do not easily open, the depressed patient looks backward and imposes the current mood on past events. As one gets a greater sense of vitality or élan vitale, the past seems less important and, in fact, seems less negative. May points out that this viewpoint attempts to contradict the notion that we are automatically shaped by our past. He summarizes the existential view on this point.

> The existential analysts take history very seriously, but they protest against any tendency to evade the immediate anxiety, creating issues in the present by taking refuge behind the determinism of the past. They are against the doctrines that historical forces carry the individual along automatically, whether these doctrines take the form of religious beliefs of predestination or providence, the deteriorated Marxist doctrine of historical materialism, the various psychological doctrines of determinism.

May's idea of "taking refuge" in the past is a very accurate depiction of what the treatment of depression often becomes. The patient has a strong yearning to delve into the past. Since most psychotherapists essentially see the task in a similar way, it is not uncommon to spend years recalling and interpreting past events. The thrust of psychoanalytical treatment, in fact, is to help the patient open the past as a key to feeling better in the present and the future. The temporal sequence I am presenting is quite different. *It is the future that holds the key to the past.* To validate this point we need only examine the changes in perceptions of the past over the course of one's treatment or, in fact, one's life. At one moment one may perceive early experiences as impoverishing. One may live with a sense of having been cheated by not being privileged enough or even by being "born into the wrong family." As one's life evolves, however, and optimism is generated by the actions one takes, the *same* past takes on a new coloration. It may be that hardships are now seen as strengthening rather than depleting and one's "humble origin" may be seen as producing a "special depth of character."

The psychoanalytic schools of thought developed the concept of resistance to explain the difficulty patients had in remembering relevant historical material. Treatment of problems such as depression would necessarily be extended, as unconscious processes subvert the primary goal, which is to make the unconscious conscious. I have found the phenomenon of resistance to be a very real deterrent to achieving the obvious goal of psychotherapy. However, I have found that depressed patients in particular, rather than resisting the past, actually exhibit resistance toward the future. I had a session with a chronically depressed but functioning woman who didn't really "know what to talk about" that day. She spoke of feeling "down" and was prodding me to do more than I had been doing to make her "feel better." She was quite comfortable when we spoke about the origin of her mood. When I began to connect her current despondent state to the absence of future images, there was a definite shift in the tone of the session. She became increasingly suspicious and began to display signs of withdrawal and anger. I failed to heed the techniques of my mentors concerning the tried and true techniques for handling resistance. Generally, we have found that it is of little value to confront resistance head on. It is better to "interpret it" by acknowledging that there are reasons to avoid the material or feeling at hand.

Later that night I got an emergency call from the same patient. She was "angry" and "distrustful" and threatened to terminate therapy. She claimed to be dismayed by my insensitivity and "unwillingness to deal with her agenda." I was, she said, "monopolizing therapy with old irrelevant issues." Often, when a therapist hits an "emotional area" the patient overreacts and goes to great lengths to steer away from the source of pain. I temporarily retreated from moving so rapidly into the future, and we were able to keep working. The continuous dialogue inherent in psychotherapy provides ample opportunities to reapply seminal themes.

In this case, I had raised this woman's awareness to the major source of her anxiety and depression. The future for this woman was experienced as simply happening. She fit a category of people who have the least futurity in the time line and are very past-focused. They tend to be anxious and depressed and to live their lives as if everything were "accidental." May has pointed out that such an individual may actually hide in the past and perpetuate the sense of despair. The philosopher Friedrich Nietzsche made an observation that is very relevant to the way out of this condition: "Man's task is simple: he should cease letting his 'existence' be a 'thoughtless accident.' Happiness is not the absence of pain, but the most alive feeling of power, and joy is a 'plus feeling of power' " (Kaufman, 1950, p. 239).

What Nietzsche did not directly discuss is that the urge to live one's life recklessly, without reference to goals, is attractive to certain individuals and tantamount to depression. These patients have a deep affinity for the past and live as if they were looking "over their shoulder." Considering the preeminent epistemology of psychology, it is very easy for the historically minded therapist to slip into the endless task of interpreting the elusive past. Ironically, when most nontherapists are faced with a depressed friend or relative, they intuitively know that it is the present and future that is blocked. The depressed person is reminded that "there is a silver lining in every cloud" and "tomorrow is another day." There is the straightforward recognition that the person who is "down in the dumps" needs to be reminded of the possibilities in life. This is especially true when confronted with the frightening possibility of a suicide from despair. Over a period of years I have had the opportunity to speak to volunteers and staff members of hot lines that were devised to diffuse acute depressions. When a telephone worker has "one crack" at someone who seems despondent, it is always advisable to steer the person away from what might have been terrible events to the prospects of a better future. The best hot line workers I have supervised, however, are those who are not burdened by too many theories. It is best when they do "what comes naturally" as they try to get the person to not accept the blame for what has happened in his life. It is then that he realizes that he can achieve a measure of control over the future.

A vexing problem is that our mental health professions have had trouble incorporating the temporal component of depression. Psychology, as Gordon Allport (1955) has pointed out, is more concerned with the antecedents of behavior than the person who is trying to figure out his future. While I suspect, based on observations derived from training tapes, that therapists *try* to lead their clients into the future, it is not done systematically or consistently. One reason for the absence of a future-based therapy has to do with the mutual anxiety that is provoked by extending forward. Psychotherapists are profoundly affected by the content and emotions aroused during treatment. Freud devoted a major portion of his theory to what he termed countertransference, which focuses on the emotional life of the analyst as he responds to the complex emotional behavior of the client.

As Minkowski has pointed out, our relationship to the future even in the "normal state" is delicate. We develop hopes and dreams that we try to cement by achieving goals. In order to realize our life plans, we must extend ourselves into the near and distant future with a sense of possibility. However, as all the existential theorists note, the future is a zone of distinct uncertainty. As we become immersed in the "consciousness of adulthood" and begin assuming responsibility, our culture points to the risks of calamity. A thirty-year-old female patient who had recently become pregnant was expressing poignant anxiety in a session. She was alarmed that she was going to give birth and neither she nor her husband had disability or life insurance. Suddenly they were fretting about becoming disabled or dying prematurely. All of us, from about age two on, begin to have intermittent awareness that the future could hold some terrifying surprises.

Sometimes it is difficult to know where or how to get an imaginary taste of the unspecified future. A newspaper story, a television show or the meanderings of our own minds can produce futurity for better or worse. A fifty-nine-year-old patient who was referred to me said that his depression seemed to come out of nowhere. One day he was cleaning out his garage and felt terrific for having gotten to a long-overdue project. The same night he began to have nightmares, he said, which were all about dreadful things happening to him. The next day he began to feel anxious and lose his robust level of energy for his work and family. When he entered therapy, a psychiatrist had concluded that this depression was the "endogenous" type, since there was no obvious precipitating cause. The patient, however, rejected the use of anti-depressant drugs. Over several months of treatment he began to see that cleaning the garage had triggered some strong reminders that someday he and his wife would have to face selling the house and making retirement decisions. He had never really thought of "running out of time" and began to see that he was terrified at the thought of "winding down" his life. After six months of psychotherapy that focused on the future, his depression lifted. The problem of coming to terms with a dramatic life change was not solved. Rather, he developed the capacity for relating to a component of life that had been "tele-pressed" or avoided.

Facing the long-range future with both its possibilities and the certainty that life will end in some uncertain way produces many responses. One of our fundamental questions is how much to care about something we will no longer have. In some sense, it's like selling our house and land after we decide to move. Shall we leave the house in good order, selling it to individuals who will cherish it the way we did? Or should we maximize our financial gain and sell to developers who will exploit the land without concern for the integrity of the community? This example is very much like life itself. As we think about life ending, we can be propelled into action with a sense of responsibility to what Thomas Cottle (Cottle and Klineberg, 1974) called the "after me." On the other hand, knowing that we are "moving out" of life can generate indifference about life beyond our own needs. Another good example is when and how people confront the business of their wills and estates. Some people, accepting life's contingencies, make out wills soon after having children. Others refuse to deal with death, make few preparations for it and leave their offspring in confusion and conflict over their inheritance. I have seen many families splinter over ambiguous instructions following the death of loved ones.

On one side of the conflict is the universal wish to live forever. Yalom (1980) points out that it is usually the responsibility of our religions to offer mechanisms for relating to life's ephemeral qualities.

He strongly argues that our prevailing religious approaches tend to foster denial and childlike fantasy instead of providing constructive help with this seminal dilemma. Minkowski (1970) dealt with the same subject in a remarkably creative way. He pointed out that contrary to what seemed obvious, most of us *would not* want to have eternal life. He brings our attention to the ever-popular tale of Dracula, who is "damned to eternal life." The only purpose to this creature's existence, you will recall, is to derive life from the blood of unsuspecting women. Otherwise, he is virtually dead, as suggested by his need to sleep during daylight hours. Minkowski makes the point that eternal life, were it possible, would be like a voyage without end. He claims the absence of the signposts that connote a beginning and end are tantamount to depression.

It is not surprising, then, that the field of psychotherapy has shied away from handling symptoms in terms of the dreadful aspects of the future. Each time a therapist sees a depressed person, it is hard enough to withstand the affective onslaught of someone who has lost élan. When the paradoxical nature of the future is tied to the current morass, the task becomes psychological and spiritual. In this sense, one has to confront such difficult subjects as the meaning of life for an individual whose life may seem very bleak. As the practitioner looks at these bleak possibilities, his own mettle is tested. We clinicians may appear to sit attentively and quietly. Nevertheless, each encounter with tragedy and emptiness has the capacity to remind us of our own future.

A young physician in his early thirties came to see me after the removal of a tumor of questionable malignancy from the area around his thyroid. In spite of a positive prognosis, he became increasingly lethargic, losing interest in his work, marriage and social life. Having just finished a residency, he found it difficult to get up in the morning and become occupied with caring for his house. His thoughts had to do with illness and a sense that he had no control over a dismal destiny. The feeling of being without control left him wondering, "What's the sense of living my life as if there were nothing wrong?" Treating this young man was extremely draining, as he worked hard to defeat any suggestion that life still held meaning. To make his circumstances even more desperate, one year after the first surgery, a second malignant site was discovered. While the second surgery was equally successful, the therapeutic challenge became intense.

After months of crying and being "stuck" in his mode of "potting around the house," we came to a pivotal therapeutic breakthrough. Using the potentially trite metaphor of a vacation, I urged him to consider how he would react if he learned after beginning a two-week trek to Alaska that the trip would have to be shortened. Would he forget about his itinerary and aimlessly wander around his lodge room, would he pick up and go home or would he accelerate and get as much done as possible? Using this metaphor as a springboard, he came to see that not as much had changed as he thought. One day he had the "startling" realization that he had always been destined to die but now knew of what. He gradually gave up focusing on how he had been "cheated out of life" and threw himself into his work and life with a novel level of intensity. The outcome of this case was extremely positive, unlike so many others. After five years, his cancer has remained in remission and his periodic psychotherapy has focused more on slowing him down than on depression.

This case clearly illustrates the powerful relationship between the perceived future and depression. The past as a determinant of behavior was certainly not irrelevant. However, as May and other writers of his persuasion have said, what *has* happened changes as a function of what it is perceived *could* happen. Helping the depressed patient open the "closed doors of the future" requires a great deal of skill and wisdom. The so-called cognitive therapies have approached this idea by seeing depression as a problem of "faulty logic." If only this were true, we could simply train practitioners to "talk people out of their depression" by persuading them to think differently. The task of dealing with our complex relationship to the future requires that therapists operate in the "realm of profundity." We must be able to use all the tools that classical psychology offers, in addition to wisdom from all sources of knowledge. Carl Jung (1916), in particular, was very keen on this point. He felt that psychotherapists needed to be deeply immersed in life and open to human knowledge from both Western and Eastern philosophy.

Jung was suggesting that it is impossible to work with people who are confronting questions of meaning in life without being comfortable with "spiritual" questions. Neither physicians nor psychologists get an opportunity, as part of their training, to confront questions of values concerning divorce, tragedy, retirement, monogamy and so forth. During my own doctoral training, some attempt was made to increase our self-awareness by mandatory participation in a group psychotherapeutic format. While this was not terribly effective, there was at least an awareness that any individual working with people's lives should start from a foundation of self-knowledge. As I supervise doctoral trainees and postdoctoral psychologists, I continue to be amazed at how naive current clinical psychologists are with respect to the role of values. Freud originally proclaimed that his psychoanalysis was to be "scientific" and free of the biases of religion. However, he did not seem to fully grasp that a value-free science is, in a sense, a religion. To propose that the therapist's values are irrelevant is to fail to understand the nature of the therapeutic enterprise.

Some examples will help illustrate the profound role of values in the everyday business of psychology. A thirty-two-year-old married woman with two young children begins to express an interest in having an affair with a colleague in her office. As the therapist begins to interpret the impulses in terms of either her marriage or historical factors, the patient rejects the interpretation. As often happens, the affair starts to develop. The therapist finds herself in the position of working with the nuances of the affair or continuing to indirectly disapprove of the affair (and risk losing her client). This is a common situation requiring the management of morality. Another common situation occurs when patients come to a psychotherapist and begin to complain about their spouses. They may paint a very bleak picture of the nonparticipating member of the relationship. Recently, a young woman came to see me in a very distraught state. She presented a picture of a husband who had detached himself from their family, which included a four-year-old child. In the ensuing weeks, she learned that he had been having an affair for two years and had used an appreciable part of their savings in doing so. When I began to lay out options, one of which was divorce, she became angry with me, suggesting that I failed to grasp that she was Catholic and would never entertain divorce.

A young colleague whom I supervise was asked to see a nine-year-old boy whose mother had died of cancer. The boy was not bouncing back after about eight weeks had elapsed. As time passed, he was becoming anxious, was having nightmares and was increasingly unsociable. The psychologist presented the case to me in terms of the boy's relationship with his mother, and his hypothesis was that the boy was angry with her for leaving him. As I listened to a tape recording of one of their sessions, I noticed that on three different occasions, the child had made some references to "where his mother was now." Sensing that the boy might need the help of a clergyman, my young colleague suggested that to the father, who indicated that they were not affiliated with any religious institution. It became clear in subsequent sessions that the boy was quite preoccupied with the afterlife. It took a great deal of encouragement on my part to persuade the psychologist to pursue this theme, as he felt that heaven was "not a subject he could relate to." When he finally *allowed* the boy to express his feelings about the afterlife, we discovered that the child had overheard his father during an emotional tirade in which he proclaimed, "There is no goddamn God." In the typical egocentric fashion of nine-year-old children, our patient personalized this remark to mean that when *he* died there would be no afterlife. Quite separate from his family, this little boy had constructed his own view of life and death, which was shattered by the combination of his mother's untimely death and the overheard pronouncement of his father. Briefly, I had my colleague schedule the father and son together so that the father could help restore his son's fragile faith in life by explaining why he had had the outburst. The depression lifted soon after psychotherapy shifted to what had been the nucleus of the problem.

I have taken such great pains to underscore the confusion over values that reigns in the mental health professions because, in a sense, the confusion is at the heart of the problem this chapter deals with. In summarizing historical and contemporary approaches to depression, I have been pointing out that temporality is a vital missing link in understanding the roots of depressive disorders. The depressed person loses the feeling that the future holds promise and turns mournfully back to the past. What has not, however, been directly addressed is *why* our culture is so beset by this "common cold," depression, which fosters the "telepression" (blocking) of the future.

The answer to this vital question does not seem to lie simply in the rise of biological correlates or in some extraordinary frequency of childhood trauma or in the faulty logic suggested by the current wave of behavioral psychologists. Rather, it appears that the underlying process of the depressed patient is directly tied to the turbulence concerning values that has characterized our culture for the last twenty-five years. The 1960s and 1970s, in particular, were marked by upheavals in the areas of sexuality, sex roles, race relations, political disillusionment and a revolution in early child care. We have seen the introduction of effective birth control, the emergence of women in the workplace and the civil rights movement. We have also witnessed the assassination of a beloved president, the resignation of another president, race riots, military humiliation, and the fall from economic supremacy. The list of cultural transformations is probably much longer. The net result of these changes is hard to assess precisely. However, it can be inferred that our traditionally cherished institutions have faded or changed, and conceptions of the good life continue to undergo constant change.

There is a definite and profound relationship between the ability to extend into the future and the presence of a viable system of values. Not having a fluid and well-established system of values prevents the establishment of a solid sense of identity. As my colleagues and I found in our research on identity and temporal orientation, the future is constricted for those individuals who have not solved the problem of identity. When life is moving smoothly and there is "momentum," values do not come into play so prominently. When momentum is broken by tragedy, fatigue, illness or simply an awareness of "uncharted territory," the doors to the future can shut and resist opening. I find that more than anything, the depressed individuals whom I encounter in practice and in the normal course of my life seem to be yearning to find "meanings" in their lives. Victor Frankl (1955), the well-known existential psychiatrist, developed an entire psychotherapy around the concept of meaning that he called "logo therapy." Living with vague values that are subject to whimsical modification is much like exploring new land without a map. It is easy when one is on a marked trail; when the markers fade it is almost impossible to navigate the terrain.

Before closing this discussion of depression it is important to note that I have mostly been addressing what could be called classical or straightforward depression. The fact is, however, that individuals respond to feelings of hopelessness in highly specific ways. While the patients discussed in this chapter exhibit the signs of a deep disturbance in their temporal balance by having a deflated mood, others develop unique strategies to cope with truncated future extensions. The chapters that follow will deal with some other variations on the theme of depression. These other individuals develop diverse syndromes that, like depression, have not been historically connected to problems with time.

IV

TIME OUT

If depression represents the common cold in our culture, then "addictiveness" must be our common virus. No issue is on our minds more than the rampant and escalating problem of drug addiction. Cocaine, in the form of "crack," has made a sudden and terrifying appearance on the American landscape and is threatening to change our social, economic and psychological outlook. Federal and local authorities are literally waging war against international and regional suppliers of all kinds of addictive drugs. If predictions are correct, a frightening new substance called "ice" (crystallized methamphetamine) is soon to find its way eastward from Hawaii into the continental United States.

In addition to these newer chemicals, we are faced with enormous problems stemming from the heavy use of alcohol and "older" drugs. Though statistics are obviously imprecise because of the fluidity of our substance abuse situation, some recent estimates provide a sense of the problem's magnitude.

According to a recent report by the United States Department of Health and Human Services (1986), alcohol and drug abuse afflict an estimated 25.5 million Americans. The estimated annual cost for treatment and indirect losses such as reduced productivity from alcohol ($89.5 billion) and drug abuse ($46.9 billion) combined is $136.5 billion per year. This economic toll is well over four times that of the burden created for society by cancer!

Despite the high profile of "street drugs," alcohol abuse remains far and away the most pervasive and serious of the substance abuse problems. The American Psychiatric Association (1988b) has suggested that at least 18 million individuals suffer from alcohol dependency and another 56 million individuals are affected by them. Excessive alcohol use is estimated to be associated with one third of all suicides, half of all highway deaths, a third of all arrests and half of all murders (Coleman, Butcher and Carson, 1984). Moreover, child and wife abuse and sexual offenses are also seen as alcohol-related, although no statistical estimates are available.

In addition to alcoholism, we have problems with other substances—other sedatives (sleeping pills), narcotics (opium derivatives such as heroin and codeine), stimulants (amphetamines and cocaine), hallucinogens (marijuana and LSD) and a whole assortment of prescribed medications, including predictable drugs like Valium or Xanax and less likely agents such as antihistamines, which cause changes in perceptual-motor behavior. Documenting the incidence and scope of these diverse problems is far beyond what can be accomplished in this chapter. It should be sufficient to say that as a culture we are becoming increasingly involved with whatever psychoactive agents our technology can produce. We discover the mind-altering properties of seemingly harmless items such as airplane glue and cough syrup. We also tap the most potent concoctions history and anthropology can uncover.

Ironically, the history of addictive substances to some extent parallels the history of medicine. Ever since a group of individuals in society were charged with making others feel more comfortable, there has been a steady supply of natural and synthetic agents to dampen the pains of both unusual and normal life circumstances. Opium was used as far back as 5,000 years ago. Galen (A.D. 130–201), the prominent physician, considered Theriaca (an opium concoction) to be a panacea for all sorts of ailments:

It resists poison and venomous bites, cures inveterate headache, vertigo, deafness, epilepsy, apoplexy, dimness of sight, loss of voice, asthma, coughs of all kinds, spitting of blood, jaundice, hardness of the spleen, stone, urinary complaints, fevers, leprosies, the trouble to which women are subject, melancholy and all pestilences. (Cited in Coleman et al., 1984, p. 388)

Though physicians have certainly investigated the use of mood-altering drugs since Galen's time, most of the current chemicals in use have been developed since the 1930s. Both barbiturates and amphetamines were developed during this period and adopted rather broadly by the medical establishment. Though amphetamines were first considered useful for the military to combat fatigue, they were later adopted as a stimulant, as an appetite suppressant and finally as a recreational mood elevator. Barbiturates were originally introduced as the infamous sleeping pill and were prescribed in large quantities as recently as the early 1980s. Despite the horror stories of brain-dead teenagers who mixed alcohol with barbiturates, it was estimated that from 1979 to 1980 33 percent of female and 22 percent of male drug-related deaths involved barbiturate use (Project Dawn, 1980).

The uses of many of the plant-derived substances are rooted in various ceremonial functions in older civilizations. Cocaine was originally used by pre-Columbian shamans to induce feelings of well-being among the Indians of South America and Mexico. Ironically, scientific support for cocaine use was provided by Sigmund Freud, who was a strong proponent of the drug. Hallucinogens were used as far back as 2737 B.C., as noted by the Chinese Emperor Shen Nung, who described the herbal properties of marijuana. Just as the ancient Chinese tended to associate drugs with curative powers, so was hallucination-inducing mescaline used by the shamans of the ancient Indian cultures in ceremonial rites and healing sessions. LSD is a product of modern science whose mind-altering properties were unexpectedly discovered when Hoffman (1971), a Swiss chemist, swallowed some of the compound by accident.

Besides the obvious rampant problems with substance abuse, we are also plagued by more subtle habits that may not be typically called addictions. With the assistance of a teenage boy newly arrived from Vietnam, I was able to grasp just how vulnerable Americans are to the development of intrusive habit-forming behaviors. The first thing he noticed here was the "fanatical" way Americans approached eating.

He was surprised, not only by the large dimensions of our population but also by the extremes in appearance. While one segment of our population clearly seemed obese, another seemed to be devoted to the "cult of undereating" or dieting. People, he noticed, didn't simply decrease their food intake in an effort to curb their weight. Rather, he pointed out, they acted like "addicts" who had to go into special programs, with special foods and behavior to decrease their body weight. The first time we visited a chain bookstore he noticed that there was a whole section of the bookstore devoted to diets and that one or two of these books were "best sellers." This seemed astonishing to a young man who had lived in a culture in which body weight was simply not a regular part of daily consciousness.

Soon after he began attending an American secondary school, he learned that some of the girls in his class had a "food disorder." This was, of course, anorexia nervosa and the related disorder called bulimia. It seems appropriate to term these disorders "addictions," as they involve behavior that the individuals seem to feel they cannot control. That a healthy individual would voluntarily starve herself was somewhat bewildering to this young person from a country where food was in chronic short supply. The business of overeating and forced purging took him a while to discover, and he was obviously as shocked by that peculiar syndrome.

While my friend had a tendency to glamorize what he had left behind, our discussions succeeded in making me aware of how profoundly addictive Americans are. Individuals develop interest in health-related activities like exercise and then seem to become obsessed with the activity. Someone who begins to jog for cardiovascular exercise soon finds that jogging becomes the organizing principle of his life. Some individuals, often women, do the same with collective efforts such as aerobics classes. They begin the activity to "get in shape" and find that they feel terrible and guilty when they are forced out of action.

These activities, which begin as life "enhancers," end by enslaving individuals. This entrapment happens in other areas as well. One of the most insidious hazards to the quality of American family life is Sunday afternoon football. Though often the focus of many jokes, the ritualized inaccessibility of grown men to their wives and children for at least 25 percent of the year is extremely problematic. If one considers that Sunday is really the only day that lends itself to family interaction, then the addiction to afternoon football is a particularly worrisome one. Over the course of my practice I have found serious family problems that included the frustration of wives and children in response to the husband's or father's television habit. In a recent case, a man whose wife was adamant about ending this "reign of terror" asked to see me in a private session. He confessed that he was terrified at the thought of giving up this Sunday habit and said that he simply "could not do it."

A particularly sad case of another addictive syndrome can be found in the quasi-glamour of settings like Atlantic City and Las Vegas. A day trip to the casinos of Atlantic City is enough to jar the sensibilities of any inquisitive person. Contrary to expectations of an electrifying and elegant atmosphere, one finds an atmosphere of toil that is usually associated with addiction. The casinos are not happy places. Just as the addicted runner, eater, or television watcher seems to derive no pleasure from his habit, so does the gambler approach his task with the same absence of exuberance. Though the climate of the gambling enterprise is supposed to be recreational, one is struck by the gray faces performing repetitious acts over card games or slot machines. While some patrons are clearly one-time curiosity seekers, there is also a solid contingent of habitual gamblers who convey the same sense of apathy whether they win or lose. It has been estimated that gambling addicts lose over $20 million each year, and the organization Gamblers Anonymous has steadily grown in size across the United States.

The list of addictive syndromes in the United States is difficult to exhaust. Despite the decade-long war on cigarette smoking, hundreds of thousands of teenagers join the ranks of the nicotine-addicted each year. While the cigarette is not as commonly found in restaurants or social gatherings as it once was, the industry continues to survive and profit. It is not hard to go from nicotine to its counterpart, caffeine. The coffee industry in the United States is enormous, with ninety-five out of a hundred adult households using coffee. While statistics are hard to come by, it is estimated that at least one third of the coffee-drinking population drinks more than six cups of coffee per day. While questions have been raised about the deleterious effects of caffeine, interest in the beverage has been high for both the regular and decaffeinated varieties. Individuals who are "coffee addicts" describe their attachment to the beverage in much the same way their chemically addicted brethren convey their need for mood-elevating drugs.

As with depression, I have found that the subject of time comes up rather directly with substance-dependent individuals. Despite the fact that temporal factors have, again, not been perceived as central to the dynamics of drug abuse, my patients have talked about their drug experiences as providing a kind of relief from intolerable aspects of their temporal experience. In particular, several patients who were addicted to stimulants spoke of their problems with the "stagnant quality of time." Contrary to what might be assumed about stimulant users, they did not get into trouble with drugs as a way of meeting the demands of their day-to-day life. In other words, they did not use amphetamines like a college student would while cramming for exams. Instead, they ran into problems when they were not involved in specific goal-directed activities associated with school or jobs. They spoke of dreading the long periods of unstructured time associated with evenings, weekends and vacations. As with the depressed patients we discussed in the last chapter, they experienced clock time as passing much too slowly. It felt, they would say, as if time would stand still when there was "nothing to do." Rather than experiencing time off from their customary roles with any relish, these patients approached holidays with a sense of dread. Almost universally, they said that when they got the craving for their stimulant of choice, the desire was to get time to pass more quickly.

Like individuals suffering from "pure depression," these addicted individuals had great difficulty with futurity. They could not plan to fill their empty time and reported that without the aid of chemical stimulation, they would slip into an alarming state of anxiety and depression. A thirty-four-year-old pathologist with whom I was working because of episodic cocaine abuse provides a good example of dreading unstructured time. Steve's pattern of cocaine use involved "lost weekends" when he would begin the process of "activating" himself with cocaine on Friday night and often not begin the "down" cycle of sleeping until very late Saturday night. In order to get to sleep, he would inevitably use a barbiturate. He would often sleep for more than twenty-four hours following the cocaine involvement and talk about the weekend as a vague but manageable "blur."

The extended "high" of cocaine sometimes involved other people, frequently women who shared the cocaine habit. Cocaine, like many other substances, acts as an aphrodisiac, so that extended sexual activity pervaded these weekends. Just as frequently, the weekends were spent in solitude, with the sense of relief associated with the knowledge that time would pass quickly. His deep problems with temporality are, perhaps, best illustrated by an episode that occurred shortly before the young doctor was about to resign from his position at a hospital. There were several weeks before his new staff position began and he called me on a Sunday to ask for support. This call was something of a turn-around in his treatment as he had always maintained a somewhat cool stand toward therapy. His attendance was somewhat irregular and he never really allowed himself to admit his cocaine dependence. He also didn't let himself occupy a dependent position; our relationship had an inadvertent collegial tone to it. The tenor of this telephone call was quite different. He said that he was really frightened because he didn't know how to handle the fact that he had "all that time" on his hands. He asked if he could call regularly to punctuate the open time with my support so that the vacation did not become an extended cocaine experience. Two or three weeks of unscheduled time for this young man was like purgatory. He needed chemical assistance to create a temporal acceleration that would transport him into the safety of structured experience.

As can be seen from Steve's RTL on the following pages, the present is the dominant time zone for him. From a spatial perspective, it occupies well over 50 percent of the time line. While he describes himself as trying to accelerate himself out of his present experience, his future perspective is extremely sparse. Note that he is so uncomfortable about futurity that the one projected experience he marked is punctuated by a question mark. Though his past is better represented, the images are primarily related to critical teenage years. This past focus has a quality similar to the "depressed" time line shown in the last chapter. The problem that Steve has with the flow of time is suggested by the discontinuity of the RTL. From the experiences he lists, there is little feeling that the past, present and future are linked by a vital thread. Rather, it appears that he lives within a broad present detached from his memories of the past and from goals embedded in a vision of the future.

A further illustration of how this man's temporal rhythm was disturbed is suggested by life-style. He had a penchant for fast German cars whose capabilities far exceeded open-road possibilities. After a few calamitous "near misses" while driving at very high speeds, he agreed to take up legitimate track racing to exercise his obsession with speed. This therapeutic step was rather successful, as he recently won his

16	18	27	[30	32	33
parents divorce	left home	gradu- ated medical school	drug problems	board certified	met Lynn

Time line of Steve, a thirty-four-year-old "addictive" pathologist

first "Formula IV" race and is content to drive a four-wheel-drive utility vehicle day-to-day. His inability to tolerate the normal flow of things is also conveyed by his unusual attitude toward the common sport of jogging. He found himself unable to run at the usual pace of recreational runners. Instead, he put himself into an unrealistic program of sprinting, which he was unable to maintain because of the frequency of minor injuries. He experienced himself as having little patience in all aspects of life. Even the preparation and cooking of food was too disturbing. He preferred fast food that required little time to "get" and less to eat. Steve still sees me on a planned, intermittent basis. He has not used cocaine for several years and continues to work with his difficulty in handling unstructured time.

Another young man who had serious problems with amphetamine abuse provides a clear example of how stimulant abusers have trouble with temporal rhythm and future extension. His wife came to see me initially because they were having marital difficulties. They were both in their late twenties and had been married for about three years. She said that when they met at a Midwestern college her husband was a "recreational speed user" but did not have a problem with addiction. According to her, he was a very analytical philosophy student whose cynical detachment she found fascinating. Coming from what she described as a typical small-town Midwestern family, she was intrigued with his anticonformity and social indifference. She said they were "lost in each other" and hardly did the "usual things" associated with campus life.

After graduating from college, they came East, got married and settled into jobs. She worked as a traveling sales representative while he took a management position with a computer software development company. While she accommodated the changes associated with leaving their college life, he did not deviate from their "cave existence"

78

34	o	34	35]	40
bought house	NOW	trip to France	remodel house	married?

except for going to work. She complained that he continued his amphetamine use, especially on weekends, and refused to socialize or become involved with planned activities or vacations. He usually became angry with her if she tried to arrange plans and would embarrass her if she brought friends home by acting strangely and in an unfriendly manner. He resented her being away from him on weekends and tried to enlist her help in re-creating the lost weekends he remembered from college.

After several months, she was finally able to persuade him to see me. He predictably was grudging and oblique in our first few minutes, making it clear this was purely his wife's idea. He tried to "outmaneuver" me with high-handed intellectual repartee, but got down to business when I hit upon his dread of the future. In fact, he wondered how I knew about this very private fear and was relieved when I told him that other amphetamine users were also tyrannized by the "business of anticipation." He conveyed the same kind of fear as the cocaine-abusing physician. He claimed to be unable to handle being alone without structured activity. When his wife was out of town or when he was alone on weekends (they separated for a brief period), he would inevitably turn to drugs. He said that amphetamines made a very long, upsetting time seem "short and interesting." Even though he didn't get to sleep because of the arousal, his sense of "lived time" changed and he felt that the flow of time was bearable.

It is curious that individuals like this young man would not plan so as to fill unstructured periods with meaningful activities. It is in this area, however, that the underlying dynamics of depression seemed to couple with the temporal rhythm difficulty. He reported that he simply could not allow himself to plan anything. First, he found that the things most people did to pass time seemed "meaningless." He would frequently ask me what I did and why it was pleasurable. He also said

79

that planning vacations or attendance at events made him very un-comfortable. Apart from his work, he could not project into the future with any success. He also added that he never seemed to have the available energy that "regular people" had. He even asked whether the yearning for stimulants was due to a "missing ingredient" in his body.

This young man is still very involved in psychotherapy. Though he has stopped using amphetamines, he struggles with the "urge" on a regular basis. His latest achievement was to take a complete vacation in New Mexico which, with great effort, he had planned two months beforehand.

If neither of these young men had found drugs accessible, their primary problems would have appeared different. Both were extremely anxious about futurity. They were also "past-oriented" and prone to depression, though they did not particularly come across as sad. In a sense, they found the "right" drugs for themselves, as stimulants served to make time seem to move faster.

Many other individuals who are having trouble with temporality are not so able to exercise selectivity in the substance they use/abuse. Alcohol, more than any of the other drugs, has been legally woven into the fabric of most societies, and it is often turned to in order to deal with a variety of uncomfortable experiences. Alcohol is available throughout the world wherever an agricultural product is available for fermentation. We have already introduced the use of alcohol at ritual occasions in our opening discussion of New Year's Eve. Wine and spirits are also associated with such diverse occasions as weddings, funerals, religious rites (such as the receiving of Communion, the Passover seder) and the standard cocktail party, and they sometimes serve as a pre-sexual facilitator. While raising one's glass in the form of a toast is a gesture of social significance, it is also a psychophysiological event. Whether one is wishing a newly married friend well, or extending good wishes to a retiring colleague or simply having a drink in order to ease the transition from the pressures of the workplace to the safety of home, the alcohol changes one's perception, thinking, and emotional responses.

Mankind could have chosen nonalcoholic beverages to associate with special events. An especially sweet, rare juice or carbonated beverage does not seem an unlikely accompaniment to significant rituals. It would seem, however, that alcohol has been universally adopted be-cause there is something in celebration that, at the same time, is "anxiety" provoking. Most special human affairs in one way or another connote the passing of time or the transcience of life. While a wedding is an inherently happy occasion, there is usually the accompanying sense of one's child having grown up. Watching one's children achieve evokes both a sense of joy and a sense of melancholy as one contemplates that life belongs to the next generation. "Sunrise, Sunset," a lovely tune from *Fiddler on the Roof*, perfectly captures the ambivalence toward watching life's dreams become fulfilled.

Alcohol had been widely used as a means for reducing anxieties of ceremony as well as those associated with day-to-day life. Alcohol's effects, however, are somewhat paradoxical. Although alcohol is a central nervous system depressant (a "downer"), its short-term effects create a feeling of euphoria or uninhibition. As a result, certain individuals discover that drinking temporarily masks feelings of depression. If we consider that depression is the "common cold" of our culture, it should not be surprising that our problems with alcohol are so widespread.

Certain depressed individuals stay "stuck" in that desperate, helpless mode while others react to the feeling and go to great lengths to restore feelings of well-being. Some data on the differences between male and female rates of psychiatric disorders provide a good illustration of the relationship between depression and drugs. James Page (1975) noted that historically, women have a higher reported incidence of problems with depression. Men, however, drink at least two times more than women at all ages, though some of these sex differences have recently dissipated (American Psychiatric Association, 1988b). Robert Cancro (1985) reported a study among the Amish, who have no significant problems with alcohol abuse. It was found that without the mitigating effects of alcohol or drug use, the rate of depressive disorder for men and women was about the same. Women, who have joined such organizations as Alcoholics Anonymous in greater numbers in recent years, have typically tended to become victimized by feelings of hopelessness and future constriction. It can also be argued that until recent changes in female sex roles, women were more acquainted with depressed moods because of monthly mood shifts as well as socialization practices that fostered a somewhat passive outlook.

In the mid-1970s, I did some work with a federal agency involved with the mental health problems of Native Americans living on reservations in Montana. Most on-site colleagues and Indian respondents with whom I spoke talked at great length about the pervasive problem of intoxication among young male Indians, who have an alcoholism rate estimated to be nine times that of the general population. Social workers and others who tried to mount effective programs were continually frustrated in their efforts to control the problem. Teenage boys began drinking heavily early on and thus became unable to function in school or family. A few years ago, *Time* (1985) reported that between August and October of 1985, nine men between fourteen and twenty-five of the Shoshone tribe in Wyoming hanged themselves. In a population of about six thousand, this tragedy represented a suicide rate estimated at twenty-four times higher than their usual rate, which was already inordinately high. It was concluded that a heavy drinking pattern was related to this rash of suicides. Drinking, then, was totally ineffective in blunting the depression associated with perceived low status, chronic unemployment and few options. On a visit I paid to a United States Public Health Service mental health clinic in northern Alaska in 1986, I found the same high rates of depression and alcoholism among regional Eskimos and Indian groups. In this setting, as in others, the problem that gets the most attention is the *symptom*— namely, the pattern of substance abuse.

In the last chapter, a strong case was made that established the connection between depression and problems with the flow of time. If the argument were extended, it would be possible to establish that substance abusers, too, are struggling with temporality, based on our premise that serious depression is at the root of many drug and alcohol problems. However, support for the relationship between chemical addiction and temporal disturbances has also been strong from the clinical standpoint. In working with addicted individuals in hospitals and as outpatients, one of the tasks has been to help the individuals understand why they become dependent on the particular substance. Most people in the throes of an addiction tend to focus on the problems caused by the substance itself. The culture of the addict addresses the habit, the procurement and the process of breaking the dependency. However, part of anyone's cure involves understanding the nature of the illness that is being self-medicated.

That depression and temporal disturbance underlie many addictive disorders is easier to see in cases involving the stimulant drugs. With alcoholism, sedative abuse and use of the hallucinogens, the relationships are not as explicit. However, the clinical evidence is very strong that problems with futurity and rhythm are associated with drug use. The vast majority of alcoholics I have worked with have a problem with unstructured time, which is similar for those who find "uppers" as the solution. Moreover, ex-alcoholics inevitably speak of the depression that seemed to precede the turn to serious drinking. In addition, I have found that alcoholics who have been sober for a number of years continue to have problems with planning. There is an emphasis on day-to-day life that is encouraged by Alcoholics Anonymous, and there is a timidity about looking at long-range goals.

As a culture, we pretty much take it for granted that drugs, alcohol and addiction are a fact of life. We are used to the idea that a large segment of our population obtains illegal substances and that others "deal" in drugs or simply become criminals in order to support habits that are physiological, psychological, or both. Our government spends a good deal of money enforcing drug laws, monitoring points of entry and even negotiating with the heads of other governments about their laxity in keeping their produce from finding its way into our drug country landscape. National and local politicians organize their campaigns against the rise of drugs and promise greater efforts at educating our young people about the hazards of these pills and powders.

All of our efforts notwithstanding, we tend to address the problem of addiction itself as if there were simply a scarcity of information. As it is, we are one of the most highly literate cultures in the world and, if anything, live with an information overload. Our teenagers, by the time they are fourteen, pretty much know "the score" concerning drugs and alcohol.

Another of the perspectives gleaned from my Vietnamese commentator was the strange process that characterizes the relationship between American parents and their teenage children. In Vietnam, as in most developing countries, children are protected by parents during childhood and then given increasing levels of responsibility early on. When I lived in East Africa, I was astounded at the competence of seven-year-olds who were caring for other children and, in some cases, spending long days shepherding flocks of goats miles away from their homes. In Vietnam, according to my young friend, children at age eight or nine perform essential agricultural tasks, which immediately gives them a sense of self-importance and responsibility.

Our children, in contrast, perform few vital functions for their families or their community. They grow up without the important feeling of being a contributor to the well-being of their social group. Their tasks tend to focus on "play," which, at best, affords the opportunity to rehearse the tasks that "real life" will demand. Besides having a ten-year-old son, I have a seventeen-year-old daughter, who was recently making a final selection of a New England boarding school with the input of her parents and school counselor. The topic on our minds, and on the minds of many parents who are considering letting their children take advantage of these wonderful educational institutions, is whether our child is prepared to deal with the drug offerings that may be presented away from home. It is not, mind you, the fact of being away from home. After all, just about every high school in the United States struggles with how to present meaningful antidrug programs to cynical and distrustful constituents. Rather, having one's child leave home galvanizes the myriad concerns about succumbing to the pitfalls of the dangerous external world.

The proper response to these fears is to remind myself that most children do not wander into serious drug problems because of lack of information or because of temptations provided by the culture. While teenagers are curious and somewhat driven to sample everything, it is pretty clear that they, like their adult counterparts, become addicted to substances when the psychological or physiological aspects of the addiction serve some need. From this perspective, considering the scope of the addiction problems we face, we must be a culture that is self-medicating in order to "treat" certain underlying problems.

Why, then, are so many individuals in our society struggling so deeply with the fundamental experience of *feeling* the passage of time? Clinical evidence has strongly suggested that the unfolding of an uncertain future is a powerful catalyst in the decision to chemically change one's perceptions. Since genetic or constitutional factors are probably not involved, the answer must be in the ways in which the person comes to terms with time in the most rudimentary way. In Chapter 3 I established that the earliest conceptions of time passing appeared during the first year of life. For the infant there is little or no awareness of time except for punctuations that are produced as needs arise and are satisfied or remain as sources of frustration. Freud was the first major theoretician to alert us to the dangers of extensive frustration during the "oral" periods. He postulated that the resulting "fixation" during the first year of life could lead to a wide range of psychoneurotic possibilities. Freud and his students spoke of "character" pathology when examining how excessive frustration affected an individual during his classical developmental stages. With respect to the oral stage, he reasoned that fixation would affect the individual's most fundamental outlook on life in terms of optimism versus pessimism. He also reasoned that the most logical disturbance would be associated with the business of "taking things in," which is at the center of the oral stage. Erik Erikson extended Freud's concept of oral stage fixation to the psychosocial realm and suggested that such an individual would have a fundamental problem with "basic trust."

Individuals who lack basic trust because of a frustrated need for nurturance are individuals who are "uncomfortable with the terms of life." Their pessimism is expressed by doubting that they will ever be able to "rise above" negative experiences. In addition to being on poor terms with the flow of time, they tend to have trouble soothing themselves with phrases such as "my blues will pass by morning." There is a tendency, perhaps derived from the preverbal state of infancy, to feel that negative experiences last an eternity. It is during these episodes of "non–well being" that the addictive person seeks a rapid change of feeling and is likely to take a drug. Once the cycle of seeking and finding relief begins, the individual with this "oral personality" seems to relish the ability to control the flow of his experience, unlike the situation in early childhood when he was "at the mercy of arbitrary forces."

Those who are well versed in the history of the treatment of alcoholics will recall that the oral fixation theory was widely accepted before the 1960s. Oral fixation theory suggested that alcoholics were addicted to the act of taking the chemical regularly in order to deal with "dependency" needs, which were insatiable. In other words, because of oral stage frustration, the alcoholic grew up with strong needs for nurturing that never seemed to be adequately met. The problem with this approach was not with its explanation for the origin of the problem, but rather with its application to treatment.

Since oral frustration theory was derived from Freud's psychoanalytic stage theory, his theories of treatment were crudely extended to the alcoholic. For the unsophisticated practitioner, this extension meant doing all the things common to psychoanalysis, including the recollection of early memories and the identification of "faulty mothering experiences." Inevitably, a sense of blaming one's mother developed, with accompanying feelings of sadness and anger at one's parents.

While this approach had a certain theoretical appeal, it was dramatically unsuccessful when applied to alcoholics and other substance abusers. The focus on the past and the opportunity to blame others for one's behavior did not lend itself to overcoming an all-consuming addiction.

The application of Freud's theory of treatment for psychoneurotic patients to alcoholics thus made little sense. Ironically, Freud never intended psychoanalysis to be used for addicted individuals. Alcoholics and other drug users were perceived as suffering from "character disorders" and, Freud reasoned, were not candidates for the rigors of psychoanalysis. Freud and his followers did not focus on problems of addiction, which were, for the most part, excluded from the body of knowledge developed on the treatment of the neuroses. Nevertheless, it is not clear that his conception of oral character pathology is entirely irrelevant to the genesis of addictive disorders. Classical psychoanalysis as devised by Freud is only one approach that could have been developed based on his observations and subsequent theoretical formulations. His followers, while often adhering to his basic stage theory, developed some dramatically different approaches to the process of changing personality.

Figures like Erik Erikson, David Rapaport, Heinz Kohut, Hyman Spotnitz and Otto Kernberg have built on classical conceptions of treatment by incorporating new dimensions that were overlooked by early pioneers. These theoreticians and others have moved classical analytical treatment toward emphasizing the interpersonal relationship as well as acknowledging the role of "responsibility" for overcoming problems. Traditional psychoanalysis had a tendency to render the patient passive by "blaming" problems on the remote past. The patient would tend to wait for the magical day when *the* memory would trigger the outpouring of emotion so that the symptoms would "go away." So deeply ingrained is this fantasy of analytic treatment that current clients and inexperienced therapists continue to expect the "outpouring" cure.

We often confuse the relationship between treating a phenomenon and understanding causal factors. If an individual develops problematic life habits such as substance abuse because of early childhood neglect, it does not necessarily follow that "the cure" lies in that remote time frame of his life. The main point here is that future anxiety may be derived in what we have come to call the oral stage of development.

However, once a pattern of fear has developed we have to distinguish between conceptualizing the origins of the problem and finding a context in which the individual can change. Alcoholics Anonymous (AA) has had an outstanding history, unsurpassed by the health sciences, in finding the right blend of factors to help alcohol-addicted individuals. Two factors that are an essential part of the AA approach capture precisely what was missing from the analytical approach to alcoholism. For one, the assumption of responsibility is central; one must accept that one is an alcoholic. While the weight of culpability is tempered by a strong belief in a Divine Being, there is a strong emphasis on taking control of one's life. The other corrective factor involves the defocusing of the distant past so that the individual can focus on the present almost exclusively. Though I'm not sure that AA can bring its members to overcome the deeply ingrained insecurities brought on by early childhood experience, their "formula" has achieved tremendous success by providing a framework for individuals to stop drinking and maintain that achievement.

In a sense, AA seems to achieve a critical change in drinking without necessarily altering the residual damage from what we are calling "oral deprivation." The orally fixated personality type is usually characterized as highly dependent. One of the ways AA succeeds is by encouraging a constructive dependency on its culture. The AA member is encouraged to attend as many meetings as are deemed necessary to meet his needs. There is no time limit on the attachment and none of the worries of "cure" or "progress" associated with the health-service-related approaches to alcoholism. Many alcoholics continue with AA for years after they have stopped drinking. They visit the "clubhouse" regularly and often stop off daily to socialize as they might have done at a tavern before they stopped drinking.

I have seen many alcoholics in treatment while they were also involved with AA. Though they did not show the overt signs of depression, they were heavily reliant on telepression as a way of dealing with their lives. AA had helped them to stop drinking by living a day at a time in the psychological present. These individuals tended to have a great deal of trouble with planning and anticipating the future. Like the stimulant users I discussed earlier in the chapter, they tended to live a "week-to-week" life, finding that extending themselves forward even for positive goals raised anxiety. Adding further support to the premise that fears of future and anticipation are rooted in the oral stage is some anecdotal information from my alcoholic patients. It seems that the largest single expense incurred by AA organizations is coffee for their meetings. Apparently AA members are extremely prone to transfer their "oral" cravings to other chemically significant beverages. One of my patients reported that most of his AA friends were very serious coffee drinkers and that most were also heavy cigarette smokers!

Another phenomenon, which also indicates that the wholesale addictiveness we see is related to problems in early infancy, is the rise of what have been termed "eating disorders." It has certainly been clear for some time that Americans are much heavier than people from other cultures and have trouble maintaining adaptive eating habits. The national obsession with dieting and weight control is not new. For at least twenty-five years we have been very concerned with weight loss, and the preoccupation with the food/health/body weight issue shows no sign of abatement.

More recently, however, we have witnessed the establishment of eating aberrations that seem more pathological than the usual overeating/dieting syndrome. Large numbers of predominantly white, middle-class young females have developed eating disturbances that are extreme and dangerous. The problems have become so pervasive that several new centers have evolved that specialize in the treatment of food-related disorders. Equally astonishing is that anorexia (loss of appetite) and bulimia (binge eating) have now become everyday terms.

It is not my purpose here to explain or theorize about contemporary eating disorders. The appearance of these disorders does, however, provide more evidence that our culture is doing something (or not doing something) to foster problems that center on the oral stage. In fact, the inability to sustain life by eating would appear to have the most direct relationship to the kind of depression that originates in the earliest part of life. The classical studies done by Renee Spitz found that infants who were not consistently nurtured in orphanages frequently lost interest in eating and were known to die from lack of appetite. This kind of depression has been called "anaclitic" and was viewed as central to the developing personality. My own experience with anorectic patients seems to support the idea of a fundamental depression that parallels that of Spitz's infants. In addition to the lack of vigor that is to be expected with malnourishment, I found the same temporal constriction as in my more classically depressed patients.

Many questions arise about why the food disorders affect such a narrow band of our teenage population. Why are race, sex, age and social class so related to the pathology that affects the ability to regulate food intake? This is a complex question that requires a detailed discussion of the psychosocial basis for "symptom selection." It is probable that this group is exposed to a unique blend of oral stage inconsistency coupled with exaggerated learned concerns about body image that are class-based. The teenage population, in general, seems to be at high risk. While our food disorder group represents a particular group of young people, other teenagers from other segments of the population are also responding with the same sense of "distrust" and "discomfort."

Perhaps the most dramatic expression of distrust and hopelessness in the future is represented by the frighteningly large group of teenagers who take their lives. Statistical data suggest that the incidence of teenage suicide has increased sharply in the past decade. Suicide now ranks as the second-most-common cause of death among fifteen- to twenty-four-year-olds (the first is car accidents) in the United States. Approximately 80,000 people in this age group will attempt suicide in the next year, and it is estimated that over 4,000 will succeed. This group is also at risk for drug and alcohol abuse (Fowler, Rich and Young, 1986). Though the impulse to stop living is not obviously related to substance abuse, the fundamental dynamics are quite similar. Suicidal teenagers share with our substance abusers a fear of the future and its uncertainties. Moreover, they are often individuals who are involved with drugs—their deaths, whether by car or by overdose, usually involve drugs.

I have worked with many teenagers who have expressed the desire to die. I have also encountered a few in my experience at mental hospitals who later committed suicide. In many respects they sounded like the others who had turned to drugs for comfort. They lacked that basic level of comfort with life that seems to derive from adequate nurturance in the early years. The terms of life were too difficult for them, particularly in bearing the responsibility for controlling the future. They seemed ill prepared for the turbulence of adolescence with its inherent pressures to control one's destiny. One of these individuals was a fifteen-year-old who overdosed with barbiturates after a relationship with a boy ended. I had worked with her while she was briefly hospitalized at age thirteen. She frequently conveyed the sense that "life was moving too quickly" and that she was unable to control the speed of time. She was preoccupied with death. On the one hand, she saw dying as salvation, as a rest from her anguish. On the other hand, she was frightened because she found that death was the ultimate symbol of not being in control. While she claimed to yearn to die as a way to "stop time," she was frightened because "it would not be on her terms." She solved this existential dilemma by dying on her own terms. She stopped all motion and time by putting herself into the infinite sleep.

Like so many others who commit suicide, this young girl, I am told, was quite cheerful and appeared extraordinarily healthy for several days before her death. It was as if she were finally free to relax and enjoy the present with the uncertainties and dread of the future resolved. This temporal component of suicide resembles the way anxiety about the future ruins serenity for individuals who do not commit suicide. I have already discussed a person who was "paralyzed" in the face of a life that seemed shortened because of illness. It is quite common to encounter people of all ages who simply cannot accept the terms of life and death. All of us have to struggle to erect and maintain the meaning of our endeavors with the knowledge that "someday none of it will matter." This theme comes up regularly in my work with my patients.

Unfortunately there is no simple answer or straightforward technique to help resolve this discomfort with life's paradox. Those who get a good start in life seem to develop the right balance of psychological defense and ability to look at life's tragic dimension. Those without this delicate perspective go to greater extremes to blunt or stop this irreversible onslaught of time passing. I have found, however, that a psychotherapeutic philosophy focused on overcoming the dread of the future has tremendous possibility. By helping the individual accept the contingencies of life in the safety of a supportive relationship, I have found an inherent possibility for a "surge of meaningfulness to life." By acknowledging and accepting the temporal flow in our lives, we gain a sense of momentum and possibility. With hard work, the impulse to take "time out" through chemicals or by exercising the ultimate control (suicide) gives way to an acceptance of oneself and the ambivalent feelings associated with anticipation.

V

TIME WARS

In the last two chapters, we have looked at reactions to the passage of time that were somewhat similar. The depressed person found the future to be without hope and turned toward the past, with the present grinding along much too slowly. Many addicted individuals seemed to be depressed and were self-medicating themselves to "raise their spirits" by creating a sense of accelerated experience. Both groups' difficulties involved temporal flow; however, neither the individuals involved nor the theorists who discuss them usually consider temporality to be the center of the problem.

The individuals whom we will be discussing in this chapter struggle more directly with time. They are acutely aware of the future and are harassed by what feels like the compression of time. Their lives are highly goal-oriented and ambitious. Unlike the depressed patient, they experience themselves moving too rapidly toward a crowded or highly differentiated future. These are not easy, diagnosable cases. They are individuals who do not fit into the labeling scheme of clinical psy-

22	25	27	[29	o	32	33]
gradu-ated college	married	moved to Philadel-phia	new job	NOW	40K	group manager

Time line for a thirty-one-year-old married woman (Lynne)

chiatry. Rather, they are groups of people who have been given popular designations such as "Type-A personalities," and "yuppies."

Lynne was always in a hurry, and usually ran late for all her appointments, including her therapy session. Though she always spoke about her life in an upbeat manner, she nevertheless appeared rushed and "hassled." Friends and family complained of her inaccessibility, as did her husband, who was extremely upset with the turn their marriage had taken. Lynne was always talking about needing to "veg out on a beach" for a vacation, but never seemed to find time for recreation. She frequently used metaphors from the only leisure activity she engaged in with any regularity—jogging. Just when you think you're out of stamina, she would say, "You push harder and somehow find a second wind." At the time she entered therapy, Lynne seemed to be having trouble finding any wind at all.

Lynne's RTL, which is shown above, was administered in the first month of her therapy. Though her marriage was in a tenuous state when she came to see me, her focus was predominantly on her career. Lynne lived a hectic life, traveling a great deal and finding it difficult to balance her business and personal lives. As indicated on her time line, she was very ambitious with an explicit "map" of her career goals. Her time line is quite different from those we have seen so far. The depressed person had a line that was clearly past-oriented. Similarly, the addictive individual lived close to a "band" around the present. In contrast, Lynne's RTL is clearly future-oriented in terms of allocated space and number of experiences. She has nine milestones located in the future, eight of which are related to her business objectives. She put a question mark next to "children," as if she recognized the improbability of achieving this goal. The four experiences she placed in the past were within a ten-year bracket of time and were, again, related to achievement.

35	37	38	40	42	45	50
75K	depart- ment manager	children?	move to regional office	125K	VP promo- tion	change careers

Lynne's treatment was paradoxical in that it rapidly became a poignant microcosm of her life. I saw her weekly for approximately two months. During this period, she was very much motivated and made extremely good use of the therapeutic process; both her anxiety and her depression were appreciably reduced. By the third month, however, scheduling became increasingly difficult. Lynne was traveling or unable to attend sessions during the hours offered. Though she did not formally stop therapy, she was able to maintain only intermittent contact, thus limiting our chances for a more complete success.

When we begin to look at the patterns of feeling rushed by the awareness of time, it becomes difficult to separate the individual from the social context in which he lives. Paradoxically, today we rush to "save" time while feeling that life is a "rat race." Our machine-electronics age has freed vast numbers of individuals from the drudgery of the repetitious tasks that are at the core of existence. The business of communicating and traveling has been made increasingly efficient. Yet the common complaint and the common observation is that we are a culture with no time. Even the man who does the roto-tilling to prepare my vegetable garden made an unsolicited observation about time-related trends. When I inquired about his usually busy schedule, he commented that business was way off. He added that most of his customers said that they "simply didn't have time for a vegetable garden this year." He took off his hat, scratched his head, and asked me, "Doc, what's going on?"

It is probably very easy to identify with the feeling of being rushed. One could easily ask whether we are addressing a problem at all or a fact of life in a complex world. To some extent, this point is well taken. Changes in family life certainly have complicated the tasks of living. Dual careers in families have made a better sense of timing between married couples with children essential. Supermarkets, laundries, and other establishments now stay open later and later to accommodate the off-hours needed to shop for food and manage other aspects of daily living. As both a parent and a psychologist, I continue to hear about (and experience firsthand) the complexity of managing careers and the active lives of growing children. Moreover, inflation has made it increasingly difficult for people to live on the income levels of other historical periods. Because money does not "stretch" as it used to, many more people must work longer hours or take supplemental jobs. If managing family and career is complex for the typical couple, it is even more difficult for the single-parent household, which occupies an increasingly greater share of our society.

In spite of the backdrop of these so-called real problems that produce more "busy-ness," there are powerful indications that many of the underlying patterns of temporal harassment are more rooted in the internal lives of people. The "time wars" I am addressing are self-imposed to the extent that individuals seem to be pursuing goals that are both unclear and unattainable within the framework of their lives. An old distinction made by Freud had to do with the difference between fear and anxiety. He explained that the experiential aspects of the two were, for the most part, the same. The difference was in the "source." While fear was based on a real external danger such as an attack by a fierce animal, anxiety was mediated by one's own mental life without specific reference to danger in the world. There is probably a parallel in distinguishing between what we might term "genuine busy-ness" and the sense of urgency certain individuals create themselves.

Perhaps the most well-known type of person who is time pressured is the Type-A personality. In attempting to discover the correlates of heart disease, Meyer Friedman and Ray Rosenman (1974) found that a striking proportion of their patients were individuals who functioned in highly stressful ways. While the concept of psychosomatic disease certainly predated their observations, heart disease had not really been seen as psychologically induced before this period. They described an individual (typically male) who was fiercely competitive, aggressive, generally hostile, preoccupied with control, and very intimidated by all kinds of deadlines, usually self-imposed. The Type-A personality is seen as the embodiment of the task-oriented, hard-driving executive whose ambition requires that he be on top of every situation.

This is the individual who works relentlessly and frequently earns the title "workaholic." Often, this individual has long workdays and is unable to tolerate leisure time. Recreational activities all too often become repetitions of the work environment. He adopts competitive sports, which, rather than being "refreshing," become alternative sources of stress. Imperfect golf scores, losses on the tennis court, or the rigors of sailboat races all resemble the competition and task orientation of this person's work life. Even less physical activities such as bridge games and various forms of subtle competition serve to raise the blood pressure of the Type-A personality. Family members of this individual often lament that the most innocuous activity can be turned into a tyranny of deadlines and goals. A family driving trip can easily turn into a race against invented deadlines. It is not at all uncommon for children to plead for a pit stop while the Type-A person (usually the father) insists on not departing from "the schedule."

Just about every form of human activity can become subordinated to the compelling drive to win. I was recently chatting with a ten-year-old boy who went on the "fishing trip of his lifetime" with his father somewhere in Florida. On inquiring about his fortunes on the trip, I discovered a certain amount of apathy and disappointment in the way he spoke of what should have been a splendid four days. He said that they caught more fish than he ever saw and that he was sick of eating fish. He conveyed the sense that the adventure quickly stopped being fun when his father insisted on fishing from dawn to sunset every day and was not satisfied until they caught the "record-breaking" bass for that day. Rather than enjoying intimate fun with his father, this little boy felt fatigued and criticized because of his father's inability to separate leisure from a competitive task with its inherent self-derived deadlines.

I have been personally astounded by a similar phenomenon in children's sports. I had heard about how Little League baseball games could become arenas for overly competitive fathers but never really witnessed the phenomenon until I myself had the pleasure of becoming a coach for the first time. As my son came of age to try his hand at the sport, I thought I would enjoy the rejuvenation of a dormant interest in baseball, as I had played the sport seriously up through the collegiate level. What began as a labor of love quickly became a tense project involving more work than originally suspected. Both my friend, the other coach, and I agreed that after a typical game, we were stressed out and felt we needed a drink. The children were delightful—eager to learn, putting their heart and soul in doing the best they could. There was, however, a noisy minority of fathers who came to "help" the coaches. In spite of all the warnings we had, we were taken by surprise at the inappropriate level of aggression and competitiveness evidenced by these fathers. Again, they were unable to keep their Type-A needs in the workplace and seemed to experience vicariously the imperfection and expectable variability in their children's talents. We coaches found we had to hold several meetings with the parents in order to remind them that the purpose of the game was primarily recreation. We also had to repeat several times that primitive yelling, criticizing and complaining about the playing time of their children was inconsistent with our objectives. In the face of losing some games, we found that this group of fathers were "concerned" about our strategy and required the frequent reassurance one might expect the *children* to need that "winning wasn't everything"!

The resiliency of the Type-A syndrome is remarkable in that it persists under the most extraordinary circumstances. Several years ago, I participated in a study of cardiac patients in which the patients and their families were interviewed during the recuperation period while they were in the hospital. Many fit the description of Friedman and Rosenman's Type-A patients and were instructed to keep their business routines away from the hospital. In spite of proven correlation between full recovery and the willingness to extricate themselves from stressful activity, many began to panic over missed meetings and the loss of continuity. They clamored for telephones and insisted on continuing the behavior that was hypothesized to be instrumental in causing the heart condition in the first place. The perplexed hospital staff found that with some of these men it was more upsetting to deprive them of their contact with their businesses than to grant the privilege. As a result, when I entered the hospital rooms for clinical interviews, I found men with blustery voices engaging in their business as if their lives were not being threatened by cardiac problems.

While the Type-A personality has been seen as vulnerable to cardiac problems and other physiological difficulties, our culture still tends to reinforce the behavior. Being tagged as a Type-A individual has a certain heroic connotation. The implication is not that one is an impatient, competitive, hostile individual who has lost the capacity for pleasure, but that one is a warrior of sorts who is willing to trade health and longevity for those countless victories in the workplace and elsewhere. When individuals whom I know personally or professionally refer to themselves as Type A's, they are alluding to a kind of "de-Latinized machismo." Without opportunities in modern society for the exercising of traditional male "power," it seems as if we have adopted the hard-driving, success-oriented workaholic as a model leader. Since we do not currently place a high value on the role of the military in contemporary Western society, this dominant behavior seems to have found a comfortable home in American corporate life.

Lawrence Miller in his book, *American Spirit: Prescription for a New Corporate Culture* (1984), points out that the culture of American business has traditionally emphasized production and power. Following a quasi-military system of values, corporations operated as the embodiment of a traditional male environment in which corporate life needed to be impersonal with devotion to the corporation being a given. Personal or family feelings were always considered secondary to effectiveness and power, so that it was not considered an asset to express too much feeling for one's colleagues or to admit that one had a mental or family life separate from the objectives of the business. When a worker was no longer productive, he was relieved of his responsibilities in the most impersonal way. This military view of the workplace was embodied in such works as Arthur Miller's *Death of a Salesman*, in which Willy Loman was fired when his productivity fell off. Other works, such as *The Man in the Grey Flannel Suit* in the 1950s, also depicted the subversion of the individual's sense of identity in a corporate culture demanding rigid conformity. More recently, in the film *Kramer vs. Kramer*, Dustin Hoffman portrayed a divorced man attempting to manage the affairs of his young son without acknowledging to his ad agency employer that he was temporarily distracted by the duties of parenting. He eventually was fired.

The militaristic value system of which Miller speaks is still evident in American corporate life. Despite the entry of women into the workplace, the "machismo" culture that disallows intimacy and fosters tireless competition in the name of success is still prevalent. In fact, in a few large corporations, one of which is at the center of the computer business, a "corporate time line" is actually provided as a basis for success. Ambitious employees are given a schedule, which suggests that they should achieve certain "success" points in a certain fixed sequence. If they do not achieve these career milestones, they are considered deviant and are generally manipulated off the growth ladder. This schedule for success seems to intimidate and promotes an at-

mosphere of subtle terror. As one might expect, feedback is often ambiguous and corporate politics leave the individual "hurrying" to
achieve the next level within the time frame.

The "heroism" associated with the workplace puts a tremendous
strain on individuals and on family life. The computer corporation I
refer to above, for example, seems to give employees the message that
"we care about you if you devote yourself exclusively to us." The
computer company requires a regular schedule of out-of-town training
conferences, particularly of new employees. It is not uncommon for
eager recruits to spend weeks or months at corporate centers studying
new products or marketing techniques.

Quite by chance I have worked with at least six families whose unity
was disturbed by an individual's conflict between devotion to corporate
goals and family life. Lynne, whose time line I presented earlier in this
chapter, enthusiastically began her career working in the marketing
division of the XXX Corporation. At this point she had been married
about four years and had lived a conservative life in a conventional
and apparently adequate marriage. She was out of town as often as she
was at home, frequently for stretches of two weeks at a time. At several
of the sessions she was housed in "resortlike" settings with new corporate recruits of both sexes. At first she was encouraged to "get to
know" colleagues, which, by virtue of the extended sessions, would
have happened anyway. She recalled feeling divided in her life. She
was developing a network of friends and experiences very different
from her customary style of life. Though she ultimately accepted responsibility for her actions, she had several extramarital relationships.
The subsequent pattern of guilt and avoidance led to serious marital
difficulties. I eventually helped her and her completely perplexed husband work out a divorce.

After the divorce, this young woman continued psychotherapy. She
conveyed that the corporate value system had played a major part in
undermining her marriage. While she was never forced to pursue relationships, she said it was almost impossible to avoid. With the strong
emphasis on maintaining close "rapport" with people who could eventually be decision-makers, she said "fooling around" was the norm
rather than the exception. Despite the "conservative" appearance of
her colleagues and the corporate reputation for being "traditional,"
there was a clear attitude that "work and play" were inseparable. It

was also very clear that the corporation, in establishing its time goals, created a conflict with family life.

In another dramatic case, I began working with a young married woman with a one-year-old child whose husband was acting "unpredictable and strange." Her husband, coincidentally, worked for the same large corporation, and just after she got pregnant, he went through a similar period of travel and indoctrination. According to her, he no longer wanted to account for his time and seemed to resent coming home from his conferences and travel. Shortly after therapy began, her husband announced that he was moving out. In the emotional interactions that followed, he confessed that he was involved with a woman in the Midwest and had actually lived with her for periods of time while attending training meetings. My client was completely traumatized by the realization, as she had believed he had completely devoted himself to the company. She was partly to blame, she said, because she gave him license to do whatever was necessary to succeed. Ironically, he was making career progress at a greater pace than anticipated.

Another business context that both exemplifies and encourages the "work for your life" ethic is the self-conscious world of law firms. Over the years of professional practice I have always had a disproportional number of lawyers or their spouses in treatment. While my legal charges were never pressed particularly to travel, there was, it seems, an overwhelming pressure to "burn the midnight oil." Young attorneys who have not yet been voted partners especially feel inordinate pressure to demonstrate allegiance to the firm and a "strong stomach" for work. Stories abound in law firms that "immortalize" the behavior of young lawyers who are willing to trade the time of their life for success in the firm. In one such story, a militaristic senior partner who heard about a young lawyer's absence associated with the birth of his first child commented, "So why isn't he here? Didn't the delivery come out all right?" A young female attorney whom I was seeing professionally was trying to become a partner in a large law firm. She experienced terrifyingly high levels of anxiety as she tried to balance the demands of a legal career with becoming a new mother. She was also married to an attorney, and life was generally hectic, with constant pressure permeating every day of the week. She felt she had no time for anything, especially herself. When her review by the firm's senior partners was complete, she received the disappointing news that her elevation to partnership was going to be delayed for another year. In spite of a successful track record, she was told that they were concerned about her dedication to the firm. Specifically, it was pointed out that she was "not around enough" after 6:00 P.M. or on weekends. A dedicated young lawyer, they said, can usually be seen in the office on Saturdays and Sundays.

It would appear that we have come to associate time pressure with feeling successful. Individuals who have experienced a sudden change in temporal rhythm often get quite perturbed when their hectic schedules become subdued. A client of mine who had undergone some setbacks in his manufacturing business would frequently say that when he was not busy he felt that he was going backward. Though he didn't speak in explicitly temporal terms, he was saying that, in the absence of goal-directed, future-oriented behavior, he felt that the time component of depression swept over him. The future ceased to feel real and he felt thrust back into the temporal past. His temporal rhythm could not tolerate the state of "timelessness." At the same time this client was disturbed by inactivity, he professed to yearn for the time to "do nothing." He would say that when financial security was finally achieved, then "I want to just watch the grass grow." It is highly improbable, however, that one can suddenly tolerate and be refreshed by a lack of external structure when life has been totally dedicated to achievement.

This ethic has even found its way into the clergy and the academic world. Spouses of ministers with whom I am acquainted ironically have the same complaint as the spouses of "high-powered" lawyers or business executives. They say that their husbands are never home and have little time for family affairs. A client came to see me because her children were getting into trouble academically and one was heavily involved with drugs. It took six weeks to schedule her husband for a consultation due to his work schedule. When we finally met, he seemed put off that I could not accommodate his schedule. He said that the demands of his church position did not permit a normal family life and that his wife was supposed to understand this when she "signed on" to be a minister's wife. I could have been talking to a chief executive officer of a corporation.

The identity of the minister had incorporated the cultural value that associates feeling harassed by one's schedule with a sense of success.

Somewhere, the notion of the cleric as the embodiment of balance and serenity had been usurped by an ideal dominated by the concept of "busy-ness." The same transformation has happened within the academic world. The image of the contemplative university professor puffing on his pipe has all but vanished. This "endangered species" has been replaced by what some have come to call academic entrepreneurs, who are driven to succeed like their counterparts in the corporate world. Success in the academic community has, for the most part, been redefined in terms of how rapidly tenure and promotion can be attained. The most influential and prestigious members of the university community tend to control large sources of external funding and are associated with the often frantic proliferation of publications. The publish-or-perish ethos seems to be an academic derivative of the overall cultural emphasis on "more in the shortest period of time."

A contemporary variation on the Type-A personality is the Young Urban Professional, also known as the "yuppie." This type of individual emerged in the 1970s as one dedicated to both material wealth and maximizing life-style. The Type-A personality strives for success almost as an end itself. The yuppie, who is usually younger, is motivated by the desire to succeed in order to achieve status and the pleasures of modern life. Thus, while the older Type A's tend to live almost entirely in the future, this more recent achiever is much more centered on the present. These individuals appear less obviously disturbed in their behavior, as they tend to function *as if* they have a more solid sense of identity. On the surface, they appear enviable: successful, sophisticated, with apparent direction. On closer examination, however, we find that this group also feels tyrannized by time. They try to crowd too much into their present and have a distinctive impatience with postponement. The future is also important but more as a means for meeting complex current needs.

A good example is a young man who came to see me about two years ago. He had heard that I had successfully worked with a friend of his who had similar problems. At age twenty-nine, he had risen to become one of the most successful retail stockbrokers in a national organization. He had been selling securities since he was about twenty-five years old and, in his best year, had already earned over two hundred thousand dollars. He appeared for treatment looking like something of a caricature of a yuppie. He wore a highly coordinated outfit consisting of a black pin-striped suit, yellow tie, pocket handkerchief and bold

18		24	25	26	[27	28
accepted into Stanford		married	started as broker	bought summer house	100K	200K

Time line of a twenty-nine-year-old male stockbroker

yellow suspenders. He drove a Mercedes-Benz convertible and spoke of owning a small house in the city and a cottage on the Chesapeake. He was very formal at first, sat stiffly in his chair, and removed his suit jacket only at my coaxing.

We spent the beginning phase of psychotherapy talking about his business, the importance of his success and his need for recognition. He noted that for the past several months he had had to try harder to maintain his unusual level of productivity. He felt pressure to maintain his high profile since the "eyes of the world were on him." He had received much attention and was usually held up as an example of discipline, perseverance and talent; he was clearly the "fair-haired boy" of his brokerage house. He said he had no idea why he had lost his "edge" and conveyed a sense that his work had become less interesting to him. It was harder to get him to talk about other aspects of his life, as he did not see the connection between his social life, recreation, his family relations and his ability to do his work. As it turned out, he had married his college sweetheart at age twenty-four and was divorced two years later. He said that she was a terrific person but turned out to be less "serious about life" than he had thought. She apparently began to resent his long work hours and complained that they ought to be freer, like some of her friends. He said they bought the weekend house and a boat but couldn't use them as often as she wanted. Eventually, she had an affair and he claimed to feel relieved when they separated so that he could concentrate on his career.

Further inquiry into his nonwork life revealed that he had few friends on or off the job. He had several acquaintances with whom he shared rigorous, highly disciplined exercise schedules involving serious long-distance bicycling. He conveyed the impression that he received a good deal of notoriety in his work but that he failed to "join the team." It seemed that holidays were difficult for him, as he became more aware of his isolation then. About two months before entering therapy, he

o	30	32]	35	40		50
NOW	go out on own	1M net	acquire major real estate	retire from broker- age business		10M net worth

recalled, a relationship with a woman had abruptly ended. They had been quite close for about six months when she became "difficult and argumentative." According to him, she felt that he was not making her feel secure about the future and she could not cope with either his work or recreational schedules. She began to feel like just another one of his calendar obligations and, claiming that she had "been through it before," she decided to leave the relationship.

This young man's time line is somewhat misleading on the surface. Just as he *appears* to be a well-balanced and a completely successful person, so does his time line indicate a fair amount of balance. While most of his "big" experiences are clustered around the "now" point, there is considerable extension into both past and future. However, an examination of the milestones indicates that his temporal scheme is completely determined by accomplishments having to do with money and success. He noted his marriage, but did not include his divorce. His extension to age fifty brought him to the pinnacle of his financial objectives and his line ended. There were some major acquisitions of real estate and the achievement of a $10 million net worth. As we discussed his time line, it became clear that he envisioned his life in a highly determined way where everything was supposed to be under his control. He lived as if everything in his life would "fall into place" if he followed the rigorous program rooted in his "foreclosed" identity. There seemed to be little recognition or acceptance that identity was a continuing project and that life would have some unexpected and tragic elements. The subject of not being in control "opened the therapeutic door" as it allowed him to deal with the parts of his life that frustrated him. He had tried hard to defend himself against the increasing loneliness and lack of nurturance in his life. Once he opened up to the non-work-related sources of anxiety and pain, he did what many individuals do whose identity is adopted. He was willing to "throw away" his career to find a more meaningful life that incorporated relationships and generosity. Needless to say, the work of therapy shifted to helping him achieve a personal identity that could incorporate his financial success and allow him to extend into a more complete sense of futurity.

One of the interesting aspects to the consolidation of this collective yuppie identity is the emphasis on economics. From my clinical work, it would appear that our young people are largely responding defensively to the "macro-dangers" that threaten their futurity. The pursuit of wealth and its accoutrements can support the illusion that one is in control of the forces of life and protected from pitfalls and calamities. This "nouveau materialism," which is intended to buttress us against other anxieties, seems to render us careless about other life choices. There is the tendency remaining from the 1960s and 1970s to think of the life cycle as infinitely extended. As William Kilpatrick (1975) pointed out, there is a sense of "endless moratorium, endless youth, endless fluidity" (p. 64) inherent in this attitude. Thus, while dedicating oneself to wealth, promotions and early retirement, one ignores, as did our young man above, the remaining components of life.

Ironically, while living a life solidly in the "here and now," there are postponements of important life choices. Somewhere in the early 1980s, a significant proportion of the group we now call "baby boomers" began to take notice of a feeling that "life was passing them by." Many of these educated and financially successful young people realized that they were in their thirties and had not yet made marital and family choices, which suddenly began to take on increasing importance. It was during this period that the term "biological clock" began to surface. Young women, in particular, began to believe that the strategy of "endless moratorium" had run its course, and they began to feel the limitations of educational and business success alone. The young women whom I worked with conveyed the sense that they had thought marriage and family were "remotely in my plans, but at some distant point." The notion of a biological clock indicated that the temporal scheme by which they were living was not synchronized with the realities of the human life cycle.

In the early 1980s, I was seeing several young professional women who were in their early thirties and concerned about their biological clocks. They had all been living the lives of the young urban professionals in that they were strongly committed to sophisticated lifestyles, which included a fast-paced leisure life in which they dined out and traveled frequently, dressed well and performed very capably. Almost as if on cue they all seemed to become worried that they would not be able to conceive and deliver children if they didn't accelerate the business of finding a marital partner, waiting a few years and giving birth to a child. One of these clients in particular, a thirty-four-year-old advertising account executive, comes to mind because of the self-defeating way she responded to her newly discovered biological clock.

This young woman had spent her twenties largely advancing her career in an unusually rapid manner. She put in long hours, socialized with people from her profession and confessed to dating men in a somewhat opportunistic manner. When she came to see me, she said she was feeling intermittently depressed and anxious about finding an "appropriate" relationship with a man. She was preoccupied with the schedule she would need to maintain if she were to conceive by her "biologically" determined deadline. She was a very attractive, well-dressed and articulate woman who seemed to exude confidence and competence. When she began therapy, she spoke of developing a family with the kind of language that might be associated with a new advertising campaign. There was a distinct sense of artificial control with an obvious underlying melancholia. As her therapy progressed, she began to express more and more sadness and the pessimistic feeling that she would never "find the right man."

Her therapy drifted into the familiar terrain, as it had for her other female counterparts, of strategies for finding and maintaining a relationship. She expressed the pessimistic idea that "all the good men" were taken and there was simply no format for meeting reasonable choices. After about one year of increasing her self-awareness and beginning to explore the temporal aspects of her identity, she became quickly involved with a thirty-eight-year-old lawyer whom she met at a friend's cookout. Both seemed eager to get on with marriage and family and they were quickly on a commitment path. She asked me to have a session with him, which would approach premarital therapy. He eagerly agreed and began therapy on his own in order to "iron out some rough spots" from his marriage of ten years before, and to deal with some current problems with "depression."

In meetings with them individually, they both expressed the feeling that they had met an "optimal" person. She, especially, felt that he had all the right credentials in terms of age, occupation and interests. He, in turn, was delighted to find a woman who had not been married before and was family-oriented, attractive and independent. In the course of working with her, we discovered that she did not have strong romantic or sexual feelings toward this man compared with previous relationships. She decided not to slow things down as I advised, saying that she wanted to take the risk because of the time constraints. In her estimation, they would have to be married within the year and she should get pregnant in about one year so she could deliver a baby before her thirty-eighth birthday. She was certain that if this relationship did not lead to marriage, she would forfeit her chance to have a biological child.

Despite my urging to explore her lack of "total feeling" for her husband-to-be, this client moved ahead with her eye on the "program" she had begun. She had the very certain feeling that her competence and record of achievement would prevail. It did not take long for conflict to emerge. They began to fight during the final days of their engagement and this continued during their marriage. They began to attend therapy as a couple and we made modest progress, mostly in diffusing the tension resulting from clashes, which occurred on many fronts.

They continued to ignore my concern and decided to conceive a child about six months into their marriage. To their surprise, after several months of "scientific sex" they were unable to conceive. She became increasingly impatient, as if it never occurred to her that things wouldn't go exactly as anticipated. Fighting escalated during this period, and they were not able to complete fertility evaluations. Almost as quickly as they "formulated" their marriage, it came undone. I continued to work with them individually after the separation even though she left therapy for several months. She initially blamed me for not stopping her from making this "irreversibly bad decision."

It should be clear from the cases discussed so far that modern society condones or even encourages "time frantic" life. Yet we know that social context does not determine how an individual will behave. Not everyone becomes a Type-A personality or a "yuppie" even when circumstances support that behavior. While some people find themselves increasingly fatigued from losing the "time wars," others achieve a sense of relative balance. As with the other syndromes I have been discussing, there are obviously individual factors that interact with cultural forces to produce these personalities. As with depression and the addictive disorders, there must be historical antecedents that make certain individuals prone to experience time as moving too rapidly, so that they feel chronically displaced.

You will recall that the depressed individual experiences lived time as moving too slowly. The time "combatant," on the other hand, has an ambivalent feeling about the flow of time. On the one hand, there is a chronic impatience. Waiting is very difficult, whether in a restaurant with "slow" service or in line at a bank window. On other occasions, time seems to be in short supply, and the days are not long enough to achieve established goals. It is this alternation in the relationship to clock time that makes this person so difficult to deal with. As the spouses of such people have said to me in practice, "They cannot stand to wait with you, and you're always waiting for them." When situations require patience and serenity, they become agitated (much like the cocaine user) and do everything to speed up the world. Under these circumstances, waiters become victims, along with anyone else who seems responsible for "things not happening" quickly enough. At other times there is the escalating sense of desperation that comes with the feeling that there isn't enough time to get things accomplished. In this mode, it appears as if the clock is racing and the day is over prematurely. This sense of racing produces a driven quality that makes it difficult for our "time warrior" to stop lest he feel that nothing is being achieved.

We are obviously describing a complex kind of behavior, so it will not be easy to postulate definitive causal childhood experiences. Moreover, it would seem that the historical factors that govern this syndrome are multiple rather than simple. There are not many studies that bear directly on the complex phenomenon we are describing. The most useful source of guidance is the "psychosocial" theory of Erik Erikson, who enhanced Freud's views of child development with social factors. As with the oral personality type discussed in the last chapter, there seems to be difficulty in the same stage as for the addictive personalities. It was suggested that many addicted individuals had difficulties in early infancy with nurturance. However, while the alcoholic individual, for example, develops a passive orientation and looks to alcohol to "lull" him, the Type-A personality responds in a contrasting way. This type of person has difficulty with passivity, as though he is repudiating the passive position of early childhood. Anticipation seems to generate anxiety, which is often followed by hostility. This sequence is evident both in children and in the adults we are addressing. Though there are no clear-cut longitudinal studies on this subject, the childhood version of this syndrome is the child who is easily frustrated by delays in anticipated rewards and who is prone to express his consternation with such self-defeating behavior as temper tantrums.

Rather than suffering deprivation in infancy, I suspect, these individuals became involved in the parents' power struggles. It is likely that an insecure parent alternates between reasonable responsiveness to the infant's needs and occasional doubts about being controlled by the never-ending needs of the newborn. This parent may seek professional "license" to hold back nurturance to teach the child who is in control. The message to be conveyed is "I will not be manipulated." Thus, early in the life of this personality type, there may be an exposure to "power politics." The problem here is that nurturance probably comes intermittently, resulting in chaotic feelings about time passing. Some support for this contention was provided in a study (Morrison, 1980) that found that many parents of hyperactive children had clinical diagnoses of "personality disorder" or "hysteria."

The prototypical child of this type probably gets through the first year of life as an "edgy" child concerned with control and power. The next stage of development is often called the "terrible twos" because of the oppositional tendencies of the period. Children, having acquired some sense of the difference between themselves and others, begin to test their will against the authority of their parents. The average child goes through a process of learning his parents' limits, and a conscience begins to develop during this confrontation. Our Type-A individual probably maintains the temporal discomfort from early childhood and adds the element of hostility from this period, so that the effect is cumulative. Rather than coming through the stage with a harmonious sense of order between parent and child, the child is burdened by a low frustration tolerance and a tendency to battle with the expectations of people in authority.

Though this is, of course, a vast oversimplification of the developmental process, the outline should convey the way in which the adult disturbance is rooted in the key stages of childhood. The task of the third stage of childhood, in simple terms, is to form appropriate identifications with parents, develop a sexual identity and develop ambition in what has come to be called the ego ideal. This stage should represent the last "storm" in childhood before the industriousness of later childhood is developed. The child in this stage is intrusive, competitive, very emotional and very interested in the politics of family life. Classical psychoanalytic theory speaks of little boys and their desire to possess their mothers by competing with their fathers, and little girls and their urge to win their fathers by competing with their mothers. It stands to reason that the fundamental distrust of the first stage and the preoccupation with control from the second stage would diminish the likelihood of a successful resolution of this stage.

By the time the child is eight years old, he is probably a tense, uneasy youngster who has not settled into the "joy of accomplishment" that characterizes other children in this age group. The child has a short attention span and is characteristically forgetful. School adjustment is typically difficult, as the child is usually overly aggressive with peers, does not accept the authority of teachers and often ignores instructions. These children are given many different labels, depending on what aspect of their behavior is dominant. Some, who are obviously intelligent, are perceived as having appreciable potential and are labeled underachievers. Others, whose primary problem seems to be attentional, who cannot wait and be passive, end up with the debilitating label "hyperactive." Whatever the label, these children are "disjointed" and show signs of being excessively driven at an early age. Drive, at this stage of life, appears as a tendency toward exaggerated behavior. Later, as the child moves into adolescence and beyond, the temporal impatience, hostility and competitiveness may unify to produce a pattern of very high achievement in the form of entrepreneurship.

It is not hard to see why our society has a tendency to romanticize the work addict. Some of these individuals, despite the disquietude they feel and spread to others, become well known for their achievements. The disturbance of the early part of their lives finds avenues for expression that may lead to positive accomplishments. Some of our great scientists, politicians, builders, inventors, artists and businessmen fit this stereotype. Nevertheless, some striking differences remain between individuals who achieve their life's goals and those who do not live up to their expressed sense of purpose, despite distorted amounts of drive. While both groups might live with a sense of urgency about achievement, the successful group is able to overcome their limitations sufficiently to extend themselves successfully into the future. In order to achieve at any level, an individual needs to have some aim for which to strive. It would appear that individuals who are driven, who feel harassed by time but never quite "make it," have greater trouble with futurity.

A logical question at this point is why some ambitious personalities seem to reach their objectives more effectively. Obviously this is a complex question: We cannot take for granted that personality factors account for all human variability. Certainly situations vary, along with talent and temperament, and there is probably even a fair amount of luck involved. Type-A personalities, living their lives with a sense of urgency, keep "plugging away" so that many successful people undoubtedly have histories of business failures. It is probable, however, that those who achieve more have less proportionate disturbance in the earlier stages of development. The individual whose subjective clock is disturbed by extremes in infancy is undoubtedly at a greater disadvantage than those whose first exposure to life is less erratic. As a result of severe inconsistencies, some individuals are probably more overwhelmed and do not smoothly resolve the tasks of the later stages of childhood. This view is consistent with the psychodynamic concept that the more severe psychopathologies are grounded in the earliest childhood experiences.

If parental inconsistency is too profound in the first stage of life, we would expect permanent psychological scarring to go beyond the temporal rhythmic area. In addition to disturbances in temporal organization, there would be disturbances in the development of self-esteem and object relations, which would lead to gross adjustment problems. It must be remembered, however, that the model I am suggesting is based on inconsistency rather than gross neglect. When there is consistently extreme neglect, the problems will probably be more pronounced, taking the form of early childhood psychosis or early (anaclitic) depression. It has also been suggested in theoretical works that profound inconsistency in the first year of life might lead to severe problems with mood, involving depression and mania. Though mania and temporal rhythm problems are related, the predominant problem with an individual diagnosed as "manic" is mood. The "time-harassed" person we are identifying in this chapter is not as severely pathological as the manic-depressive.

Another kind of temporally harassed person is the superachiever, who makes a special mark in his or her lifetime. Whether we are speaking about Marie Curie, Benjamin Franklin, Mahatma Gandhi, Martina Navratilova or John D. Rockefeller, we are dealing with individuals whose accomplishments have a place in history. In order to have attained their goals, they most certainly must have operated on a frantic work schedule. I suspect that in some ways these unusual people resemble some of the cases I have addressed in this chapter. They probably live each day feeling that time is short and they must consolidate their efforts to realize their aims. A major difference, however, is that they do finish their tasks in spite of day-to-day feelings that might suggest the contrary. Unlike the individual who is humbled before the flow of time, these combatants, living as if with Nietzsche's "sense of urgency," manage to apply their extraordinary talent and get things done.

So far I have identified developmental history as the basis for distinguishing varying degrees of success in goal attainment. Perhaps the fundamental difference in level of achievement, especially in light of the thesis of this book, has to do with the ability to extend into the future with some very definite goals. One of the impediments to future extension, you will recall, has to do with the discomfort most of us feel around the long-range extension. We have suggested that all humans have a love-hate relationship with the distant future as it connotes the end of one's life. It would appear that our "trailblazers" have a very definite sense of the finiteness of life and respond with a sense of mission. Life is lived in order to fulfill one's destiny and often to leave behind a monument in the form of a great accomplishment.

Pyramids, castles, books, music, wars and religions have been created as testimony to the lives of extraordinary individuals. When we stop and take note of these, we marvel at the creators and accept them as historical heroes. It is important to recall the romantic conception of the creative artist, which embodies a powerful theme of personal suffering. One view of the romantic artist has him suffering like Toulouse-Lautrec, living on the edge of poverty in lonely solitude. On another level the superachiever may suffer from a kind of tension derived from a blend of genius, effective planning and extraordinary drive. The few great men and women whom I have interviewed in my office conveyed a perspective that shed considerable light on their work and its relationship to lived time. One of these people was an actor of national acclaim. He originally came to see me as the result of a career setback that left him in a prolonged state of depression. He reported that usually he would quickly rebound from setbacks and find his old level of "workaholism," but this time his depression seemed different; he was not so interested in resuming his work or the accompanying habits. After a short period we began probing his personal history. He claimed that "as far back as I could remember I was a very anxious person." Even as a young man he felt that the "predators would soon come knocking on my door." He felt that he needed to be more successful than his peers to satisfy what seemed to be deeper levels of fear. Further exploration revealed that he became somewhat preoccupied with death as a young child. He claimed that his family's explanations, rooted in the Presbyterian religion, never put his fears to rest. As he grew up he recalled vacillating between despair over the inevitable end of life and a race to use his time while he had it. He lived his life as if he were running a race. He felt out of synchronization with both time and other people.

In the course of therapy, he made the not unusual realization that his achievements were not making any difference to the way he felt. The more acclaim he received, the less it meant to him. In one of those rare, precise moments in the therapeutic process, he commented, "Even though my work has an immortality, my life is not going to go on forever." He began to grasp that the race he was running had no real finish line. He began to realize that all those days when he was in bad spirits because of the "time war," he was alienating his third wife and his two children. He found, like other extremely ambitious people, that the people closest to him became fatigued from his skirmishes with life and the many crises over deadlines and imperfect productivity. They suspected, he reasoned, that his pursuits were self-serving after all, and that all that effort and worrying only detracted from their life.

This client's battle with his ambition and the time constraints of his life can be directly traced to a particular period of childhood. He recalled worrying about dying "just about all my life, starting at about age four." In Chapter 2, we discussed the universality of children trying to come to terms with death and how their families frequently obstruct this effort. This man, like so many others, remembered becoming psychologically fused with several of the comic book variety superheroes. He remembered wondering if he could possibly be a variation on young Clark Kent (Superman) and would read the comic book depicting Superman's boyhood over and over. As he grew up, he remembered that he grudgingly gave up this fantasy but retained the feeling that he was "special." He recalled that this special feeling had both served him and brought him to the brink of personal tragedy. He grew up with the appearance of great self-confidence and bravado, which he learned to convey in his work on the stage and in film. However, in his early twenties he recalled doubting his uniqueness and feeling he had to go to great lengths to support the idea of his not being just "another mortal." By the time he was in his thirties, his life's rhythm, he said, was colored by a definite quality of racing against the clock to live up to his childhood fantasy.

This client's time line was unique in that it was almost all located in the near and distant future. The imbalance in his temporal organization was indicative of an identity that was not based on the integration of his life experiences. Rather, his view of himself was totally tied to his achievements. As a result, his sense of balance was completely connected to the volatile nature of his occupation. As we came to see in the course of his treatment, he never got over the fact that "all the king's horses and all the king's men couldn't put Humpty Dumpty together again." He was victimized by an inordinate fear of death, which he handled by a combination of denial and the superperson overcompensation. He lived his life trying to convince himself and others of his specialness by overproductivity. Despite a very successful careeer, however, he was always aware of his life "slipping away." Aging was very difficult, and the more he became aware of growing older, the more he felt he had to achieve. We are still working together in psychotherapy. As he puts it, he is beginning to "enjoy just being another mortal."

As we try to outline the dynamics of the time-harassed individual, there is a tendency to focus too much on the high achievers. However, the experience of feeling pushed by elusive goals and being constantly disorganized is widespread. I hear about it on all levels, from ordinary social situations to professional practice. Recently I received a call from a friend who was confirming a dinner meeting for the following week. When I asked how he was, he said he was incredibly rushed and had no time "for himself." When we sat down to dinner the following week he continued in this vein, claiming to feel overwhelmed by his work and needing more hours in the day. This interaction with a friend is not an isolated event. I hear similar comments from many people, including teenagers who have become victims of the sense that there isn't enough time to live their lives. I have already discussed how that disordered temporal experience often leads to drug interest for our young people.

Our culture has begun to produce products and services that relate to the problem of temporal disorganization. Though psychology has been slow in incorporating temporality within its body of knowledge, the business sector has reacted to a widespread need. You have undoubtedly noticed the recent proliferation of all sorts of new personal "organizers." Whereas we used to carry small pocket-sized appointment calendars, there are now exotic devices that come in all sizes and shapes. I have been astounded at both the quantity and the number of types of these organizers as they surface at various meetings. It is not uncommon, in the process of trying to arrange a meeting, for someone to haul out an enormous book with separate sections denoting different time units. I recently fell prey to one of these systems myself, only to find that organizing my schedule was adding an unwanted burden to my existing routine. Others with whom I have conferred tend to agree that these sophisticated time organizers intimidate by their complexity and sheer weight.

Time management seminars have also sprung up throughout industry to increase efficiency. In the sales field, in particular, experts boasting new systems for organizing and "prioritizing" one's obligations are commonplace. From my experience with an industry spokesman, these seminars have achieved such popularity because so many managers, executives and salespeople experience temporal disorganization. Most attend these classes on the premise that greater scheduling efficiency will lead to increased productivity. Because temporal harassment is so universal in our culture and omnipresent in the business world, it is not hard to find candidates who identify with the problem as outlined by the program developers. I attended one of these seminars, given by one of the most respected time management "gurus" in the country. I also had the chance to speak to several of the participants in the context of a corporation for which I served as a consultant. Inevitably, the students seem to leave the seminar on a very high note, feeling that their new materials and system have given them a powerful new tool.

The fallacy in this approach is, in a sense, the fallacy of naive behaviorism. It is assumed that the way to get people to experience their life differently is to tell them how to behave differently. Though the goal is for the individual to approach his scheduling differently, the problem is more centered on temporal fluidity. The person who is unable to effect a work schedule that leads to designated goals frequently has trouble with the relationships between present behavior and its consequences. Inevitably, most individuals become discouraged in the face of poor results and drift into temporal disorganization. As we have seen, however, the inability to generate future images connected to relevant past and present behavior is a complex problem involving experience and structures that defy simple behavioral "tune-ups." As might be expected, I have not heard of any long-term miraculous changes resulting from a new time management book.

When considering the main personality type within this chapter, it is easy to assume that we are dealing primarily, if not exclusively, with men. The notorious Type-A personality who is driven, competitive, fascinated with the time "crunch" in sports and prone to great achievement is generally a male stereotype. We traditionally have not been apt to think of women as being temporally harassed, preoccupied with productivity or hopeless workaholics. This common presumption is probably in error in two ways. First, women have and probably have always had Type A's among them. I suspect, however, that the view that only men are victims of temporal flow stems from a bias that places a higher premium on a man's work than on a woman's. Before the entry of women into the workplace, their only contexts for the expression of drive and achievement were in the home and in community service. With respect to household management, there is no question that there was and is great latitude in how one handles daily tasks. While some women maintained the flow of their work in an even, effective way, others felt overwhelmed and behind and often could never stop working. The difference, however, was that while men's excesses were often glamorized, an overzealous housewife was seen as matronly, cumbersome and dull.

The same can certainly be said in the arena of volunteering. Women's service groups have been the long-standing supporters of most of our cultural institutions. Our museums, orchestras, ballets, zoos, hospitals and many other highly visible social entities could not have endured without the fund-raising acumen of a large number of very successful women who have never worked for a salary. Despite the absence of financial motivation, the energy expenditure, dedication and work habits are quite similar to those of men in the workplace. In the context of these organizations, women certainly exhibit ambition, competition, impatience and the propensity for overextending themselves in their mission. They also show a wide difference in ability to achieve goals in a harmonious way as opposed to feeling the tyranny of temporal pressure in all aspects of their lives.

The second basis for the mistaken assumption that "time combat" is a male trait has to do with the emergence of women in the workplace. Up until the 1960s, paid jobs typically did not allow women to express their drive, since they tended to be in nonmanagement or nonexecutive positions. That has certainly changed dramatically. Women now occupy positions in all levels of the corporate world and are entering the professions in greater and greater numbers. They are also appearing in greater numbers in medical schools, law schools, doctoral psychology programs and business schools. It is not hard to find women in financial services, computer industries or management positions struggling with the temporal organization in the workplace in a way we have usually associated with men.

It would appear that women are not only expressing their temporal difficulties as men do but are also showing similar signs of the "wear and tear." The Type-A personality, originally a male prototype, was linked to heart disease. It has now been extended to correlate with other psychosomatic disorders, ranging from ulcers to hypertension to general immune system deficiencies. Heart disease rates are on the rise for women along with the rapidly rising rate of addictive problems that were traditionally male. It is not that the trait of temporal disorganization did not exist before women's entry to positions of high visibility in the workplace. Rather, due to the complexity of the business context, including evaluation by others and lack of total control, the working woman may be subject to higher stress. It is also true that many women who work are subject to greater stresses, since they typically shoulder greater domestic responsibilities than men.

A young female physician came back to see me professionally after an absence of about three years. I had worked with her over a period of two years while she was in medical school. She was an extremely animated, energetic and ambitious young woman. She spoke primarily about her difficulties in her relationships with men, and especially of finding herself out of synch with their "levels of energy." She seemed to "move faster" and required more social and cultural stimulation. She was very close to the Type-A configuration in most ways and was prone to psychosomatic attacks, which usually took the form of acute skin rashes. During the course of therapy she made the transition from being a nutritionist to attending medical school. The greater challenge of becoming a physician helped channel some of her drive as long as she worked on ways to dilute her sense of temporal discomfort. She learned to pace herself better, she came to understand the origins of her impatience, and she selected a male who complemented her behavior. In the past, she had become involved with driven men like herself, resulting in an intensification of her struggles. Through therapy she eventually married a "low-keyed" individual who did not "add fuel to her fire." Rather, she said, he taught her the art of "letting time pass."

She came to see me shortly after having a baby. Like many modern, educated women, she chose to nurse her baby for about three months. After the second week, however, she became extremely agitated, began to panic and came to see me in a state of crisis. She apparently found the unexpected and extended periods of inactivity extremely difficult. She was unable to handle the extensive needs of the nursing baby, which she had assumed would adopt one of the idealized pediatric schedules immediately. Her anxiety raised tremendous fears of failure and an inability to nurse her baby successfully. She had come to view nursing her baby as another goal that she was not prepared to fail to achieve. After exploring alternatives, we decided she should stop nursing and let her husband become more involved in the feeding of the baby. She did this for a few weeks, during which we were able to help her regain her sense of control and confidence. She increased her involvement with feeding the baby and in a few months felt that the baby, like her husband, was giving her the "gift of serenity."

It is impossible to discuss the subject of activity levels without getting into the question of inherited constitution. To be sure, as far back as 2,500 years ago, the eminent Greek physician Hippocrates postulated his well-known "humoral theory" to account for differences in mood and behavior. Hippocrates essentially claimed that classifiable disorders occurred when one of the four vital substances (or humors) of the body was present in excess. Those who suffered from mania, for example, were thought to have too much red humor (blood) in their body, while melancholics were thought to have too much black humor. Modern constitutional theorists have certainly gone beyond the typologies first developed in ancient Greece. Nevertheless, the results are not of particular value in terms of the phenomena we have been discussing. In the case of extreme manic-depressive disorders, compelling genetic data (Allen, 1976) suggest biochemical transmission. However, in the less pronounced "mood" disorders under consideration there is no such data. With respect to the agitated, restless, and time-harassed person of this chapter, it is possible to speculate about the neurotransmitters that were identified in discussing depression. However, there is no evidence that the syndrome has a measurable biochemical basis. Even if we look to the hyperactive child as representing an extreme temperamental type, research findings strongly suggest that hyperactivity "fades" somewhere in adolescence (Saterfield, 1978). In summary, while it is naive to assume that there are no differences in inherited constitution, this area of inquiry is not apparently relevant to temporality and behavior.

Further evidence that this temporal rhythmic problem is not inborn is suggested by the susceptibility to change. While "decompression" is difficult, imposing a situation in which usual behavior patterns are disrupted often leads to at least short-term changes in time comfort. Confinement during periods of illness, unstructured vacations and even various kinds of incarceration can be pivotal in letting people experience themselves in greater synchronization. Near tragedies such as averted plane crashes continually get individuals to question their life pattern and rethink the crowding of goals into the near future. Finally, a kind of psychotherapy designed to break the vicious cycle of early childhood experience and time war can be a profound experience for those who are willing to examine the coordinates of their life. In the final chapter I will talk about such psychotherapy in greater depth.

VI

PRECIOUS TIME

So far, we have been looking at our society and individuals who are in the prime or in the middle of their lives. From a time line perspective, the yuppies, Type-A personalities and substance abusers are largely individuals near the middle of their life cycle and tend to mark the present at the center of the line. There is, however, a large and vital segment of our society who are well past the midpoint of their lives and who are having their own particular difficulty with temporal organization. More so than individuals who are in their forties, for example, those who are over sixty have a great deal of trouble extending into the future.

On pages 120–21 are the time lines of two women in their early seventies with whom I have had contact. Both are articulate, healthy women who had reason to seek professional help for a brief period. I selected these particular lines because they are, in a sense, typical of the kind of temporal perspectives we will be discussing. "A" is a woman who lives "one day at a time," has a crowded life in the present and has a high diversity of experience in the past. There is obvious telepression

	5	16	25	30	35	45	52
Woman A							
	got a house	sweet sixteen	married	first trip abroad	Bob's new business	graduates	first grand- child

Time lines of two women in their seventies

	10	16	18	24	35	51	57	60	65
Woman B									
	first sum- mer in Maine	sister died	vale- dicto- rian	mar- ried	hus- band starts own busi- ness	son plays profes- sional tennis	MFA degree	first grand- child	trip to Alaska

of her future, as she manages to extend ahead only about two years, and has not indicated that her life will end. Goals are not well represented in the future; this person is living as if there were no particular reason to rush ahead. She complained of anxiety, sleep problems and a growing loss of interest in everyday affairs. On closer examination, "A" was not unlike many younger counterparts whose futurity seems blocked; she was depressed.

Person "B" is probably representative of a special breed of elder individual who is fully engaged in life and thus is part of a minority. This person's time line indicates that life is still ahead of her, although her extension into the future brings one to "the end of the line." Death for this woman is a motivator rather than a suppressor of goals and objectives. The acceptance of death as a "punctuation" point in the life cycle signals her to "crowd" the future with the unfinished business of her life. The past and present are not unrepresented, since this person can move into the future realistically only if she draws on the meaningful parts of her past and present life.

Although these two women are approximately the same age, they obviously view their lives quite differently. The first woman seems to have little in her future to look forward to. She spoke in her therapy as if there were simply "nothing in the world worth doing." The second

60	68	[69	o	71	72]
husband died	mother died	major surgery	NOW	Bermuda cruise	new volunteer work

67	68	[71	o	72	73	74]	78	80	82 Die
husband dies	recovered from hip injury	started therapy	NOW	sell house in Maine	open book store with daughter	travel to England	start bookmobile for inner city	a last trip to Europe	work on book collection

woman actually sought therapy because of a problem she envisioned would *unfold* in her future. She envisioned family conflict over the sale of her large house in New England and sought ideas about how to manage a potential conflict. The differences in their connection to the psychological future did not stop with their time lines. They almost seemed to be from two entirely different generations. Woman A made frequent reference to aging and was considering moving into a "retirement community." Woman B spoke with a sense of urgency and planned to "work until it hurt too much."

Both women remained in treatment for less than four months. The outcomes, however, were quite different and not unexpected. Woman A did not find the task of self-exploration very easy and complained that she was looking for some definite ideas. She was, however, resistant to most suggestions about future images, which, she said, "weren't her." After about ten sessions, she asked for a referral to a psychiatrist, who prescribed antidepressant medication. Woman B was one of those clients who make the work of a psychotherapist a really gratifying experience. She focused her energy on her family relationships and her concern about selling her large home. She was open, discriminating, and definite about her therapeutic goals. She completed therapy after fifteen sessions, expressing a great deal of gratitude. I received a Christmas card from her in which she mentioned an interest in resuming psychotherapy of a "less specific nature."

Increasing numbers of mature adults are finding their way into psychotherapy. Though it has not been traditional for individuals beyond the middle years to enter psychotherapy, that has begun to change in recent years. It was probably the psychoanalytic movement that established the original bias against working with the psychological difficulties of older adults. Otto Fenichel (1945), in describing who should be included in the psychoanalytic enterprise, put most individuals who were over forty off-limits. Seeing psychoanalysis as a youthful endeavor requiring an extraordinary commitment to far-reaching personality change, he did not believe that middle-aged individuals would have the "libidinal resources" to undertake the project.

This age cutoff was reinforced by both the psychiatric establishment and older patients themselves. The original Freudian bias, coupled with the predilection of medical people to see the problems of the elderly as organic, created a tendency to not see this group as needing psychological service. My own early experience with this "over sixty" population came largely from referrals by physicians or the children of the potential patient. Though I often found an obvious functional basis for their complaints, they tended to resist the idea of a long-term therapeutic relationship. They acknowledged the problems and were intrigued by the chance to "explore their psyche," but thought that it was generally too late in their lives. The attitude was exemplified by the comment of an older acquaintance who said, "Why should I buy another tuxedo when I will get to wear it only a few more times, at best?" This statement reflects a feeling of being on "borrowed time" without an extended future. Though older females typically had less of this feeling of a curtailed future, they too, did not make willing candidates for psychotherapy even when the indications were quite positive.

In the last ten or fifteen years, there has been a decided shift in our collective feeling about the last fifth of the life cycle. This change in outlook has undoubtedly been brought about by dramatic changes in life expectancy. The demographics of aging have changed dramatically, with impact on just about every aspect of life.

According to the *Register Report* (1988), 10 percent of our population was over 55 in the year 1900. By 1986, over 20 percent of our population was over 55. The same report projects that between the years 1980 and

2030, the 85-plus part of our population is expected to quadruple. One can already sense the profound increase in that segment of our society. In the same vein, the United States Department of Health, Education and Welfare (1978) reported that our life expectancy at birth has risen from 47.3 years in 1900 to 72.8 years in 1976. Perhaps most profound in terms of our current discussion is a conclusion drawn by a United States Senate committee on aging (1987–1988). They reported that the expected number of postretirement years changed from 1.2 years in 1900 to 13.6 in 1980, due to the large change in life expectancy.

It is rather clear that human consciousness does not always keep pace with sociological and technological changes. We are still suffering from the growing pains associated with the computerization of society. We have not yet solved the problem of adolescent productivity in the modern industrialized society. The emergence of women in the work-place has altered the nature of sex roles and our framework for caring for young children. The twentieth century, the last twenty-five years in particular, has seen radical changes that will eventually "push" our values and ideals to new positions. The extension of human life is certainly one of the transformations that will require a re-examination of our views concerning life beyond the arbitrary age of sixty-five.

One of the indications of shifts in our attitude toward aging is the degree of conflict inherent in modern society. Human history is replete with variations on the theme of searching for the key to eternal life. Since the beginning of recorded civilization, societies have usually worked toward the extension of life through government, religion and, eventually, science. Both traditional medicine and, more recently, scientific medicine have dedicated themselves to prolonging human life. It was taken for granted that keeping people alive as long as possible was inherently good, and that the aging themselves certainly would want the maximum length of time in which to fulfill their destinies.

In some older societies, achieving an older age entitled one to a special status. Aging was seen as a process of adding stature and wisdom that required respect, and naturally placed the elderly (especially men) in the position of family and political leader. This phenomenon was exemplified in ancient China, where the Confucian philosophy explicitly required that the elderly be treated with special deference. This "gerontocratic" trend was quite evident until recent times throughout most of the world. Leaders like Winston Churchill, Charles de Gaulle, Nikita Khrushchev, Golda Meir, Marshal Tito, Mao Tse-tung, Jomo

Kenyatta and Dwight D. Eisenhower all exemplified the sense of trust associated with the notion of being led by our elders.

However, the period following the 1960s saw a dramatic shift in our beliefs about the elderly. We became a youth culture, believing that the "prime of life" was located much earlier in the developmental cycle. During the turbulence of the sixties, the warning "Don't trust anyone over thirty" became fashionable. In the same vein, our fascination with athletics reflects the notion that one can be old by age thirty. We see tennis stars peaking in their late teens and football players "cut from camp" because they are considered expendable at age thirty-two. We also see, particularly in yuppies, a strong emphasis in our culture on "making it" before one is thirty-five years old.

A comparable shift has occurred in our views concerning aging and competence. Government leaders, particularly since John F. Kennedy, have tended to be increasingly younger. This trend has continued, with elected officials becoming more concerned about appearing youthful. Even President Ronald Reagan, who is in his seventies, was very interested in appearing vigorous. He was often depicted as an ageless cowboy, as contrasted with an aging Eisenhower, who always seemed to be "out on the golf course." Though I have no statistics available, it also seems that heads of corporations are increasing younger. It is not uncommon for CEOs to be in their mid-forties, as compared to the much older image connected to this position in the 1940s. In the same vein, intergenerational dynamics have also changed. Grandparents are not often perceived as sources of authority, and parents, in general, do not exercise as much control over the lives of their children. Generally speaking, it is not typically assumed in contemporary society that greater knowledge or competence comes with deepening maturation.

The critique of gerontocratic idealism is typified by Sidney Hook in writing about man's quest for immortality.

> It is clear, not only after a moment's reflection, but from a study of the representations of immortality in all ages and in virtually all the visual arts, that when human beings desire immortality, it is not eternal life they seek or yearn for, but eternal youth. (Hook, 1988, p. 22)

Hook is arguing against the glorification of old age. He sees the aging process in "realistic" terms as representing the decline of the individual. He recalls the British philosopher Bertrand Russell saying before he died, "Hook, don't let anyone tell you about the great satisfactions of old age" (Hook, 1988, p. 25). Hook's view is a direct reaction to a recent resurgence of the position that views aging as a part of the overall evolutionary process.

For about the last ten years, there has been a growing movement within psychology, sociology, religion and the field of gerontology, which has identified the latter stage of life as *different* from but *equal* to other stages. The model of the eight stages of life created by Erik Erikson (1963) has been revived, since it holds that growth and challenge continue throughout each stage of the human cycle. Erikson sees the developmental cycle in terms of the task at each age. Thus, while he sees "intimacy" and "generativity" (giving back) as critical to early and middle adulthood, he sees old age as providing the opportunity to achieve another level of wisdom, which he calls "integrity." Erikson's theory, then, is "epigenetic" in that there is the implication of critical sequence and of a building process that leads to the higher level of existence. It would appear that integrity for Erikson represents a kind of global thinking, probably synonymous with the wisdom inherent in traditional Oriental views of old age.

D. J. Levinson (1978) represents a refinement of Erikson's approach to adult aging in that he differentiates four stages of adulthood ranging from early adulthood (17–45) to middle adulthood (45–65), to late adulthood (60–85), to late, late adulthood (80-plus). Levinson's theory attempts to define each stage in terms of a period of stability followed by a transition period that leads the person into the next stage of adult life. He sees individuals as evolving in an "actualization" process of creating and re-creating the structures of life. It suggests that adults continue to appraise their lives as they progress and, after sometimes turbulent periods of evaluation, begin to create new structures. Though this theoretical orientation tends to focus on middle adulthood, it implies that there is potential for growth into the final stage of life.

Research programs that began in the 1970s tend to support the notion that life after sixty-five is not necessarily dismal, despite the position that Hook exemplifies. J. L. Lachman and colleagues (1979), for example, could not find significant differences in the ability of different age groups (44–53 versus 65–74) to retrieve information. Asking questions like, "What was Muhammad Ali's original name?" they found that the age groups were not really distinguishable, thus dispelling the myth that memory of this type is bound to deteriorate in the older group. J. L. Horn (1978) and his associates go beyond suggesting that the "decline" theory may not be completely evident. He develops the concept that as we become older adults, we begin to make changes in that *kind* of intelligence which is dominant. Horn calls the ability associated with younger people "fluid" intelligence, which is related to the ability to solve problems. Older individuals, according to his research, develop an intellectual capacity called "crystallized" intelligence, which uses the knowledge accumulated over a lifetime. This distinction in intellectual skills tends to align itself with the adult developmental theories of Erikson and Levinson. Erikson, in particular, sees the achievement of "integrity" as associated with the type of "wisdom" that can develop only from the perspective that is *possible* for older individuals to achieve. For Erikson, the achievement of this wisdom is not automatic, since it requires the continuous management of identity and temporal concerns.

One of the other traditional views of the aging process concerns the human capacity for passion, sexuality and romance in the later years of life. In *Human Sexual Response* (1966), Masters and Johnson attempt to dispel some misconceptions about sexuality in older adults. They reported that individuals can and do maintain sexual behavior into old age and describe the qualitative and quantitative differences. This finding runs against the grain of conventional feeling about aging, as there is a tendency, especially for young people, to cringe at the idea of their grandparents engaging in sexual activity. It is hard enough in our sexually conflicted culture for many young people to consider the sexuality of even their parents, who might be in their forties. The Masters and Johnson finding has probably served as both a source of information and a source of encouragement for our older population. Sexuality, after all, is not unlike other behavior, in that it is shaped by cultural beliefs and expectations. Just as cultures have "rites of passage" that suggest a time framework in which to begin sexual activity, so do we possess "rites of egress," which suggest when behavior should draw to a close.

The notion of a changing but continuous sexual drive is consistent with the other developmental approaches, in that the structures of life are seen as evolutionary. Though there are detractors from this viewpoint who see positive views of aging as more inspirational than real, there are certainly many supportive indications. A favorite example is a woman whom I saw professionally several years ago when she was in her late seventies. After the death of her younger sister, she became increasingly depressed and, with the encouragement of a good friend, decided to try psychotherapy. In the process of exploring her life, we arrived at the subject of love and romance. I must admit, being subject to the usual biases myself, I almost ignored her cautious attempts to discuss a rather uncomfortable subject. In spite of my clumsy handling of her first thoughts about her love life during the past ten years, we managed to develop a lengthy dialogue about a relationship she had with a man when she was seventy, several years after her husband had died. She described this relationship as the greatest love affair of her life, which she pointed out was not without a fair range of relationships, both in and out of the United States. Consistent with the tendency to deny sex at her age, I assumed she was speaking about intimacy and companionship. She set me straight by letting me know that while she was speaking about intimacy, she was primarily speaking about a sexual affair.

Her elaboration on the "affair of her life" takes us right back to a discussion of temporality. I was astounded by her ability to speak directly of the connection between sexuality at her stage of life and her sense of an intensely expanded present. She said they felt like reckless adolescents because they were unencumbered by the need to project the relationship out of the "moment" they found themselves in. There was no talk of commitment or marriage, only of discovery. The absence of goals within their relationship and the absence of external life pressures, she felt, made "time stand still." Both had few other responsibilities, so they could focus on communication, the sharing of intellectual interests and lovemaking. When I discussed temporal rhythm earlier, I noted that the sense of pacing of time is directly affected by how much the activity is future directed. These two individuals happened upon the oceanic feeling of timelessness in the context of a love relationship devoid of temporal flow.

The view of aging embodied in romantic tales of "love in the seventies" represents one side of a very large conflict in our culture. On the one hand, there is the large contingent of older adults for whom it is important to believe that life is not finished after age sixty-five. The life cycle developmentalists within psychology suggest that human growth is a continual process which does not end at some age. There is also the continued impact of the human potential philosophy, which happens to concur with the psychological view that humans

127

have the potential to grow into new levels of intellect, spirituality and wisdom as they near the end of their lives. The "death and dying" movement typified by Elisabeth Kübler-Ross (1974) extends the human capacity for sustained growth right through the actual process of dying. I will discuss the death and dying perspective more extensively later in the chapter.

A recent cinema series called *The Karate Kid* explores, perhaps in a coincidental fashion, the relationship between a troubled adolescent boy and an older Japanese man skilled in the art of karate. Though the first film's primary focus was on the woes of the besieged boy in need of some instant martial arts training, the sequel moves more fully into the adventures of the older gentleman. While grandfatherly characters have often appeared in our art forms, it is unusual to depict an older person as wise in addition to possessing a superior physical skill. Mr. Miagi is actually a better fighter than the young foes of our teenage hero. As I am blessed with a ten-year-old son, I have had ample excuse for continuing my investigation into the martial art movie form. Again, one of the peripheral aspects of many of these films is the reverence for the intellectual, emotional and *physical* ability of the old master. In the past, this element of geriatric admiration was to be found only in Oriental films, where the cultures tend to regard aging as "seasoning" rather than "rotting."

Despite the wave of thought that attaches a high value to the final stages of life, we are a culture with deep conflicts concerning how older adults should function and the resources that should be made available to them. One of the concerns has to do with the allocation of health-related resources, which are obviously very costly for older adults. In a recent book, *Setting Limits: Medical Goals in an Aging Society* (1988), David Callahan argues that we need to direct our finite economic resources to the younger segment of our society. He argues that after a person has lived what he tries to define as a full life, we should not expend our resources on that individual. According to Callahan: "After a person has lived out a natural life span, medical care should no longer be oriented to resisting death" (Callahan, 1988). Callahan is confronting an ethic that has long been central to Western medicine. Though questioned in recent years, the Hippocratic oath calls for the physician to extend human life whenever possible.

As Callahan attempts to define his concept of the "natural life span," he stumbles into some complex philosophical terrain. He reasons that it is possible to evaluate when a person has finished what, in Callahan's scheme, is a complete life. He makes a strong attempt to define the vital parameters of the life span and includes such categories as love, procreation, work, raising a family, social relations, the pursuit of moral ideals, and the experience of beauty, travel and the quest for knowledge. Stopping short of endorsing euthanasia, Callahan suggests that we must find an equitable way for the health services system to judge when medical efforts are wastefully attempting to extend a life that has completed its course.

On one level it is not hard to sympathize with Callahan's argument. We obviously spend an inordinately large portion of our health dollar on complex life support equipment whose cost is exorbitant. There is a growing consensus that it is inadvisable to devote ourselves to those patients, young or old, who will never regain consciousness, especially patients who have been pronounced "brain dead." The problems with any implementation of the "natural life span" criteria to real lives become insurmountable when they are applied to the myriad "gray" situations. How is it really possible for any "expert" to decide when someone has achieved the lofty goals Callahan has outlined? Paradoxically, if we were to apply his criteria, we would be searching for a rare breed of "Renaissance person" and would probably not effectively curtail health costs at all. While it is hard to disagree with the essence of Callahan's criteria for achieving a full life, the achievement of "beauty" and "wisdom" sound rather class-laden. It is hard to imagine a panel of physicians trying to decide whether a seventy-year-old coal miner with an eighth-grade education had experienced sufficient beauty or pursued enough morality to warrant granting medical services.

The idea of a working "cutoff point" for our older citizens, then, is virtually inapplicable. However, it does demonstrate the extent to which we are in conflict over the role and "value" of individuals in our culture, once they have passed the "working age" of about sixty-five. Over the last ten years, we have seen our laws reviewed and modified to deal with the problem of our burgeoning older population. On one level, the legal issues of retirement deal with the broad-scale socioeconomic problem of how to make room for an increasingly educated younger generation, whose grandparents and parents "clog" the routes to good jobs. On the other hand, as our older adults become increasingly vital, having benefited from years of good medical care and nutrition, there is a greater reluctance to simply step aside when one has many more productive years remaining. A good example of this conflict is the recent changes in the rules governing the mandatory retirement of college professors. In the next few years, federal legislation will require that the age cap be lifted so that faculty members will not be forced to leave their posts at the current age of sixty-eight.

As age discrimination laws are enacted, reviewed and debated for other industries, many issues will be generated. It will become increasingly difficult for industries and institutions to accommodate their younger staff members, and the non-age-related criteria will become harder to articulate. The tension between the aging individual and those who witness and are affected by his decline will force us to deal with this vital issue. Particularly in the professions, it becomes extremely difficult to ascertain when the wisdom/execution balance is thrown off sufficiently that an individual should retire. Unfortunately, it is usually the affected person who is least in the position to make that judgment. Professors, lawyers, judges and administrators at various levels perform functions that can easily defy simple measurement. Complicating the matter further is the tremendous range of differences in how individuals approach the inevitable end of their work life.

From my vantage point as a psychologist, I see our cultural conflict over aging being played out increasingly on an individual level. I listen to my friends and patients who are in their forties begin to address the business of the latter stages of their lives. They attempt to make linear temporal extensions, which include how they will finish their work lives. Many of the time-harassed, Type-A personalities of whom I spoke earlier are in a great rush to solve the financial riddle. They frequently speak of wanting to reach a point where they "don't have to work" at a relatively young age. When we discuss what they intend to do with their lives on the other side of this economic nirvana, they are most often at a loss. The future, for them, has a final goal of making their fortunes, so they can "get off their treadmill" and begin a life of unspecified other activities. I see a similar pattern in my contact with individuals who are in their fifties. They seem to yearn for the time when they are free of the hassles of the "busier" time of life. Their work or careers may have lost their luster, and they begin to anticipate an end to pressures, schedules and the feeling of not being in control of their own destinies. Women who are not in the workforce and who have devoted themselves to raising children experience the conflict in a similar way. They anticipate an end to the confinement of raising a family with a good measure of enthusiasm, only to find that the real "emptying of the nest" leaves a void.

With individuals who have entered their seventh decade, the extension into their future becomes more enigmatic. On the one hand, we have the "mainstream" concept that finishing work will provide the transition to another stage of life, which frequently includes relocation to a retirement community. The post-retirement living arrangement, in this scheme, is usually a simpler environment, which may be near one's community or may involve moving to another more "hospitable" part of the country. The tremendous growth of the Sun Belt in the last twenty years is directly related to this move toward simplicity in a more temperate climate. In the last decade we have also seen the rapid growth of retirement communities that offer varying concepts of "total care," so that the residents can have their medical and social needs met with different levels of structure as they age.

Embodied in this concept of retirement is no definite image of how the individuals will spend their time. On the positive side, one envisions a comfortable, safe environment dedicated to the special needs of the aging individual. In this context, one is spared the stresses associated with population congestion, urban complexity and crime and the discomfort generated by the proximity of younger families with children. The more affluent of these full-care communities have begun to attract residents with in-house gourmet menus and social programs, which include high-quality entertainment such as lectures, dinner theater and musical performances. On the negative side, this model of the later years frequently embodies the feeling of dislocation that comes with severing ties with familiar surroundings, relatives, friends and institutions. Individuals who make the complex pilgrimage to places like Florida and Arizona often report a disturbance in the continuity of their lives. They may find that while life has become simpler, it has also lost an element of meaningfulness as goals become less compelling. It is both common and ironic that individuals who have elected to live in these detached communities find the age homogenization bothersome. They are not always pleased to interact with people who are in the upper strata of age, and even miss some of the turmoil associated with the presence of noisy grandchildren or neighbors.

Coexisting with the simple approach to older life is an idealization associated with the "growth" models. At the same time that a large majority of our retired citizens are opting for relocation and lives largely dedicated to more leisurely pursuits, we tend to grant individuals who defy this trend a kind of "folk hero" status. I am talking about those relatively few men and women who continue to be enterprising and energetic throughout most of their lives. They either maintain their momentum in their primary work and activities or, some time in later life, embark on a new course that generates the sense of heroism. This dedication to meaningful work in later life is not just satisfying, but might also be life extending.

It could as well be possible that individuals who are endowed with the "right" genetic makeup may simply be more energetic into older age, but those who maintain their élan vitale into the later stages of life seem to go beyond simple biological luck. Certain people who maintain their health sustain their careers because they have both freedom and motivation. Someone like comedian George Burns, for example, is able to continue his work in entertainment because there is no mandatory retirement, and he seems to enjoy his work thoroughly. Bob Hope, another comedian, has generated a great sense of *momentum* and *purpose* in his joint role of comedian and morale builder for our armed forces. The maintenance of élan throughout life requires active work as we make frequent choices, sometimes avoiding taking the easy paths life affords.

The heroes we are discussing are undoubtedly admired because we know they have worked to maintain their life's momentum. Throughout our lives we make critical choices that continue to affect our personal futures for long periods of time. Many young people from economically deprived families, for example, face difficult choices in high school. They must decide whether to drop out of school so that they can buy the clothes or car that become so important during those years. Unfortunately, some choose the seemingly easy route of getting a job with short-term rewards while putting tremendous limitations on their lifelong options in the workplace. Such points of decision occur throughout life and seem to differentiate the adventuresome from the lethargic throughout the life cycle. One of the common themes among depressed adults whom I see in my practice is the deep sense of regret for not "stretching oneself" at different life stages.

A good example of an individual who has made difficult and bold choices is a woman whom my wife and I have come to admire. We met her in New England, where we have spent every July for the past fifteen years. We became acquainted with her through her activities in the Audubon Society. At the time we met her, she was involved with a conservation project that required her to capture and band birds in a rugged place near the ocean. The job required long hours, physical endurance and a devotion to the creatures she stalked, temporarily restrained and marked for further study. At the time we made her acquaintance, she was just over eighty years old. After spending considerable time with her and marveling at her energy, skill and dedication, we learned something about her life. (It was impossible for two psychologists to ignore this "rare breed" we had discovered.) She told us that she had not always been involved with birds or with conservation projects. She became involved when she was in her seventies, shortly after her husband and close companion had died. She said she struggled with how to spend her life beyond her husband's death. Ignoring the advice of her children and friends, she became deeply immersed in the conservation of birds, something she had been interested in but had neglected. What was most exciting about this extraordinary woman was not only the work she was so highly invested in, but also her courageous plans. She indicated, in the most matter-of-fact way, that she was well on her way to being awarded a federal grant to continue her work in the Rocky Mountains.

Another person of this kind is the grandfather of a very close friend. When he was about seventy years old, a widower and recently retired from a long career in a manufacturing plant, he suffered a stroke of appreciable proportions. After some intensive physical therapy, after which he regained sufficient strength to become mobile, his family began the usual process of taking control of his life by trying to decide what would be best for him. After a long, painful process, they decided that he should live in a graduated-care community that could meet his projected physical and social needs. He surprised them by announcing that, after his rehabilitation period was over, he planned to buy some land and fulfill the lifelong dream of doing some profitable farming. His children could not envision his becoming a pioneer at the age of seventy-three, especially with his physical limitations. They were convinced he had lost his lucidity and tried to get him to see a psychiatrist. He summarily dismissed the idea and embarked on his plan to purchase land. He continued his physical therapy while searching for the right farm. Despite the best efforts of those around him, he ended up getting his farm in upstate New York, where he lived productively until he was ninety-three years old. I was fortunate enough to talk to him on two occasions and inquired about that period when he struck out on his own. He said his great achievement was not farming in his eighties. Rather, he claimed that overcoming his infirmity was the greatest challenge of his life, and that it was the possibility of fulfilling a life's dream that give him the strength to press on through a painstaking rehabilitation program.

The future for older adults poses the same dilemma it does for individuals of other ages. To consider the future, to project oneself forward, is a source of anxiety. For people in the middle of their lives, the future is hopeful but uncertain. In a sense, we would all like it to somehow "happen to us and come out OK." On the other hand, not to deal with the future forces us into living on a day-to-day basis or immersed in experiences and memories that are more appropriate to another time in our lives. We have already seen that the failure to achieve a personal temporal formula that includes an extension into the future is hazardous. However, the source of future anxiety is rather different for individuals as they approach the later stages in life. For them, telepression is not based on uncertainty, as it is for younger people. What is uncertain is how and when one will die; what is certain is that one's life will surely end.

It is not that the awareness of dying is not with us for most of our lives. We discussed earlier how little children begin to struggle with how to go on with life, knowing that it is destined to end. Often, while they are close to making peace with this existential imperative, cultural concepts distract them and put the resolution out of reach. As we pass into the seventies and beyond, however, it becomes increasingly difficult to ignore the thought of death. Our bodies become less hospitable, and the obituary column begins to include increasingly familiar names. Though elderly people often find a way to not address their own death, it is virtually impossible to telepress on the most private level without a serious rupture in mental functioning. I am told that the most common topics of conversation in retirement communities are the illnesses and deaths of other members. Nevertheless, it is rare to find someone who is capable of addressing the end of his own life as part of his planning.

As peculiar as it may sound, one of the serious problems affecting our older population is the inability to know how to think about death and dying. Several centuries ago, the great philospher Baruch Spinoza exclaimed that the only reasonable way to deal with death is not to think about it. Both the psychoanalytic and the existential writers have indicated that Western man has, for the most part, attempted to implement Spinoza's recommendation. Freud, especially, was fond of viewing religious ideas of afterlife as a childlike fantasy that served to minimize the anxiety associated with contemplating death. The existential writers discussed earlier essentially agree with Freud. In any event, with or without the support of systematic religious dogma, modern adults, by and large, continue to live by Spinoza's suggestion. Though I do not have systematic data on elderly adults, preliminary time line results suggest that a majority of individuals do not include the *end* of their lives as a *part* of their life blueprint.

I have found that individuals given the RTL tend to espouse an "I live one day at a time" philosophy. Frequently, they say that they arrived at this view on the advice of a physician or clergyman. They often add, "At my age I'm happy to wake up and get through another day." They say this with a surprisingly strong sense of conviction, as though it has come to represent a contemporary spiritual (or unspiritual) approach to life. It is our older generation that frequently makes evaluative comments about the "now generation," which I discussed in the last chapter. Ironically, however, they seem to be caught in the same psychohistorical processes, since living a day at a time is not very different from being stuck in the narcissism of the "here and now."

The "one day at a time" approach to life has had an interesting effect on transgenerational family life. One of the most common complaints I have heard in the past ten years is that grandparents refuse to accept their role. Specifically, young married couples are finding that their parents are rarely available to help with children and often seem "put off" when asked to babysit. They do not seem to take the traditional interest in the progress and welfare of their grandchildren and seem to need prodding to stay involved. In fact, one of the most distinct pressures on the modern nuclear family is the breakdown of the extended family as a support system for dual-career parents. The defense one hears coming from the senior generation is that life, nowadays, holds more possibilities for the retired person. In the past, they say, the aging adults didn't know what else to do, so they relegated themselves to the task of raising their grandchildren. The prevailing feeling is "I have worked hard all my life, now I'm going to live for myself."

How one should spend the remainder of one's life is a volatile subject that generates substantial reaction from our elderly citizenry. The suggestion that a life dedicated to self-oriented pursuits does not appear healthy sparks defensiveness and anger. A sixty-eight-year-old female patient recently told me that she will not allow her children to turn her into a maid and housekeeper. She said, "I have worked hard all my life raising three children with two different husbands and deserve just to take care of myself." She did some "light" babysitting but was careful not to let them get used to depending on her. She told me to wait until I was her age to see whether I wanted to maintain responsibilities, or whether I would want to devote myself more to a life of leisure and pleasure. We got into an extended dialogue on the subject, and she eventually opened herself up to consider the values she was living by. We were able to break through her defensiveness by considering the question, "What would you do if you were told you had a few weeks left to live?" Ironically, she immediately thought of the significant relationships in her life, especially with her daughter's family, and planned to redirect her priorities. After considerable therapeutic repetition, she began to steer away from her present-centered approach. She was the first to note that as she became more involved with the milestones of her grandchildren, it was inevitable that she also projected her own futurity. Through this process of exploring her priorities, she eventually achieved a new temporal balance accompanied by a stronger sense of purpose.

On some level, it would be nice to be able to heed Spinoza's advice about not thinking about death. It would also be nice not to have to convey what sometimes seems like a ponderous existential message demanding that we be serious and responsible at all stages of life. Yet the evidence at hand suggests that ultimately life does not appear satisfying or socially valuable when approached as an opportunity to be free of responsibility. First, trying to live one's life without the awareness of death is virtually impossible. Ernest Becker (1973) has developed the idea that death is a major concern at all ages and that efforts to deny the associated anxiety ultimately do not work. Second, living "a day at a time" leaves a person vulnerable to the insidious kind of demoralization our older population is experiencing. A chronic effect of guilt comes from turning from family and community involvement. In addition, I have witnessed a striking loss of self-respect when individuals no longer feel useful to society as a whole. From Erik Erikson's perspective, the failure to achieve "integrity," which involves "giving something back," leaves the individual in a "neurotic-like" state. Finally, it does not seem that our society can afford to lose the skills and resources of so many people.

You will recall from the discussion of Minkowski's view of depression that he saw death as a critical "punctuation" point on an individual's life line. Without the capacity to deal with life's end, he reasoned, the individual cannot extend temporally into the future with a sense of realism. Consequently, there is little opportunity to achieve the kind of temporal balance I have been discussing throughout the book. Most of the "heroic" older individuals to whom I have spoken did seem able to relate their current and future life to their eventual death. They spoke about their goals and life as though they were aware of having to live within the constraints of a somewhat uncertain schedule.

The important realization was that someday life would be over and that one had to incorporate the end into any life design. Using our vacation analogy once again, it is highly improbable that the time available to us would be well used if the boundaries of the vacation were not sometimes considered. If one is not cognizant of when the trip or holiday is over, there is the sense the experience has somehow slipped away.

There is no perfect solution to the temporal problem for the older person. The paradox is that life at any stage cannot be meaningful without the presence of self-generated goals that give form to the future. Yet we have seen that goal-directed behavior tends to produce temporal racing, so that one feels the clock is moving too fast. On the other hand, living with no futurity is tantamount to psychological depression, in which the individual feels that time is standing still. By blocking the awareness of death, one blocks the future, so that there is no vital sense of forward flow. Obviously, one cannot live one's life at any stage by thinking about death regularly. Constant awareness of death would undoubtedly produce a kind of paralysis toward life.

Kübler-Ross (1969) approaches this problem by theorizing that humans are best served by stripping away the mystique so that death and dying can be incorporated into the life plan. Focusing primarily on the end of life, Kübler-Ross thinks that the process of dying is as important as any other part of life. In a sense, she is saying that the way a person dies will be a reflection of how that person has lived his life. An individual who has confronted life's complexities head-on will tend to confront the end of his life in the same way. No matter how much time is left and no matter what one's condition, while there is life, there is still potential for meaningful behavior. The only way to prepare for death, according to Kübler-Ross, is to consider it as part of the life process. When death is confronted successfully over the course of life, it is more likely that one will be able to work through the difficult stages this theory postulates and achieve a final acceptance.

We attempted to test some of these assumptions on an older population of individuals who were living in a retirement community and were willing to participate in a study. Two of my students collaborated (Fossler et al., 1989) and used the RTL in conjunction with a scale that measures death anxiety and another scale that attempts to assess how much "purpose" an individual felt was in his life. Though the group data made some of the results difficult to interpret, the findings tended to support the direction of our thinking. Those individuals whose lives were imbued with a sense of greater meaning tended to be less anxious about dying. That is not to say they had no death anxiety. It would be pathological to approach death totally without apprehension. Rather, the distinction is more like the difference between fear and anxiety that Freud originally made. In this case, it is considered reasonable to have a certain amount of fear of death. Death anxiety, however, might be considered a different reaction in that it could involve an attempt to repudiate or deny the fact of dying. Thus, those subjects who found greater meaning in life and who were relatively less anxious also demonstrated a greater futurity in that they had greater extension on the time line. Conversely, those subjects whose life had no strong sense of purpose tended to be quite present-centered.

The student who collected the data and interviewed the older individuals reported that it was difficult to get them to do the time line. While they "griped" about the other tests, the time line was especially unnerving. This observation was entirely expectable since we were prodding our subjects to look into their future, even if they couldn't "mark" the line accordingly. Some of these subjects complained about the line being too big, with too much space. Ironically, some of the subjects who were able to extend into the future complained that the twenty-four-inch strip of paper was too confining. This is a fascinating response, in that they might have been saying, metaphorically speaking and considering their future goals, that life felt too short. The present-centered group, which struggled with the line being too long, seemed to be saying that the unstructured future forced them into taking refuge in the day-to-day life of the present. The individuals who were successful in confronting temporality portrayed the future as spatially shorter than the past, with the anticipated goals uncomfortably crowded into a smaller line segment. They tended to move the "now" point on their time line clearly toward the right, thus accommodating the notion that they were in the final stage of life.

I have been finding people in their sixties and seventies increasingly fascinating to work with in psychotherapy. The relationships between "purpose in life," death anxiety and the planning of one's life are clearly at the core for many of our older citizens. As I said earlier, once we get people over the bias that it is frivolous to be in therapy at these ages, the fact is that it is a perfect time in life to confront the nature of one's existence. There are usually ample time, focus, and financial resources to face these critically important issues. However, as with patients of other ages, the path to self-exploration is often indirect, especially since individuals over sixty really haven't "grown up" with the notion that one can seek professional psychological help for certain life difficulties. There is often a heightened sense of embarrassment and a feeling of overindulgence in my older clients.

A sixty-four-year-old woman was referred to me by her daughter, whom I had seen several years earlier. The mother was quite reluctant to come to my office and had to be personally escorted for the first session. Her daughter had told me on the telephone that her mother was having "panic attacks" and that both she and her sister were worn out by their mother's continual need for reassurance and attention. The daughter portrayed her mother as a person who had always been very "solid," a hard worker who had had a change of personality in the last few years. It was particularly disturbing, according to the daughter, to listen to her mother's preoccupation with the various male relationships that consumed most of her time. She also said that her mother had become a "frivolous" person who spent most of her time on "beautification" in shopping malls or at her salon, where she would spend hours on her face, hair, nails and body tone. It was clear from the daughter's depiction that she and her siblings were, like many other adult children nowadays, very disappointed in the behavior and apparent values of their mother.

The patient needed to be reassured by me in our first session that this was necessary and appropriate. She spoke of her "spells"—intermittent anxiety episodes that were apparently triggered by her anticipation of being alone "without something to do." At the same time, she was clearly searching for a dependent relationship. She also frequently expressed doubts about whether I could help her. She said that her family physician had referred her to a psychiatrist about six months before, and that he had prescribed sedatives. She said that while the sedatives helped her sleep at night, she didn't like the effect on her energy level. She was active in golf and bridge, and found her concentration to be adversely affected. We overcame her focus on whether to commit to therapy by agreeing to eight sessions, which seemed to relieve her apprehension about decision making. In the subsequent sessions, she spoke mostly about the frustrations of her relationships with the men in her life. She was aware that her concerns sounded "adolescent," but she was totally preoccupied with meeting men, analyzing each relationship and responding poorly when their behavior did not indicate that they "wanted to get serious."

Though noticeably embarrassed about talking to a younger man about her "silly love problems," she nevertheless continued to fill her hours with "men talk." She said that both her doctor and her psychiatrist had told her not to worry about the disapproval of her children. She had given enough years to them and it was time to enjoy herself. She had not heard that response from me, and somewhere in the fifth or sixth session pressed me for feedback of that type. I gently inquired how she would react if I were to disagree. We looked at her time line and spoke of the void in her futurity. She was quick to pick up on the direction of my thoughts and said, "You're absolutely right, I should be doing more serious things with my life." I was impressed with my strategy, patted myself on my back, and suggested she give some thought to *filling* her time line. There was only one problem in my treatment plan. She did not appear for the next session, explaining on the telephone that she felt much better and wanted to "try it on her own."

Several months passed before I heard from her again. Her daughter telephoned saying that her mother wanted to see me again but was afraid I wouldn't want to "waste my time with someone like her." I suggested that her daughter tell her I would be delighted to see her, and she resumed her therapy. This time, she said, we would not need to put time limits on our sessions, as she was more ready "to work." This was certainly helpful, since my failure to keep her in therapy the first time was probably due to the pressure of the time constraints that pushed me into not managing her telepression carefully. She said that a very powerful dream had brought her back to see me. In the dream, she found herself in a dark, unfamiliar room and was frightened that she was going to die. A sinister-looking woman in black was laughing and saying that it was time to "come over," since her life was of no further value. She said she could not tell if she started a new dream or if this one continued, but she screamed to her deceased husband to help "save her." She screamed "get my pills" over and over again until he finally appeared, saying, "Don't worry, I'll get your medicine." She recalled that he appeared at her bedside with the look of "some sort of sage" with white hair and white beard. He said, "Here is your medicine," and when she reached for it, instead of medicine, she grabbed what appeared to be the body of her oldest grandchild. She said what terrified her was that her grandson looked like "one of those starving Ethiopian children."

That dream offered the opportunity to look at her anxiety in a more expansive context. Over a period of about one year, she came to see that she had been frightened of aging and eventually dying, and did not know what to do with the rest of her life. She had defended herself against these fears by developing the obsession with men who would "save her" from having to confront the difficult task of deciding on a meaningful life course. She had the insight that in her dream "even death was laughing at my life." She eventually understood why I had not supported her "life at play." The guilt she was feeling was not something to be discounted or ignored, but rather a signal that she was not engaged in meaningful activities. The image of her starved grandchild led her to see how she was contributing virtually nothing to anyone's life, especially those who were counting on her. In the process of making these discoveries about herself, she seemed to forget about men. That is not to say she stopped enjoying heterosexual relations, sports and bridge. However, these aspects of her life began to recede into the background as the foreground of her life took on a sense of urgency. Her new anxieties were much more palatable to everyone, especially herself. She began to worry about time being *precious,* and about how she would find the time to do everything that suddenly was becoming important. She has recently begun to explore whether the Peace Corps would consider accepting someone her age. She is making the transformation from what Heidegger called a "forgetfulness of being" to a "mindfulness of being."

VII

Timely Theories

In the last five chapters we have looked at specific kinds of behavior from a temporal perspective. It should be clear by now that the individual problems we have examined are directly and inextricably related to the way time is experienced over the human life cycle. Temporal orientation must be viewed as an important personality trait in its own right and must be understood as a primary element in the development and maintenance of psychological disorders.

It was Minkowski more than any other writer who was responsible for the development of my own thinking and the direction of my research methods. When I first discovered Minkowski's *Lived Time*, I was exhilarated. I had already been thinking of time as the unifying thread of human existence. Minkowski presents compelling case and theoretical data that suggest that disturbances in the way individuals live with time constitute the basis for understanding psychopathology. The more conventional approach both during his period of work and now is to view temporal disturbances as mere *symptoms* of other problems. For example, in his extensive analysis of melancholia (depression), he noted that depressed individuals do not project themselves forward in any positive way. They shrink in the face of the future and tend to muse about lost time and opportunity. The dynamics of depression have not changed, as individuals diagnosed as depressed behave in much the same way today. However, Minkowski points out that the temporal problem is *primary* to the disorder of mood rather than secondary. In much the same way, he discusses the phenomenon of schizophrenia, in which there is fragmentation of the personality. One of the common approaches to the diagnosis of this major psychological disorder is the "mental status" examination frequently used by psychiatrists. They attempt an interview with the patient, one part of which focuses on orientation to time. The patient is asked about the date and the recent past in order to get a sense of whether he is aware of major current events. If there is serious time disorientation, the patient is considered psychotic and possibly schizophrenic. Other possibilities include biologically based temporary or longer-term mental disorders. In this instance, the temporal disturbance, again, is seen as a manifestation of the more central problem, schizophrenia. Minkowski, however, tends to view the temporal disorganization as at the root of the problem rather than a peripheral indicator.

Sometimes there is a tendency, even among great thinkers, to miss the obvious. Though it is abundantly clear that thoughts about time infiltrate our experience over the life cycle, there is surprisingly little attention to the subject in mainstream psychology literature. Reviewing psychology and psychiatry research for the past twenty-five years, one finds a few scholarly research programs by such individuals as Thomas Cottle, Joseph Rychlak and more recently, Philip Zimbardo. For the most part, however, the subject of time has been the domain of experimental psychology, which has emphasized the perception of interval clock time or time estimation.

Perhaps the most limiting aspect of psychological science can be attributed to the behavioral movement typified by B. F. Skinner. In that tradition, only observable behavior is studied on the premise that subjective or experiential phenomena are not appropriate for scientific study. This view, now called "radical behaviorism," has at times generated absured debates centered on whether human thinking is "measurable" and at times on whether it exists at all! Fortunately, behavioral scientists have softened their stance and begun to acknowledge thought as relevant, in what is currently being called cognitive behavioral psychology. While the shift is certainly welcome, it is rather preposterous that it has taken so long for our science of man to acknowledge the "internal" life of man.

Temporality is certainly one of those psychological characteristics that are deeply buried in the self of the individual. For that reason, it has not been easy to translate into paradigms that could be studied using our contemporary models of research. An early approach, typified by the research of E. Douvan and J. Adelson (1966), was to do national surveys with American adolescents. The findings yielded ratings of temporal orientation derived from questions concerning significant life events, plans, goals, commitments and the associated feelings. Generally the findings indicated that those adolescents with the most positive extension into the future were "healthier." They had a stronger sense of self as measured by other scales. Another approach, used by A.E. Wessman and D.E. Ricks (1966), was to take a standardized psychological test, the Thematic Apperception Test (TAT), and adapt it for studying temporality. The TAT employs a set of picture cards that portray individuals in various ambiguous emotional and interpersonal situations. The subject is required to tell a story about each picture and is evaluated in terms of the projections he makes onto the ambiguous situation. The researchers analyzed the stories in terms of the time span used and whether the character was depicted as recalling the past or moving into the future. General findings tended to agree with the survey results in that future-oriented subjects were found to be less anxious, be higher achievers and have clearer goals. The "retrospective" subjects were found to be more vulnerable, less open to the future, more frightened by prospects of change, and generally less "well-adjusted."

While these research efforts were establishing important links between psychological well-being and the temporal dimension, their assessment of lived time did not really correspond to what we mean by temporality. In order to provide some background for the direction of our current research, it is worthwhile to review some of the ideas generated by Minkowski, whose ideas are pivotal to current approaches to understanding and measuring subjective time experience. For Minkowski there are two components to temporal experience. The first is the dynamic élan vitale. The other component is connected to the élan vitale and has to do with an individual at a particular moment in time experiencing the spread of his own life. Both Minkowski and Heidegger employ the spatial metaphor of a horizontal line to describe the spread of time and of a person's life as lived over time. Implicit in this model is the idea that, at any precise moment, the past and the future are spread out before us in an ever-shifting set of successive points. The past and the future can, in turn, be further subdivided into zones of varying distances from the present, each of which is experienced differently. Basically, Minkowski sees this time line as extending forward and back from the present in a dynamic process. Using the line as a frame of reference, individuals may vary with respect to the "accessibility" of and the "value" placed on their past experience. They may differ in their awareness of their activity in the present, their capacity to experience continuity between time zones and the extent to which the future is experienced as open or closed, accessible or blocked, empty or full.

The first American researcher to use Minkowski's concept of the "time line" was Thomas Cottle. In the late 1960s and early 1970s Cottle (1969) and his associates developed what they called the Lines Test. Subjects received a horizontal line of a fixed length as a representation of "life span." They were then instructed to designate birth and death points on the line, as well as past, present and future time zones. Cottle had also devised a somewhat different measure, which he called the Experiential Inventory of Time Perception. He asked subjects to list ten "important experiences" on a time line and to judge each one as belonging to one of five time zones: distant past, near past, present, near future and distant future. Cottle used a technique that allowed for the averaging of a series of numerical values culminating in a measure of "primary temporal orientation."

When I first discovered the work of Cottle and his associates, I was excited, as they had begun to explore the very phenomena that fascinated me. A network of studies was done during the early 1970s that used the above measures on large and diverse samples. Cottle and Klineberg (1974) summarized the results of these studies in a book that cites studies on such populations as school-age French children, American Indian adolescents, Austrian schoolchildren and a large sample of American naval recruits. Their results were encouraging in one respect and discouraging in another. On the positive side, the direction of the findings supported general hypotheses about the relationship between temporal balance and other indications of adjustment. They reported that the presence of temporal integration correlated highly with factors such as higher intelligence, lower anxiety levels and personal achieve-ment. They also found that when the person's "time zones" did not seem integrated or "connected" to each other, the individual was usu-ally anxious and lacked clear achievement goals. Another very impor-tant finding demonstrated that future orientation had different meanings for different age groups of children studied. For young chil-dren (ages ten to twelve), the findings indicated that a future orientation was associated with poor adjustment. As children reached adolescence, however, a future orientation was more indicative of well-being and seemed to correlate with the consolidation of identity.

The problem with the body of information generated by the Cottle studies was that it was based on several instruments, leading to findings that were not always comparable. Psychological research has generally suffered from this problem of data proliferation without essential and useful integration. At the risk of impiety, I must say that I have always felt that the bulk of psychological articles that appear in a wide as-sortment of specialized journals is not justified by the findings gen-erated. Typically, the results of single experiments using diverse measures on different populations appear in a wide range of professional journals with differing editorial policies. Cottle and Klineberg did, how-ever, attempt to integrate their work by writing a book summarizing studies in the area. I am grateful for their effort and think that we need more such work in the social sciences, in general, and in psychology in particular. The growth of psychology as a science requires a healthy balance between theoretical developments and subsequent experimen-tal research.

Before embarking on my own research program, I was faced with a dilemma, which I would like to share. Obviously, I did not want to make the errors—which as I noted have plagued modern psychology—having to do with proliferating, marginally connected research stud-ies. It was also not clear whether such a deep, experientially based phenomenon as temporality could be measured using the method-ology of Western psychology. A purely theoretical work based on phil-osophical concepts, clinical observation and deduction would run the risk of becoming another esoteric explication of existential and phe-nomenological thought. In other words, as I began to study lived time, I was very concerned with having a measure of impact on the field of psychology. The most productive path was to first demystify the existential notions of time. This meant translating Heidegger's and

147

Minkowski's ideas into the metaphorical language of experiments and statistics. While pure phenomenologists object to analyzing human experience by using numerical reduction techniques, I feel, as did Cottle, that the group data format is best in terms of linking developments in the area of temporality to the mainstream in psychology. I did not plan to simply improve on this measurement process and generate the usual bulk approach to research.

The plan that evolved was to build on existing research by developing a straightforward and "robust" assessment of temporality that was simple to administer and interpret. While studies were being produced, the plan called for the integration of theoretical ideas, research methods and findings and observation from the clinical world. The remainder of this chapter will, then, deal with the evolution of my thought and the development of the Rappaport Time Line (RTL). Now that you have examined the RTLs of several different types of individuals, it should be useful to examine the construction of the measurement tool.

The time line approach, conceived by Minkowski and first adapted to the experimental context by researchers like Cottle and Rychlak (1972), was the approach I thought had the most promise. However, there were several critical problems in the way the line had been developed and applied. First, there were problems in the degree of "structure" inherent in the original Lines Test. Procedures that use ambiguity as a means to get an individual to express thoughts or feelings are usually called "projective techniques." Such traditional tests as the Rorschach ink blots and the Thematic Apperception Test rely on the fact that stimuli with no intrinsic meaning can serve as catalysts in understanding the individual who "imposes" structure on the unstructured situation. When people look at an ink blot from the Rorschach series and see a bat or people or insects, they are projecting, because there are no such characteristics inherent in the cards. A skilled interpreter is able to derive a great deal of information about an individual from such factors as how many figures are seen, where they are located, their nature, how the perceptions were formed and what actions the projected characters are enacting.

When people are given a piece of paper that represents the "line of their life," they are being asked to project a portrayal of their life onto the empty page. At a given moment, they will be filled with memories, current circumstances, and images of the anticipated future. On Cottle's "Lines Test," the subject was asked to indicate "birth" and "death" as points on the line so that the formulated "zones" would use the beginning and end of life as boundaries. While this procedure produced a certain commonality in the lines, there appeared to be a violation of the spirit of projective tests. If a test is really going to show the experience of time as it is felt by the individual, there should be as few cues as possible. When birth and death are predetermined experiential anchors, temporal experience has been shaped and influenced by the test. Feelings about death are induced by making it a structural element of the task. As we later discovered in the development of a revised time line, when consciousness about death is raised, some individuals become anxious and defensive, thus changing the manner in which they address the task. We also found in subsequent work that when left to their own devices (on an unstructured task), some subjects omitted either birth or death, or both. Failing to include the most distant reference points for one's life involves an obvious loss of valuable data.

The second problem with the original approach to the line assessment of temporality was that the individual was asked to think of past, present and future in the abstract. All of us in the business of psychotherapy know that it is not very productive to ask our patients to describe their past without reference to specific situations. If we can elicit what Marcel Proust, in the novel *Swann's Way*, describes as the experience of the "petite madeleine," then the past will explode with life. In other words, when our thoughts come to a memory that is highly invested with feeling, then we are powerfully pulled into our histories. By the same token, when we anticipate the future, it too comes to life when images of what is expected are imbued with personal feeling. In psychotherapy, we guide the individual forward and back by exploring recollections and anticipations. As we began administering lines under various instructional sets, we found very different outcomes to the organization of a time line when it was filled with events.

What we did, then, in the development of the RTL was to combine the essence of two procedures. We adopted the lines test without the structure of birth and death and added the task of the experiential inventory. Unlike the experiential inventory, this procedure did not require people to produce, nor were they limited to, ten experiences. You will recall from Chapter 2 that the subject was also asked to make a "dot" to indicate the "now point" of life, with brackets around the experiences that they felt embodied the psychological present.

When developing ground in new scientific areas, it is important to tie new theoretical concepts to established theories. One way to do this is by conducting research along conventional lines. While the group format is far from optimal, the statistical summaries permit us to study temporal properties in the experimental context. A second important step in the development of a new approach to measurement is to establish what are termed acceptable levels of validation. One way to ascertain if such assessment tools as the RTL are "valid" is to see how they behave in relation to certain more established measures of psychological phenomena. Similarly, if a relatively new concept like temporal perspective can be shown to relate to other established concepts, then a level of "construct validity" is said to exist.

As we developed the RTL in the late 1970s we began to consider the question of what a "healthy" line would look like and what other existing psychological concept it would correlate with. Drawing on the clinical examples in the last five chapters, we would expect that an individual's temporal perspective would be balanced. All three zones should be represented if an individual is centered. A good metaphor that emerged was the playground "seesaw" with equal weight on either side of the fulcrum (present). An individual with this kind of balance was seen as psychologically "open" to past, present and future experience. Defensive processes for this individual would not necessitate cutting off the past or the future. We would expect him to extend himself forward or back with equal facility.

This idealized conception of temporal functioning ironically comes very close to a concept of the psychoanalytic tradition. Erik Erikson was instrumental in developing the concept of ego identity, which he believed was as important in our era as sexuality was in Freud's. Erikson emphasized that this sense of identity is achieved in terms of an individual's sense of personal continuity over time and in terms of a continuity between the individual's perception of himself and the self as it appears to other people. Erikson conceptualized the process of achieving an identity as the central task of late adolescence. Each stage in his eight-stage life cycle theory has an inherent conflict that requires resolution. The particular problem for the adolescent involves the polarity of identity versus identity confusion. The conflict becomes a "crisis of wholeness."

The wholeness to be achieved at this stage I have called *a sense of inner identity*. The young person, in order to experience wholeness, must feel a progressive continuity between that which he has come to be during the long years of childhood and that which he promises to become in the anticipated future. (Erikson, 1968, p. 87)

In addition to the achievement of this sense of sameness over time, the adolescent must tackle the job of making serious life choices and commitments. Values having to do with education, religion and occupation must be confronted.

New identifications are no longer characterized by the playfulness of childhood and the experimental zest of youth; with dire urgency they force the young individual into choices and decisions which will, with increasing immediacy, lead to a more final self-definition, to irreversible role patterns, and thus to commitments "for life." (Erikson, 1959, p. 11)

In terms of our objective, which was to connect the RTL to another known psychological construct, ego identity seemed perfect. The adolescent who has achieved the sense of personal identity of which Erikson speaks would, in a sense, "know where he's been, where he is and where he's going." We expected such an individual to show a balanced time line. At the opposite pole is the individual who is identity-diffused. This person, who shows an inability to establish commitments to occupation, relationships or belief systems, would not be expected to show temporal balance or to have the ability to extend into the future. This confused profile is correlated with other kinds of psychological symptoms such as anxiety, depression and overall emotional instability.

As one might expect, Erikson did not see the achievement of identity as an all-or-nothing affair. He developed intermediate categories to handle the individuals who fall between the identity achievers and the diffusers. An interesting pattern is the one he called the "foreclosed" sense of identity, in which the individual maintains rigid commitments, which are often imposed by others. This person tends to adopt a "way of being" that is prescribed by a parent or a culture and in a sense avoids the "crisis" of identity. In Erikson's system, this foreclosure leads to a "totalism" (closed system) characterized by rigidity, as opposed to "wholeness" (open system), which is characterized by fluidity and adaptability. We expected such types to behave like those who achieved identities but without the overall sense of temporal balance.

Recognizing that the full achievement of identity is not commonplace within this adolescent group, which covers ages from sixteen to about twenty-two, Erikson suggested that many young people are in a state of "moratorium." While they are working toward the establishment of an identity, they often postpone the final choices. This individual has a sense of who he is, as opposed to the diffuse person, who is somewhat lost. However, there isn't the sense of certainty that may accompany the foreclosed person. Thus, the time line associated with the moratorium period might show neither the balance nor ability to extend into the future of a true identity achiever.

To assess the extent to which our theoretical assumptions were valid, we devised a study that would allow a measurement of the correspondence between Erikson's levels of identity achievement and the temporal perspective dimensions. In this case, college students were appropriate subjects, as they were allegedly in the midst of resolving their personal identity. A system for classifying eighty undergraduates into categories of diffusion, foreclosure, moratorium and identity achievement was adopted from the earlier work done by James Marcia (1966) and his associates. After a period of extensive pilot research, Marcia found that the best way to assess the extent to which a young person had achieved an identity was with a semistructured interview format. In order for the individual to have a subjective feeling of continuity with the past, meaning in the present and direction for the future, two factors had to be present: commitment and a crisis. He found that those students with the strongest identities were explicitly committed to both an occupational direction and a form of ideological or religious conviction. The crisis, which was roughly defined as a period of doubt and indecision, was necessary, Marcia (1975) reasoned, to distinguish the individual who achieved an identity from the one who had adopted someone else's. Career choices and ideology are certainly not the only indices of commitment that one could connect to a solid sense of personal identity, but they are, or should be, the primary concerns for this particular age group. Moreover, during the late 1960s and 1970s, when the research was being conducted, these were subjects that seemed germane to the majority of college students. This was a period of marked political activity and cultural upheaval, which involved an intense scrutiny of cultural and national values. It is probable that the interview format, if it were to be used in the late 1980s, would have to be modified to reflect a decrease of interest in those areas. Marcia notes, however, that ego identity is basically a subjective phenomenon, so that it is not very important exactly which barometers of underlying values are used to ascertain levels of ego identity achievement.

As in other studies that used "lines" approaches in studying temporality, we found that subjects in this age group used a disproportionate amount of linear space (duration) for the present and time zones near the present. (For this study we used a highly refined statistical methodology that included near and distant components for the past and future.) Overall, the findings tended to support our expectations concerning the relationships between temporal behavior and the levels of identity our subjects had achieved. We found that the identity achiever group had the most future orientation (density of experience) and the most balance between zones. The diffusion group, on the other hand, was extremely past-oriented and showed little balance in temporality. The moratorium group in the midst of the "crisis" of identity was also oriented toward the familiar past but showed greater balance than our "identity-less" (diffusion) group.

The foreclosure group, who had not gone through a process of personally "choosing" their identity, produced findings that were somewhat surprising and rather important. We discovered that this group was the most future-oriented in terms of the percentage of experience they allocated to the future and in terms of their extension into the distant future. On the other hand, this foreclosure group showed considerably less balance than our identity achievers in that they did not draw heavily on the distant past. In line with Erikson's notion that foreclosed individuals have a totalistic and closed identity, it appears that for these individuals the future is pictured rather lucidly. The lack of balance in their experiential inventory indicates, however, that the projections into the future may not be solidly grounded in their own past experience. In other words, the identity they have adopted does not appear to be based on the sum total of their own empirical experience.

Thus we found that temporal perspective is strongly connected to the degree to which an individual has evolved personally relevant values. The individual whose identity is ill-formed and whose values are vague cannot formulate goals and retreats to the security of past experience. The identity achiever, on the other hand, has a certainty about who he is, which facilitates the mapping of significant life milestones in the future based on the accumulation of prior experience. It is this retrievable past that is applied to the formulation of personal identity. The moratorium group was the most frequent (twenty-seven) in our sample of eighty, and the identity achievers the least frequent (thirteen). I suspect that this ratio may persist well beyond the late adolescent stage and into adulthood (preliminary research seems to support this notion). These moratorium individuals are approaching the development of a viable life scheme derived from personal experience, but they face a crisis that becomes magnified in proportion to the need for clear-cut choices. While they show a fair amount of temporal and value balance, they are nevertheless anxious and unable to extend themselves effectively into the future.

The finding that the foreclosed subjects extended into the future more significantly than our identity achieving group illustrates a phenomenon that makes a great deal of intuitive sense. The ability to extend into the distant future is not, in itself, an indication of psychological health. In fact, individuals whose temporal perspective is dominated by images of the distant future are often plagued by severe problems (for example, workaholism) in achieving balance in their lives. Like the foreclosed subjects in our study, their aspirations and behavior are probably determined by values that have been adopted rather than chosen. Much of their lives is determined or "programmed" by distant goals, at a great cost to spontaneity and flexibility. As we saw in the chapter on Type-A personalities, goal-directed behavior can be all-consuming with little capacity for the pleasure associated with "getting lost" in the present.

A series of studies was begun several years ago to see how futurity would be affected by raising consciousness about the sad state of the world's resources. It was postulated that individuals who were systematically exposed to frightening news about the global ecological situation would become defensive and exhibit "telepression" or a constricting of their ability to project into the future. In this study we wanted to demonstrate firstly that the RTL was a viable research tool. Secondly, we wanted to create a paradigm in which we could induce a state of defensiveness about the future. We thought that creating a constricted feeling about the future would cause a shift in temporal orientation back to the past.

We used standard experimental design with more than fifty college students. In the "ecology" group, a psychology class heard a lecture that dramatized the shrinkage and contamination of the world's essential resources. The lecturer prophesied population overgrowth, energy shortages and the pollution of the air and water supplies of the industrialized world. In a comparable psychology class, the standard psychology lecture for the day was given. At the conclusion of each lecture, the RTL was administered. Afterward, the students in the "ecology" group were "debriefed" and told that the lecturer had intentionally exaggerated the ecology issues for purposes of the research.

The study produced some expected and some unexpected results. The data for the two groups were different but not entirely in the way we anticipated. It was not easy to document "telepression" on all the temporal dimensions. Both groups showed minor futurity, which indicated a certain level of future constriction without the experimental procedure. As I will discuss later, our whole culture may be living with narrow future possibilities. The ecology group did, however, show less inclination to extend into the future compared to the control group, meaning that they could not project themselves as far forward into their lives. This finding supported our prediction about future defensiveness.

Perhaps a more dramatic finding was the way in which the temporal balance of the ecology subjects shifted toward the past. The past became the dominant temporal zone for these subjects on all of our temporal measures. They placed more experiences in the past, allocated more space to the past and extended further back to earlier ages of their lives. Besides dampening their future extension, this "temporal retreat" also had an impact on their present orientation. Subjects in the ecology group experienced the present as a much smaller component (duration) of their time sense.

Thus, in the face of seeing the future as problematic and frightening, our subjects did a temporal "about face" and retreated to the security of the past. They telepressed their current and future sense and accentuated the known and predictable.

Outside of the "laboratory," we have witnessed similar phenomena. Following periods of social unrest or war there is often a resurgence of traditional and conservative values. Even in war-torn countries where the future appears bleak, we see people continuing to propagate as if having families continued to make innate sense. In our more immediate environment, a strange effect was noted after the energy crisis in 1973. Once the immediate effect of the higher gasoline prices was over, a Gallup poll showed that there was a resurgence of interest in large "gas-guzzling" automobiles. A similar trend occurred not long after the crisis of 1979. It did not take long to put the long gas lines out of consciousness and de-emphasize fuel economy. The mid-1980s, in fact, has seen another sharp rise in larger high-performance vehicles with little concern for what is still a shrinking supply of petroleum-based energy.

The studies cited above are samples of research conducted using the RTL. They have, I hope, provided a solid feel for the way the instrument can be used in psychological research and provided a familiarity with the time line itself. Other studies have used time lines, and we are now using the RTL in some diverse and fascinating areas. For example, a doctoral student is currently running a study using the RTL in an evaluation of a program that deals with the homeless in Philadelphia. Another doctoral student is using the RTL to help clarify the difference in the way men and women establish personal identity. I have been corresponding with increasing numbers of researchers around the world who are attempting to connect temporality to other significant theoretical variables.

I have also been extending the concepts associated with the time line to areas that have not yet been researched. It is also important to recall that the ultimate efficacy of our temporal perspectives is derived from multiple sources. First and foremost, temporality is a philosophical and psychological concept. We can safely say that the RTL has validated the notion that lived time can be approximated by the spatial metaphor of a line. To some extent, then, the theories I have been developing are based on empirical studies. However, many of the inferences that have been established are based on the more complex interplay of clinical data, sociocultural observation and deductive processes. The complexity of our subject matter necessitates that we go far beyond the data of laboratory studies.

VIII

SIGNS OF THE TIMES

As I begin this chapter, it is ninety-nine degrees in Philadelphia and the media are filled with dire news from the Midwest.
Comparisons are being made to the "dust bowl days" of the 1930s and
there are alarming forecasts of higher food prices and an economic
ripple effect that will probably affect every American as well as individuals in countries that rely on our crops. Perhaps more ominous is
the resurgence of scientists' projections about changes in global temperature patterns into the twenty-first century. James E. Hansen, the
chief of NASA'S Goddard Institute for Space Studies, has already made
headlines (Weisskopf, 1988) by suggesting in a congressional hearing
that the "greenhouse effect" is upon us. He claimed that fossil fuel
emissions are shrouding our environment and causing an increased
tendency for droughts and higher temperatures, which will continue
into the next century. Other scientists have been in substantial agreement, noting that 1988 is the warmest year on record since modern
statistics have been compiled.

It is very difficult to relate to the dire forecasts that suggest that our global temperature will rise as much in the next fifty years as it has since the end of the last ice age (four degrees Fahrenheit). The subject is not the focus of sustained conversation as there seems to be little direction for dialogue. On local news, for example, neighborhood fires and crimes were given about as much attention as the Midwestern drought, which is being talked about in calamitous language. Ted Koppel, I am told, had a guest on his *Nightline* show who used a computer simulation showing how the earth's temperatures would become unpredictable and hotter, with specific reference to how our temperate climate might shift so that our abundant agriculture could not be taken for granted. I was told about the television show by a patient who said, "The whole thing gives me the creeps." She later added, "I guess you can't do anything about things like that, so you might as well live it up." Others I have talked to tend to respond in a similar way. At first they acknowledge the seriousness of the ideas by exploring the immediate consequences of a sustained change in environmental conditions. They then seem to shrug the events off, as if they were too far removed or too abstract to really grasp. It is, however, the kind of information that cannot help but have some impact on the way we feel about our life and imagine the future unfolding.

It is fairly obvious that there are interactive effects between prevailing cultural factors and individual behavior. In addition, different periods of history can be identified by certain major motifs. Of course, when historians make reductions or abstractions, like other scholars, their goal is to enlighten through highlighting what appears seminal. One must, however, remain cognizant that a "reduction in data" has occurred for purposes of elucidation and that all elements cannot be perfectly portrayed. In attempting to understand an era, I am sure, historians do something akin to what a psychologist might do in evaluating an individual. A theoretical perspective creates a template that covers the subject of one's analysis. If the template is robust, it will help portray the object of study in such a way as not to lose the more subtle or less obvious aspects of the subject.

As we explore the temporal behavior of individuals we must always examine the interplay between individual and sociocultural forces. This is an ambitious approach to psychological phenomena but nevertheless essential if we are to understand why certain phenomena occur in epidemic-like proportions. Such psychoanalytic writers as Erich Fromm and Karen Horney corrected some of Freud's early "culture-bound" conceptions by pointing out that the individual and society cannot be understood separately, but rather must be seen in a dialectical relationship. The individual is shaped by his environment and, in turn, shapes it.

In approaching the significance of temporality issues in particular, it is necessary to take this two-tiered approach. First, difficulties on an individual level such as depression and addiction must be addressed in terms of their various manifestations. However, we must carefully consider the dramatic sociocultural trends that are equally a part of the dialectical temporal fabric. In fact, there are very strong indications that conflicts relating to the management of "lived time" are so omnipresent as to represent a major underlying psychological determinant of behavior in the second half of the twentieth century.

For example, most people in the United States who are over fifty-five were deeply touched by the Great Depression. Even if they were not personally victimized by the shrinkage in job markets, they were certainly influenced by a climate that was not full of high expectations and emphasized caution toward spending personal resources. While the economic future was not bright, there was no dire global consciousness that led one to fear that the world and its resources were finite. On the contrary, in this pre-television, pre-telephone, pre-jet age world, the planet earth seemed vast and permanent. This was a period when our current mature adults learned that one could not have everything in life and kept a steady, patient attitude. The concept of delayed gratification probably typified the psychology of this period, buttressed by both religious and familial perspectives. For the most part, people grew up with a feeling that "someday" they would have the important things in life and that waiting for them was a virtue.

Though the onset of World War II brought the West out of the economic depression, there was not a discernible shift in attitude during the war years. Values remained somewhat constant and familiar during this period. The war effort required a strong work ethic, and even though money began to circulate again among the depression victims, goods were in short supply, as was leisure time. In the period following the war, particularly the beginning of the 1950s, there was an explosion of change, which has continued into the 1980s. It is extremely important to note that the changes were not necessarily negative. After the war ended, there was a resurgence of the American economy. Consumer goods and disposable income became interdependent as the industrial gains of the war years were consolidated. Telephones, automobiles, washing machines, vacuum cleaners and eventually televisions began to find their way into a greater number of homes. Inexpensive development housing and the availability of "cheap money" put home ownership within the reach of many renters. National pride rose as America emerged as a world power and became a military and economic leader. A rapid growth began in higher education, supported by the philosophy that a college education should be available to anyone with the intellectual tools and the desire.

I was ten years old in 1950 and retrospectively remember the times as being very uneven. The end of the war undoubtedly left everyone extremely relieved, and the country was probably on the verge of becoming lighthearted or even frivolous through the 1950s. That's what apparently happened in the "Roaring Twenties," the "devil-may-care" period following World War I. The popular music of the 1950s was nondescript, bordering on the silly. Songs like "Aba Daba Honeymoon" and "Jambalaya" were common and early television featured vaudevillelike comedians such as Milton Berle and Sid Caesar. Other favorite television shows were wrestling or game shows like *Charades*. Contrary to the superficial frivolity, undercurrents of disturbance were developing. Juvenile delinquency was extremely prevalent along with teenage gang hostility, which dominated adolescent life during the period. Certain masculine cinema heroes (for example, James Dean) were introverted, angry and disconnected from mainstream society. The seeds of the strife associated with the civil rights movement became evident as the 1950s drew to a close.

This summary of the 1950s is sketchy, as I am not a historian, nor is this work the place for a comprehensive analysis of the period. However, the thirty years before our current observations are unique in human history. Anyone who was at least ten during the 1950s will remember the rapid descent from the celebration of the Allied victories into the Cold War. Almost immediately after the Japanese surrendered in 1945, the United States and Russia undertook a long, ominous path of ideological and geopolitical warfare. The Korean "conflict" was the beginning of a new kind of war, dedicated to "stopping communism," in which there was neither winner nor loser. Following the tenuous peace that followed, the world was treated to a decade of rapid nuclear armament, highlighted by the frequently televised exploding of atomic and hydrogen bombs before national audiences. It was during this period that the mass buildups of nuclear arms began, along with the first human awareness that the potential destruction of the planet was within man's control.

During this era, we saw our government behave with apparent paranoia in the inquisitionlike McCarthy era. Even after this dreadful episode finally came to an end, we felt the threat from irrational authority toward normal people and their beliefs. As a country, we began to act as if a nuclear war were inevitable, and we prepared schoolchildren with weekly drills on how to behave during a nuclear air strike. The business and ideology surrounding the personal air raid shelter evolved with debates on whether to permit an "unprepared" neighbor into one's family shelter. There was a frightening quality of absurdity to the seemingly unavoidable crash course upon which humanity was embarked.

Indications of psychosocial disturbance began to appear during this period. College students began to deal with the predicament of trying to plan a life and future in the Cold War world. I was in college at the time and recall attending a few meetings of a group that I think was an early version of the Students for a Democratic Society (SDS), which later became radical during the Vietnam War. This was clearly a fringe movement of students who were beginning to get an activist feel about them. However, they made their case in conventional ways, through pamphlets, speeches and satire. Most of us listened to these positions and accepted that they had some merit, but went on with our lives. Nevertheless, a ground swell of literary and political dissent was growing out of the feeling that life and the future were being jeopardized by generals who, since the McCarthy period, were no longer given unconditional approval. It was difficult enough to solve the riddle of how to make life meaningful knowing that one would die a natural death someday. The idea that death could come because of a soldier's intoxication while at the radar screen or as the result of a politician's megalomania directly impeded any thinking about the future.

Cynicism began to appear on many fronts. The idea of "dropping out" of society showed up in the Beat movement with such spokesmen as Jack Kerouac, Allen Ginsberg and Lawrence Ferlinghetti. As we entered the 1960s it became increasingly acceptable on college campuses to be "anti-establishment." Avant-garde theater, which emphasized the absurdity of the human condition, was finding its way to New York with plays by such writers as Samuel Beckett and Eugene

161

Ionesco. Terry Southern's comic satire *Dr. Strangelove* (1964), which treated the possibility of nuclear war and the madness of our top-level military, became an accepted symbol of a growing antimilitarism. Within the social sciences, individuals such as Paul Goodman (*Growing Up Absurd*, 1960) and C. W. Mills (1960) inspired students with their attacks on the contradictions inherent in society and the need to become more active in changing our social and political institutions. Even preteenagers during this increasingly volatile period read *Mad* magazine, which saw life in the United States as a basis for cartoon parody.

By the early 1960s "lines" were being drawn throughout the culture based on political ideology. The intellectual/academic community was beginning to vehemently attack our politics and we became aware of the emergence of a distinct "counterculture." One of the early spokesmen was Herbert Marcuse, a philosopher whose opening statement in *One-Dimensional Man* sets the tone for the period:

> Does not the threat of an atomic catastrophe which could wipe out the human race also serve to protect the very forces which perpetuate this danger? The efforts to prevent such a catastrophe overshadow the search for its potential causes in contemporary industrialized society. These causes remain unidentified, unexposed, unattacked. (1970, p. ix)

The deep level of distrust inherent in Marcuse's comment was deeply reinforced by the assassination of John F. Kennedy in 1963. In fact, more than any single event, this tragedy accelerated the loss of faith in established government by a whole generation of youth. While the Warren Commission report on the assassination attempted to establish reason and order, it never succeeded. The Vietnam War escalated during the Johnson presidency, and the schism widened between an enormous segment of college-age students and established society. The sense of cynicism and anger was multiplied tenfold when other mainstream leaders were struck down. The assassinations of Robert F. Kennedy and Martin Luther King, Jr., left the country demoralized and angry. When Eugene McCarthy lost to Hubert Humphrey at the Democratic convention in Chicago in 1968, the country was torn apart as many young people felt as if there were no legitimate avenues open to express their fear and distrust.

Mass demonstrations and urban riots gripped the United States as a community of academicians and students continued to develop the consciousness of a counterculture. In the process of confronting the traditional sources of information and power, there was the simultaneous rejection of conventional cultural values and a great emphasis of the expression of personal freedom. What could not be achieved in the political arena was seen as possible in the social and personal arena. The mid-1960s saw an explosion of styles ushered in by a wave of new music, new ideology and new behavior. Thus, while the young were demonstrating against the military and the government, they were also participating in a revolution in personal consciousness.

The Beatles introduced a new metaphor in music and triggered a revolution in appearance and dress. Long hair and bell-bottoms appeared at the same time as Eastern philosophy and a fascination with the unfamiliar. Those who grew up in this period remember it as a time of frenzy and excitement. The "sexual revolution" seemed to begin during this period, facilitated by the new music and the availability of the birth control pill. As sexual expression became associated with the new movement, men and women began to reject traditional roles and dress. Women, in particular, responded to the new sense of possibilities, and a modern feminist movement rapidly developed. New norms were established for sexual expression, premarital cohabitation and the relationships between sexuality and commitment. At the same time, the homosexual community responded to the climate of freedom with the large-scale public disclosure of sexual identity.

This was a period marked by contradictions of all sorts. While the growing activism fueled a sense of new political and social possibilities, there was also the sense that things would never change and that irrational historical forces would prevail. It seemed that the greater the level of underlying hopelessness, the greater the radicalization of ideology and behavior. Another contradiction involved the disparity between the exhilaration of involvement with and commitment to the larger goals of the period and the tendency to slip into more egocentric behavior involving personal expression and satisfaction. This was the period when psychedelic drugs appeared as part of a philosophical landscape that suggested that "personal transformation" was somehow the key to the salvation of our society. Writers such as Norman O. Brown (1966), in attacking the psychohistorical roots of irrational Western thought, advocated a new kind of sexuality free from the goal-oriented philosophy of Calvinist, capitalist society. At the same time, a mood evolved in psychiatry that suggested that mental illness was a response to insane conditions in the society. Ronald Laing (1972), a British spokesman for this viewpoint, saw serious mental problems such as schizophrenia arising from conspiratorial forces in family life and our culture. Something of a "prophet" during the mid-1960s, Laing and his South African counterpart, David Cooper (1972), suggested breaking away from traditional values and conventional notions of family life. Laing, in particular, turned to "Eastern" sources of wisdom, and his ideas served as an attractive justification for the emerging drug culture.

The seeming contradictions of the period can be understood by looking at much of what happened as a defensive process. The convergence of all the factors I have been discussing left a large segment of our youth frightened, confused and, especially, with no clear sense of personal future. Under these conditions, I have noted, the process of telepression can prevail and unbalance temporal organization.

In *Future Shock* (1970), Alvin Toffler addresses what happens when changes in a culture accelerate beyond a certain point. It becomes difficult to retain a sense of continuity with the past; history becomes increasingly distant and meaningless. According to Toffler, the same is true for the future. Endless change makes the future alien and unpredictable. In the face of accelerated social and technological upheaval, it is difficult to project into the future and to plan. There is certainty only in the present, which is immediate, comprehensible and concrete. While the shift to this present-centeredness evolves from fear and defense, eventually we reify present experience and search for philosophical justification.

In the 1960s, young people were adversely affected by the conditions Toffler cites in his work. Though outwardly many seemed deeply involved in activist politics, there was frequently personal confusion derived from the inability to anticipate a gray future. Kenneth Keniston saw youths in this period as suffering from "historical dislocation." Their inability to find connections with either past or future gave them "the feeling of unrelatedness, of being adrift, of not being able to catch hold of anyone or anything in our rapidly changing society" (Keniston, 1965, p. 240). This difficult state is something akin to what we have been referring to as a diffusion of identity. The individual cannot use what *has* happened in order to shape what *will* happen. Thus there is a weak defensive alignment with the present or an attempt to escape the terror of not having a solid identity.

In a state of weak ego identity, individuals or collectives of individuals are prone to adopt personal identities offered by those in positions of prestige. Thus, the 1960s were marked by an intense search for self-definition, which did not seem to develop by simply living one's life. Rather, the business of self-discovery and awareness was elevated to a quest. Hallucinogenic drugs were perceived in the early 1960s as a way of achieving higher levels of being. Eventually, the drug experience became entrenched as a means to achieve enlightenment, social acceptance and personal efficacy. Intertwined with the rapidly rising drug culture was the emergence of what was later labeled the "human potential movement." Originally a "California phenomenon," this movement saw the convergence of threads of European existential thought with American humanists such as Carl Rogers and Fritz Perls. Methodologies such as encounter groups, T-groups, sensitivity groups and marathon groups evolved as contexts in which to heighten self-awareness in what came to be called the "here and now."

It was presumed, based on the legacy of the thinkers of the "beat generation," which emphasized personal freedom and rebuffed conventional wisdom, that we as a culture needed emancipation from the shackles of temporal considerations. The combination of impersonal nuclear anxiety and the more immediate fears concerning the omnipresent draft appeared to prove that our elders and figures of authority were misguided and leading us to potential collective and personal doom.

Social science seemed to lend support to the idea that our capacity to experience simple, honest emotions such as love and commitment were hampered by socialization that emphasized conformity and the achievement of prescribed goals. The result, it was reasoned, was an ad hoc ideology that suggested that new, more viable identities could be formed by shifting life's focus from striving to personal exploration and the pursuit of satisfaction in the context of one's current existence.

While the focus of the late 1950s and 1960s was on critiquing Western society in order to avoid political and social absurdities, the focus of the human potential movement was primarily personal. The aim of the workshop experiences was not to revolutionize society, but rather to achieve the transformation of self. This shift of focus from large-scale concerns to the small-scale issues of personal existence is extremely important to understanding the activist period as well as our current concerns about "yuppie" behavior. While many of those who lived through the turbulence of the "antiwar years" feel totally dedicated to the cause of peace, it is critical to examine the processes on another level. I have been making the argument that much of the impetus for the sociological patterns of the period came from personal and collective fear of the future. Yet, when analyzing historical events, it is difficult to address the motivational factors that are not readily available to individuals within the historical period. The college students who marched for peace, for the most part, believed they were dedicating their lives to the cessation of "Western imperialism" in the Third World. Most of them (author included) could not conceive of living one's life without a deep and fundamental commitment to political processes. The tension between this "enlightened subculture" and the political establishment would conceivably go on indefinitely.

Yet, as the Nixon administration brought American involvement in Vietnam to an abrupt end in 1973, interest in ideological and political matters waned dramatically. At the risk of offending many activists of this period, I must point out that when the threat to our own safety and comfort was eliminated, our attention to the affairs of peace in the world at large seemed to ebb. Even though turbulence and bloodshed continued on a massive scale in both Vietnam and Cambodia, the ending of our military draft saw our interest in the affairs of Southeastern Asia disappear except for a small, dedicated contingent. In addition to shrinking from geopolitical awareness, our interest in local politics declined. The revolutionary zeal of the activists of the Vietnam war years dissipated almost all at once.

It would seem, then, that much of the churning of the 1960s was generated by a futurity anxiety, which was psychologically handled by the many collective activities we have noted. When the obvious and immediate threat ended, the larger anxieties about the future of "the world" did not cease. The Cold War continued and, almost immediately, we began to enter a period of dramatic "ecological apprehension." The first oil shortage began in the mid-1970s, accompanied by astounding increases in the price of oil and gasoline. I had been out of the United States between 1970 and 1973 and was shocked to find that the price of gasoline had reached a record fifty cents per gallon on my return. For all the time that I had driven a car before this period, one could fill a gas tank for three or four dollars. The gasoline shortages and rationing were something Americans were not used to and, though brief, served as a stark reinforcement that the future continued to feel uncertain and dire.

In addition to nuclear, ecological and Cold War anxieties, there is still another dimension of contemporary existence that cannot be ignored. Marshall McLuhan (1965) saw a profound relationship between the rise of electronic media and man's relationship to himself and others. Known for his maxim "The medium is the message," McLuhan has made a compelling case that from a historical perspective, man creates media and that media, in turn, have the power to transform man. His theory is germane to our concern with both temporality and identity. He explained that the "print" (books) and "mechanical" (clocks) culture that arose in sixteenth-century Europe was intricately related to the way man experienced time. Books and mechanical clocks fostered a linear experience of time flow, which structurally biased man toward a future temporal perspective. McLuhan is not referring to a balanced temporality, but to a tendency to see life as predominantly in the future at the expense of the present. This analysis would be applicable to Victorian society, in which life's pleasures were postponed as reward for living life virtuously.

The act of reading, according to McLuhan's thinking, is a totally private experience in which the images produced are highly subjective and variable. In addition, the codification of facts and experience into the printed word produces a sequential and fragmented sense of experience. Combined with the effects of print was the enormous impact of industrialization, which, for McLuhan, was symbolized by the clock more than any other machine. The clock was revered by the great thinkers of the period, such as Isaac Newton. The development of a uniform standard of relating to the passage of time was critical to the industrialization of society. However, the breaking up of the flow of temporal experience into seconds, minutes and hours had a decidedly negative effect on man's relationship to himself and to natural cycles. "The acceptance of such fragmenting of life into minutes and hours was unthinkable, save in highly literate communities," McLuhan wrote (1965, p. 153). Industrialized man became tied to the clock and developed a stilted view of time.

McLuhan welcomed the liberating possibilities of the electronic age. He thought that the "hot" medium of television, in particular, would reverse the negative temporal identity of industrialization by what he called the "recultivation of the immediate." In live television and radio, images and sounds are generated instantly with all observers receiving a collective and instantaneous message. The sense of immediacy inherent in this medium, McLuhan argued, would offset the future-oriented temporal perspective associated with the print-mechanical culture. In addition, the collective perception would move the individual away from the "less useful" private identity toward a greater immersion in the group, which he refers to as "retribalization." The electric-age person, then, would be much less individualistic and more grounded in a so-called global community.

I have discussed a very important theoretician in this brief manner in order to simply outline the main thrust of his thoughts. His writing was seminal to the intellectual climate of the late 1960s, as he was able to formulate the complex and subtle relationship between human temporal experience (including identity) and the media. His ideas were extremely compatible with the mainstream of the human potential movement, as he was eagerly anticipating the transformation of a future-oriented, self-centered society into a less introverted, socially committed group. His emphasis on the virtues of being immersed in the present certainly fit the ethos of the post-antiwar period. His conception of the erosion of individualism also converged with the ideas of other thinkers, such as Brown and Laing, who were advocating a society less driven by personal, capitalistic motivation.

McLuhan's theories were controversial at the time they were written and they continue to raise questions. It is obvious that he runs the same risk common to all theorists who try to overextend their ideas to diverse phenomena. Just as Freud and Marx tended to reduce history and personality to single concepts, McLuhan may have overestimated the role of media in shaping human history. Nevertheless, at many levels, McLuhan's forecasts have materialized. Television, stereo and the computer revolution (not technically part of his theory) have certainly had a dramatic impact of human consciousness.

In my research, I have been tracking ways in which there is a contemporary bias toward a present temporal perspective. In addition, ample evidence suggest that our young people are growing up without the power of introspection that McLuhan claimed was a by-product of the print culture. The impervious nature of the drug culture certainly points to the power of the group, as opposed to the individualistic capacity to reason that McLuhan saw as disappearing.

Both the McLuhan approach and the main thread of this book suggest that recent historical forces have interacted to produce a contemporary society organized for living in a narrow slice of the time line, the "now" zone. While temporal theory has traced the origins of the shrinking temporal band to a spectrum of psychosocial processes, McLuhan focused on media impact. Beyond the differences in how causes are viewed, there are also fundamental differences in how the more present-oriented individual is assessed. McLuhan, in concert with the humanistic wave which swept the United States, emphasized that immersion in the present was an essentially liberating experience that would be beneficial. Temporal theorists, drawing on the more disciplined existential philosophers from Europe and the United States, argued for a balanced temporality, which as I have said must include past, present, and future.

The difference in the two views is not as great as might first appear. During the height of the turbulent 1960s, humanistic thinkers were calling for the plunge into "now" as a correction for what they saw as a society with its eye on the distant future. It was presumed that as a society we were "one-dimensional" in the way we mortaged our current lives to the promise of future security. The stereotyped Protestant ethic, which advocated hard work for distant rewards, came under heavy attack. It was reasoned that when one delays the critical experiences in life, one also loses the capacity to relate to those experiences. A typical example is the individual who says he has always wanted to travel extensively but never felt he could afford the time or that he "deserved it." By the time such an individual "comes of age," he is usually much older with limited mobility and an eye that will not see the world with the excitement of youth. This future devotion represents a kind of temporal insecurity that is organized around the maladaptive theme, "If I save time now, I will have more later." Thus, do not do today what you can delay into the distant future.

Our temporal approach to human behavior would not suggest that this overdetermined future perspective represents an ideal. It is critical, however, to point out that the now orientation that has evolved in our society as a "correction factor" has overcompensated, so that we find ourselves encountering problems related to the absence of a viable futurity. McLuhan believed that the electronic age would somehow render individuals less private, with a greater affinity for the group. Ironically, as a society we seem to have become heir to only the negative part of that prediction.

Media have, in essence, created a collective identity where ideas, fashions and even jokes have a frightening uniformity throughout the

United States. The addition of satellite communications has undoubtedly brought us closer to a truly global identity. Thus, while being more shaped by common images and perceptions, we have nonetheless emerged as a society of self-oriented individuals. Frightened by an uncertain future and given license to live in the here and now, young people in particular have developed an alarming self-centeredness. Christopher Lasch elaborated on the developing pattern of exploitive, opportunistic behavior in his book *Culture of Narcissism* (1978). Consistent with Lasch's description, the *Diagnostic and Statistical Manual* of the American Psychiatric Association (*DSM-III*) introduced narcissism under the general heading of "personality disorder." The insertion of this syndrome into our diagnostic nomenclature underscores the widespread nature of the behavior.

Lasch spoke of this narcissism as the absence of real convictions other than the advancement of self. The diagnostic approach sees narcissism in terms of the failure to behave in an appropriately reciprocal manner in interpersonal relationships. The spoiled child who puts his needs above anything else is used as a model for this individual. However, what Lasch is saying is that we are not simply speaking of a few "neurotic" or "spoiled" individuals. Rather, our culture has developed an implicit ideology that sanctifies the perpetuation of self. Consistent with temporal theory, Kilpatrick (1975) sees the problem in terms of a tenacious clinging to the vicissitudes of adolescence so that adult identity is neither sought nor achieved. Kilpatrick speaks of an "endless moratorium" in which "Adolescence," which used to be a staging area for the assault on adulthood, has more become a sanctuary that adolescents don't want to leave, and that adults want to re-enter" (pp. 63–64).

Kilpatrick was writing about the state of our culture in the 1970s. In this period we saw the reification of this adolescent self living for present pleasures and avoiding the commitments that had typically characterized adulthood. Relationships, career and identity were cast into moratorium while individuals pursued the satisfaction of current needs. Adults, too, he noted, were caught by the "don't postpone" philosophy of the period. This period saw a tremendous destabilization of family life as women began to deeply question their roles in the family and men became unsettled in their career pursuits. Long-standing marriages and careers were threatened and often ended as we became gripped by an epidemic of "midlife crises." As our fascination with the apparent freedom of adolescence grew, our ability to sustain commitments faltered. It was during this period that family life in the United States suffered as adults began to feel entitled to the pursuit of their "own space." Consequently, family therapy seemed to arise dramatically in concert with these complex pressures on all members of the family.

By the late 1970s and early 1980s, there was a distinct change of climate in the country. Colleges and universities were noting that students seemed different in their bearing, drifting away from social activism, liberalism, cynicism and idealism. Perhaps coinciding with a shift in presidents from Carter to Reagan, their concerns moved from issues of social justice to economics. During this period, MBA (Masters in Business Administration) programs saw unparalleled growth, and students in other graduate programs rejected traditional areas to specialize in applied business theory. Not only did celebrated activists like Jerry Rubin and Tom Hayden pursue "establishment" careers, but the new generation of college students were also shifting dramatically in their values, outlook and even appearance. The counterculture look of the activist years gave way to striped suits and suspenders for men, and women returned to traditional fashions including the "made-up" look that had lost some appeal during the preceding ascetic years.

The yuppie years were born around the same time we quietly decided to abandon the digital watch in favor of the more customary sweep hand watch. The digital watch came upon us very suddenly as an obvious extension of McLuhan's electronic age. It was different, inexpensive and, most important, changed the way we interacted with our time tools. While the older watch face gives a sense of past and future, the new digital upstart speaks only for the moment. The digital phenomenon seemed a likely correlate of the now-centered society that had become entrenched by the middle 1970s, and digital sales skyrocketed for several years. Young people and more established individuals had a decidedly different look about their wrists, and we were all becoming accustomed to those unsettling beeps that punctuated so many meetings. Just as rapidly as digital watches grew in numbers, they have begun to fade. While some people continue to use them, they seem to have become a recreational tool used in walking, jogging or rowing where computation and pace are important. Teenagers have clearly abandoned theirs in favor of the colorful, inexpensive analog watches that give the user the essential sense of "before" and "after."

171

It was apparently no accident that digital timekeeping gave way to the more linear and traditional method at the same time we saw the resurgence of interest in business and success. The collective perspective that emerged had a partial future focus that seemed largely based on personal success and monetary programs. The narcissism and self-centeredness did not fade away. The achievement of economic success was highly valued as a means to achieve the best possible lifestyle. The other dimensions of this contemporary identity have not kept pace with the business component. Apart from anticipating the future in terms of financial viability, there is still a decided tendency to live close to the "now" point. The achievement of an identity in late adolescence involves more than the development of a career plan. The essence of one's ego identity ought to be an accumulation of one's life experiences, which serve as a navigational system for a future that one projects into. When Erikson, in particular, wrote about identity, he was considering a hard-fought composite that covered all the bases of "humanness."

The contemporary present-centered identity is not predicated on a solid temporal base. In Erikson's approach, the identity is foreclosed to the extent that it derives from the culture's current trend. It does not arc back to one's personal past and tends to extend forward in a one-dimensional way—working. The spoils (money) generated by one's work provide immediate rewards in the form of "toys" or are used to keep a record, which becomes the measure of personal success. It is this self-serving drive that has made these values the subject of ridicule and sarcasm. In a sense it epitomizes the narcissistic person who has mastered a particular way to achieve economic success. Others who work in close proximity to this "new breed" often react with alarm as they feel they cannot compete with the highly "programmed" nature of the behavior.

In the linear scheme of time, the past is irretrievable, so that Westerners live with the good feeling that we are moving toward something new and the somewhat frightening feeling that we cannot move backward. In a way, this is another basis for defining the Western concept of progress as one of change. Our ambivalent relationship is predicated on our thirst for novelty coupled with the melancholy associated with lost experience and opportunity.

It is very difficult to step out of one's customary way of experiencing something as central as the flow of time. Our language, syntax and values are intrinsically connected to our linear view of temporality. Westerners also suffer from a tendency to view other models of experience as less advanced.

I have encountered this problem before in my studies of traditional medicine in East Africa during the 1970s. In examining the skill, efficacy and meaning of healing as practiced by shamans, I had trouble naming what I discovered to be a very relevant, dynamic and unique approach to healing a very broad range of human maladies. For want of a better term, I used the term "prescientific" to convey the philosophical roots of the practice. The prefix *pre*, however, in our Western framework implies *before* and connotes a lesser level of progress. I did not intend this connotation and probably should have used the term "nonscientific" to suggest that the system I was studying represented an alternative rather than a historical antecedent of our contemporary approach to healing.

Time has traditionally been symbolized in Oriental writings as circular rather than linear. In order to sense the difference between the Eastern and Western views, it is useful to consider the linear view of time as an arrow traveling in a linear trajectory and disappearing somewhere ahead. As with the notion of progress, the arrow moves forward in an irreversible way, so that its path will not be repeated. The idea of life moving on a "one-way" line has inherent anxieties, which accounts for much of the stress of modern Western society. The circular notion of time, difficult to grasp for Westerners, incorporates the notion of time and life as occurring in potentially repeating patterns. From this perspective, time is not "lost" as it is in the linear scheme, but is simply moved to another point in the cycle. Before rejecting this model as arcane and irrelevant, consider the breakthrough in the laws of energy in the late nineteenth century. Helmholtz's conservation law posits that energy cannot be destroyed but only transformed into another state. If we add Einstein's theory of relativity, which poses some complex paradoxes about the passage and speed of time, there should at least be some consideration of circular patterns, or nonlinear depictions of time's flow.

Anthropological research has told us that some cultures have no terms for past, present and future. Melges (1982) speaks of the Hopi Indians who tend to place memories and anticipations in the same experiential bracket. Again, it is difficult for us to comprehend experiencing our lives without our customary causal sequences. "Nonscientific" cultures like those of the Hopi Indians and the Trobriand Islanders tend to see the passage of time in holistic patterns where the meanings are the unifying factors rather than the linear connections. In these cultures there is a fatalistic outlook in which causes and consequences are not part of the experience loop. The emphasis in life is not on effecting change but on being a part of the spiritual, natural and social fabric of the culture.

Perhaps it is easiest to understand the differences in temporal perspective by pointing to a yearning within Western society to seek the wisdom and experiential "purity" of these nonscientific cultures. When we speak of "getting away from it all" as a way of replenishing ourselves, we are generally referring to retreating to a place or set of behaviors where the usual goal-oriented behaviors don't exist. We go to the seashore, visit mountains and travel in order to use our time in a different way. Without the past-present-future line of goal-directed behaviors, we find time more friendly. Our lives are not dissipating as if controlled by something other than our own will. It should suffice to say at this point that nonlinear time experiences are essential to human well-being. I am not saying, however, that our scientific approach, which uses the past to formulate plans so that we can envision and achieve goals, is malevolent. Rather, we need to understand alternative ways of relating to the experience of time in order to be more fully at peace with ourselves. Our scientific approach to life has created and continues to create endless possibilities. It is probably that knowing how to experience time in alternative channels represents the strongest basis from which to live our lives.

One of the dimensions of "Old World" life to which Americans always react is the great sense of tradition. Europeans, in particular, are often held in awe by Americans because they appear so immersed in routines of life that suggest a great deal of quality. We in the United States seem to value change yet crave the comfort and familiarity of tradition. In America, however, we find vast differences in different regions of the country with respect to the degree to which tradition governs day-to-day life. Certainly we cannot think of Californians and New Englanders as similar in terms of traditional interests. Californians are, for the most part, a transported populace of individuals who perhaps personify the kind of changeability I am discussing. New Englanders, on the other hand, are a largely indigenous group with a specific dialect and a fairly deep immersion in the history and geography of the region.

Europeans often find us naive, with a tendency to adopt every new trend or fad that happens our way. While I am not certain who recently suggested that walking was a better form of cardiovascular exercise than jogging, it has definitely become a new "sport." I cannot help but wonder what the reaction of an objective observer would be to our new infatuation with "serious walking." One sees small groups of these new devotees, with set chins and arms pumping, moving about our streets and parks with a righteous sense of determination, armed with the latest walking shoes and often with exotic stereo headsets. I have no quarrel with exercise or trying new approaches to mobility. The peculiar aspect of such phenomena is how quickly individuals "get into" new trends and how tenaciously they advocate them for relatively short periods of time. The large share of our manufacturing businesses devoted to advertising is testimony to how malleable our buying habits are thought to be. As a result, our marketplace is in a constant state of flux: our clothing, cars, ideas and perceptions are, for the most part, easily manipulated.

Sometimes the adoption of transient ideas can be associated with more serious matters. During the early 1970s when there was great concern in the industrialized world about the depletion of natural resources and the overpopulation of the world, voluntary sterilization became fairly widespread among the educated affluent class in the United States. Many women and men who had "reproduced themselves" were having tubal ligations and vasectomies. The decision to end the reproductive part of their lives was often made as a gesture to a larger global conciousness. Some people who could not face the future in such a "shrinking environment" could not envision having children. The relevant issue, here, is that so many individuals irreversibly altered their biological endowment based on a set of compelling ideas, which seem to have faded rapidly. Not only have the fears of overcrowding receded from the headlines, but the trend toward smaller families has also been reversed, so that demographers have recently been speaking of a new baby "boomlet." Ironically, I have seen several men professionally who deeply regretted their sterilization decision and have tried reversals with mixed success.

During what have come to be called the "Iran-Contra" congressional hearings, I was most struck by how volatile the opinion polls were with respect to the key figures. Lieutenant Colonel Oliver North, in particular, went from an "unreal John Wayne"–like figure to a nationally admired hero in a matter of days. In the same vein, there was a dramatic rise in support for the Contra cause as a function of the remarks made by Lieutenant Colonel North.

Americans are changeable for at least two distinct reasons. The first has to do with an absence of the deep sense of roots that characterizes people in the more "charming" cultures. America is a nation of immigrants, the oldest dating back to the seventeenth century and the newest arriving daily. When we look at the degree to which there is a distinct set of values that govern a group's life, it is ironic that the oldest and newest "settlers" are probably the most solid. The early settlers have been here for several centuries and have had the time and resources to solidify a viable sense of values. New immigrants, such as the Portuguese, tend to bring Old World values that remain intact so long as the pluralism of the majority culture has not produced the inevitable intermarriage that comes with exposure. The groups in between have frequently changed regions, have intermarried and have been subject to lessening degrees of control from such traditional sources of values as the extended family and religious institutions.

As Vance Packard (1972) pointed out in *A Nation of Strangers*, we are a migratory nation tending to live in unfamiliar places with unfamiliar people. This dynamic pattern tends to produce a constant sense of uncertainty about one's value structure. Without the deep inner sense of identity that seems to be associated with continuity, the individual is very externally oriented, scanning the environment for help in making life choices having to do with education, dress, career and even how to eat. The absence of what Erik Erikson calls a clearly defined historical identity leaves the individual with a "low-grade" sense of inferiority, so that Americans who suffer from an unclear sense of identity will be those most likely to "try on" a new wardrobe of values.

Lest I paint Americans in a lopsided manner, let me note that there is another side to our tendency to be changeable. As a nation of pioneers, we are a more adventuresome and open culture than most in the world. We are always seeking novel approaches to problems and have had a love affair with the scientific approach to knowledge and problem-solving. During the years I worked in East Africa, I was struck

by the differences in decision making and willingness to adopt experimental approaches as compared with my counterparts from European
universities. Our culture, including our rock music, jeans, Coca-Cola
and cinema, are compelling and attractive to even the most insulated
nations of the world. A deep sense of optimism and a problem-solving
orientation have personally served me and other Americans in the
world arena.

We do, however, pay a great price for our absence of a coherent
national set of values along with our tendency to perceive change as
virtuous. The large proportion of Americans who are touched by these
factors find themselves in a state of turbulence. Without viable values,
it is not possible to project oneself into the future in a meaningful way.
If the achievement of an identity does not occur in early adulthood,
no such value system is possible. In the absence of these "signposts,"
there can be no workable futurity and, therefore, no temporal balance.
Thus, the changeability of which I am speaking is only the outward
manifestation of a deeper problem. When one's time line does not have
any form in the future, there is a tendency to develop the kinds of
symptoms that I have discussed in this book.

IX

HEALING TIME

The annual vacation is a useful metaphor for addressing the universal temporal dilemma. When a vacation begins, one looks forward to the novelty and the accompanying sense of freedom and pleasure. At some point in the vacation, however, the awareness sets in that the respite will end and one must "go back to real life." Dread becomes so powerful in some individuals that they lose enthusiasm about the second half of their vacation or adopt some extreme frenzy. In neither case is balance achieved.

I have heard from many of my patients over the years that Sunday is a difficult day for precisely the same reason. Great anticipation of the weekend fades by Sunday morning to the awareness that in one more day, the "grind" will resume. As a result, Sundays are fraught with intense and distracting feelings for these individuals.

The achievement of sense of balance is one of the most essential and difficult tasks of life. In a way, the quest to immerse oneself in the present while anticipating, planning and fearing the future constitutes one of life's most difficult paradoxes. The future simultaneously represents possibility, destiny, hope and an inescapable burden. In spite of our best efforts to plan and control our destiny, each future moment is fraught with an immutable sense of deep uncertainty. Expressions like "Who knows what tomorrow will bring?" and *"Que será, será"* (what will be, will be) capture the sense of helplessness about the future. Moreover, the prayers recited by millions of individuals of many religions around the world all attempt to bring some divine support in maintaining or creating well-being. Certainly the fascination with astrological forecasting, whether for entertainment or more serious planning, also indicates the wish to bring a level of predictability and order to what is experienced as a potentially capricious future.

Individuals in our culture are having trouble with the future. That is not to say that the repression of past traumas is no longer relevant. Theory builders have always known that the subjects they theorize about are more complex than the models we construct to understand them. If we are to understand the afflictions of people in the latter half of the twentieth century in industrialized society, we will have to add a concept like "telepression" so that we can include the future in our analysis and treatment of the individual.

I strongly suspect that most readers of this book will have attempted a personal time line by now. It is probably impossible to consider the approach that others cited in this book have taken without tackling the task. The difficulty in taking such a "test" is that when one knows how to interpret an instrument it is difficult to complete the task genuinely, without considering the "right" answers. This is a common problem when giving psychological tests to individuals with varying levels of sophistication with the tests. One way to cut through the problems of prior exposure and knowledge is to ask someone to give you more responses than you might ask of the uninitiated respondent. In giving a psychologist a Rorschach ink blot test, for example, one might want to consider only the last bunch of responses in an attempt to screen out all those responses that "belong to other people."

On the assumption that you have at least tried your time line many times over, I will urge you to try one the "right way" by following the directions in Chapter 2. Actually get the twenty-four-inch strip of adding machine paper (or a facsimile) and try to delineate the milestones of your past, present and future. Remember to note the "now" point, bracket the present and include a notation of your age at each significant "mark" on the line. Try to put the prototypes and idealized lines out of your mind and simply reach into your own experience to arrive at your temporal perspective. If you pay careful attention to your tendencies and feelings as the line is marked, you will be amazed at the explosion of self-awareness. Try to complete the line in one sitting in a period of no more than about thirty minutes. Before continuing with the rest of this chapter, I suggest you try the time line. It is, however, not mandatory!

The suggestion to do a time line is intended to sensitize the reader to the potential intensity of this exercise. As I have said repeatedly, I almost always have trouble getting people to do the line because the task of stepping back from your life requires considerable effort and durability. Most individuals without much input from me begin to comment immediately on what they have discovered in the process of creating this life "blueprint." One of the first observations that people make is how hard it is to summon up experiences that they consider important. There is the urge to be stereotypic, which, after all, only suggests that many of us have similar endowments and views of what is important. It does not take long to realize what pieces are missing from the blueprint. Forgetting selective past experiences such as the death of a certain loved one can be startling. Trying to label the pursuits of one's immediate present life can be equally memorable, as one ponders what keeps one feeling so rushed when there is no adequate language to describe what one does day in and day out.

The most telling part of doing a time line will be the conclusion drawn about temporal orientation. The most obvious dimension of the time line is a spatial one, in that we can see how far in length we have strayed from the "now" point on the line. The density of experiences within a particular time zone is usually connected to the physical space allocated to that zone. Of course, doing a personal time line, which is self-evaluated and provides the opportunity for introspection, will be as valuable as the actual completion of the line itself. Parts of the temporal spread will be easier than others, as there are periods in life that are not well recalled and there are anticipated periods that are not easily amenable to imaging. Most people who reflect on this experience find the future to be the most difficult, though that does not necessarily indicate that they are not future oriented.

The natural question in response to the identification of a personal pattern is, What do I do about it? or, How can I change? Americans are both very arrogant and very impatient. We read the myriad self-help books and sometimes delude ourselves that we can change ourselves in any way we choose if we put our mind to it. The fact is that change is a slow, difficult process, which requires focus, energy and commitment. A good place to begin, however, is with an understanding of what is wrong. It is fairly clear that one of our temporal problems (which we noted earlier) is our tendency to want everything to happen immediately, usually because we "have no time." I hope that readers will come away from this discussion with a new sense of how to account for this distress and some ideas of what directions to take personally and interpersonally to break out of the limiting temporal patterns.

One possible result on the time line is the problem that I theorized resulted from too many goals in the near future, especially for a person who is under fifty. This excessively goal-directed existence seems to be endemic among Type-A personalities. This is an enduring pattern of behavior that seems highly resistant to change by self-help. It seems that people have to have an "Ivan Illyich" level experience to jolt them into gaining the ability to reorder their life so that they can control their time. I am referring to the life-threatening event that leads to the inevitable question, "What's it all about?" usually followed by a declaration that new priorities are in order.

By far the most common temporal pattern I have found involves a defensive telepressed future. Though there is insufficient data, the norms would undoubtedly indicate a trend in the United States, and possibly the entire West, of temporal imbalance. When we do find individuals who achieve sufficient levels of futurity, it is usually from a relative perspective rather than a case of a well-balanced time line. In other words, most people have a much better perspective of the past or present than they do of the future. While one might conclude that our approach to measurement is not valid, in the sense that our idealized norm is in the minority, there is reason to suspect that the problem lis not with the testing approach. For one thing, interview results tend to correspond to what we find with the time line. Individuals, particularly in therapy, who cannot project themselves forward and who complain of having no direction in life seem to produce time lines that correspond. In addition, there *are* individuals who seem to have the kind of temporal integration associated with other indices of health, such as ego identity.

Individuals of all ages and from all walks of life who recognize that they have the kind of problems we have identified do various things to confront their difficulties. Some energetically and enthusiastically set out to conquer their own limitations. This is obviously the best course as it is indicative of a kind of personal strength that is somewhat lacking in the modern industrial society. Some have or are given the gift that allows them to *work at* their lives while fully *working in* their lives. Such individuals expect that there will be periods in life that will tax their resources more than other periods. They simply "dig in" and make the internal and external adjustments essential to moving forward. I suspect I am speaking about an "endangered species." It is obvious when we look at our culture in terms of its reliance on both legal and illegal drugs that many of us are not equipped to deal with the complexities of modern life.

Our society has certainly become "psychologized" over the last twenty-five years as we have gone through the various spinoffs of the human potential movement (which was briefly summarized in Chapter 8). The love affair with professional "growth" programs has teetered during the last decade as EST graduates have become either less evident or much less vocal. At any rate, I rarely find friends, patients or students speaking about new self-awareness programs, though I do find an increasing emergence of fundamentalist religious affiliations. Professional "growth" programs have been somewhat replaced by a ground swell of self-help organizations that have attempted to rekindle that old Yankee ethic of self-reliance. Though the spirit seems commendable, I have been distressed by the wave of "self-help" experts who have emerged in the last ten years. It has unfortunately become commonplace for troubled individuals to own a veritable library of inspirational and self-help books, from which they frequently quote. I was surprised to see a whole section of a well-known bookstore labeled "Self-Help." Though there is certainly nothing wrong with finding new perspectives and behavior, this movement has taken on a slightly absurd quality, as slogans and clichés dot the psychological landscape. Once again, one senses a disquieting search for simple recipes that serve our well-established impatience for quick cures.

Despite the self-help movement, many of the problems that I have outlined are being treated by professional psychotherapists. Moreover, because of changes in the conception of how to manage serious psychological disorders, inpatient treatment has increasingly given way to care in the office. Every major American city is well supplied with psychiatrists, psychologists, clinical social workers, pastoral counselors and other individuals who are trained in specialties such as marital and family therapy. California in particular has developed professional schools of psychology that are graduating huge numbers of practitioners, most of whom will end up in private practice. As indicated before, the majority of these outpatient practitioners fall into two or three basic camps in approaching the therapeutic task. The so-called traditional schools, which dominate psychiatry and clinical social work, are basically derivatives of the psychoanalytic approach. Psychology has increasingly adopted behavioristic and neobehavioristic approaches to treatment, even though a few programs in psychology continue to emphasize traditional psychodynamic (psychoanalytically oriented) views. Some therapists from each of the disciplines focus more on family factors and marital processes and are usually considered system theorists. Finally, we cannot overlook the psychiatric practice of medication, which is supported by the other professions, which usually make referrals when verbal treatment is ineffective in controlling severe symptoms.

While there are no approaches that focus on temporality explicitly, recently there has been some positive development in the behavioral field that has incorporated the cognitive life (thinking) of the individual. The focus of cognitive behavioral therapy is to get the individual to think differently about herself by changing pre-existing thought patterns. The behavior therapist looks to break stimulus-response patterns so that the individual can become free of response tendencies rooted in past associations. This might involve learning new phrases to define oneself in order to influence one's overall outlook. In this sense, the development in the cognitive therapies is, to a limited degree, beginning to move the experience of the patient to the future. This is especially true for the treatment of depression, in which such theoreticians as Beck attempt to break the cognitive cycle of pessimism and self-fulfilling prophecies.

The system-oriented therapies are much like the psychodynamic therapies in that symptoms are conceptualized in terms of patterns of experience and behavior that have their roots in a patient's significant interpersonal relationships. These systems are often historical, but the analysis from this perspective can move to the present temporal frame, since individuals often respond to pathological communication that is current, as well as to historical relational conflicts. This is particularly true in the marital therapies, which are used to deal with problematic marriages or as a framework to understand children's symptoms. It has become increasingly common to treat children's adjustment problems by looking at the conflicts in a marriage that affect the psychological life of the child. Again, however, there is no specific reference to temporality and particularly no framework for dealing with future extension as an element in a systems conflict.

Finally, at the risk of explaining what appears self-evident, something should probably be said about drug treatment. I should state clearly that I am not unequivocally opposed to chemotherapy. I occasionally will refer individuals I have seen for psychiatric evaluation. However, in no case do I view drugs as curative, as they never do anything like destroy bacterial or viral infections. Psychotropic drugs suppress symptoms and allow people to function better, and in that sense, should make them more amenable to psychotherapy that aims at underlying causes. From the temporal perspective, drugs certainly have an impact on present behavior and can even raise expectations of the future. If someone who has been tyrannized by thought problems, as in the case of schizophrenia, can experience a sense of being back in control, there is often an immediate lifting of the spirit, so that the future brightens. However, as with other contemporary approaches to mental disturbances, any temporal considerations are coincidental rather than overt.

The overriding reality is that, with few exceptions, the dimension of time is not systematically treated in our contemporary approaches to human conflict. Despite the fact that so many of our seminal thinkers in the West have identified time as *the* essential coordinate of human experience, temporal theory is, for the most part, "missing in action." Having sounded that alarm, it is not difficult to conclude that we need to consolidate the groundbreaking work of individuals like James, Bergson, Heidegger, Minkowski, Sartre, Binswanger, Ellenberger and May. While these thinkers are not ordinarily connected to the development of treatment methodologies, they all addressed temporality as central to the task of understanding and treating human conflict. Minkowski, more than any other, stressed that in order to make any progress with patients, we would have to find ways to help them unblock their personal future.

There have been some attempts to introduce temporality into the modern American array of psychotherapies. Rollo May, James Bugenthal and Irvin Yalom have certainly incorporated temporality into the framework of their conceptions of treatment. Perhaps the most significant work to date that has recognized the essential value of time is that of Frederick Melges (1982), who has actually outlined a methodology of treatment labeled future-oriented psychotherapy. Future-oriented psychotherapy is a breath of fresh air in that Melges devised a behaviorally oriented approach to unblock the future through a combination of relaxation and visualization. His approach is simply to deal with the defenses erected against future anxiety by using a well-accepted practice common in the behavior therapies.

Melges's work is a welcome departure from the current methodologies in psychology. His use of behavioral methods should be of great value in that it serves to demystify some of the more esoteric, philosophically oriented approaches to which I have referred. Yet, to my knowledge, his future-oriented approach to treatment has not had a broad impact. That is not to say that it is not being used by some of his associates. However, it has not captured the interest of mainstream psychiatry or psychology. When a new idea comes along that has impact, it rapidly moves to the forefront in both the academic and the applied community. Family systems theory is a good example of an approach that was quickly embraced and had a strong impact on the practice of psychotherapy. Another, though much more short lived, was Eric Berne's transactional analysis. TA, as it came to be called, introduced some novel concepts involving "relational games" and has had a residual effect on at least the language of the psychotherapist.

Future-oriented psychotherapy, it would seem, has not taken hold because its methodology and world view are in "apparent" conflict. As I have indicated above, the constituency within clinical circles interested in temporality in general, and futurity in particular, comes from a very definite side of psychology. The best reception I have found in proposing the inclusion of temporality in personality and psychopathology models has come from existential and certain psychodynamic theorists. Terms like futurity, temporality and density do not have much appeal to the parsimony-driven behavioral community. The former group, I sense, is ready to embrace a psychotherapy that moves beyond the mechanistic limitations of psychoanalysis and behavioral treatment. Though Melges's model for working with the future is not purely behavioral, it nevertheless has the feel of a methodology that is philosophically close to contemporary "cognitive behavioral models." The problem, as I have suggested, is that the future is not an acceptable epistemological realm for mainstream American behaviorism. The part of Melges's theory that is more dynamically focused ironically draws on transactional analysis, which I suspect will not appeal to behavioral, existential or psychodynamic clinicians. In a sense, while I am highly sympathetic to and interested in this model, it will probably not heavily affect the therapeutic "marketplace."

Innovation in any field of applied science, in order to gain a level of recognition, has to be well timed (no pun intended) in terms of its ability to address some existing void. There is no question that the broader intellectual climate in the West suggests that the field of psychology should soon be ready to accommodate the temporal dimension. It is heartening to see a plethora of books appearing that deal with time from very different perspectives. As we approach the end of the twentieth century, quite naturally the sense of time elapsing is reaching threshold throughout the world. Books such as *A Brief History of Time* by Stephen W. Hawking, *The Body in Time* by K. J. Rose, and *Time Wars* by Jeremy Rifkin have all surfaced within the past two years. These works reflect an increased awareness within the fields of astrophysics, biology and history of the human experience and capacity to relate to time.

There is little question that a void exists in the theories that serve the varied fields of human counseling. Time is clearly on everyone's mind. When I lecture on temporality, from almost any perspective, members of the audience, graduate students or colleagues almost always respond with a resounding "Yeah." They mean that they are acutely aware of time, both as a fact of life and as a frequent enemy. They, like their patients, struggle with the passing of time. Yet several colleagues whom I have supervised for state licensing were initially reluctant to admit that they worked heavily in the future zone of their patients' lives. They had gotten the idea in their training that one simply did not deal with the future in any prescribed way. In the same vein, doctoral students are almost always reluctant to have the recordings of their sessions played back to supervisors. In addition to the usual performance anxiety, they have a distinct feeling that they have been doing their therapy a little differently than the theories they have mastered have prescribed.

The fact is, as Gordon Allport originally said, that the patients (and I think the new therapists) yearn to move their dialogue into the future. However, the "power of positivistic thinking" is so insidious that the fledgling therapist feels inhibited, sensing that to address the future is not "real" therapy. As I have said before, even patients of mine have resisted the idea of addressing "tomorrow," because it did not feel like real therapy. It seems that we need a revolution in the way we think about growth and change. Despite the emergence of the "actualization" theories of therapy, it appears that we have receded to notions of change that are still attempting to undo historical associations and connections. One of the most obvious yet elusive large-scale errors we make in our approach to dealing with psychological problems is the confusion over cause and treatment. Even in the "mechanistic" medical model of illness, it is understood that it is not necessary to go back to the contaminated water in order to effect a cure for cholera. In my work with a Holocaust victim, I learned that lesson the hard way. Together, the patient and I struggled to purge all the hideous memories and feelings that had been cut off from consciousness. At some point it ironically became clear to my patient that we were "beating a dead horse." We needed instead to help rebuild his forward momentum by opening the door to the future.

The idea of future possibilities pulling us forward is what had led me to the idea that psychotherapy must be construed as a process of achieving temporal balance. Though I agree with Melges that we need a psychotherapy that focuses "forward" to the future, it is crucial to consider the full breadth of "lived time." In attempting to bring a depressed or telepressed individual into experiential touch with the future, there are strong obstacles to overcome. Future images, goals and possibilities do not come easily, just as the remote past can be sealed from memory. It can sometimes take years to uncover traumatic memories when efforts are completely oriented to the past. In the same way, it is naive to assume that we can get the individual to simply "figure out" the future.

Virtually all psychodynamic clinicians have respect for what has commonly been called "resistance." Individuals want to achieve change experientially and behaviorally on one level, while they are, on another level, ambivalent. Thus we have the well-known caricatures of the patient forgetting to attend sessions or coming late to see the therapist. These stereotypes are based on reality, at least to the degree that we recognize that we tend to be in strong conflict about embracing change.

It is this inaccessibility and the accompanying resistances that led me to formulate an approach I have labeled Temporally Oriented Psychotherapy (TOP). I have been developing this model over the past ten years and hope to soon be ready to publish an independent description of the approach. I will try to outline the main elements to TOP here to clarify the direction of my thinking. Before giving a name to this psychotherapy system, I was in conflict on two points. First, I was reluctant to develop another "school" of therapy. Both the academic community and the layman have a difficult time as it is selecting from the broad, sometimes confusing "menu" of options. Second, I was torn about not including "the future" in any new school, since it has been this time zone that has been most excluded. To be sure, most of the problems I have addressed have involved the overcoming of a telepressed future.

However, to describe the system of work that is essential to overcoming these complex problems, a "future treatment" completely disregards the fundamental laws of temporality. The separate zones of time—past, present and future—operate in an indivisible synergism that is irreducible. Just as we cannot study the water in a moving stream without considering its direction and speed, so is it impossible to study any specific moment on a time line without referring to what comes before and what will come after. The future, then, does not exist as a separate entity, but derives its vitality from what has happened and what is happening. The past too does not exist in an inert state but draws its balance from how the individual sees life evolving. As indicated before, the same past can be seen as dreadful and negative or as a serendipitous source of "character" and motivation. Ironically, whether deprivation is seen as an encumbrance or catalyst depends on the success of the individual.

The future, however, is the most significant focus to TOP and represents the target of change. That is not to say that I do not conceptualize problems in terms of other time zones. Many of the traditional symptoms treated by modern psychology clearly involve an analysis of the past. Traumatic stress reactions, specific phobias, heavy use of the defense of repression and many other symptom patterns involve historical material and memories. In addition, some of the cases used to illustrate temporal disorders certainly don't involve the future alone. The "now" generation is a metaphor for individuals whose lives are defined by the present. Type-A personalities are often overly productive with respect to future goals so that they experience time as "flying."

However, every human problem is in some way directed at the future. The person with flashbacks of a terrible trauma is anticipating more trouble with unwelcome memories. The future is construed in terms of intruding images that might terrorize the vulnerable individual. A strong case can be made that all symptoms, in fact, are deeply connected to the individual's projections that the future is not controllable and that many traditional disorders represent defensive strategies for dealing with unexpressed futurity anxiety.

It is virtually impossible to conceptualize any behavior without reference to what I have termed the irreducible synergism of the temporal zones. TOP represents a departure from many other approaches to psychotherapy in having an explicit format for addressing the temporal flow of an individual at selected points in therapy. The time line and the construct it represents afford the opportunity to use temporal integration as a yardstick of health in trying to ascertain the relative progress of a given patient. In many instances we are not treating a single symptom that is cured by the therapist. The cases I have been citing are complex and do not easily lend themselves to deciding when the work has been "finished." Most schools of treatment with which I am familiar have a difficult time deciding on that critical end point of therapy. Though behavioral approaches often involve short durations such as ten sessions, the problems being addressed are quite different and the goals decidedly less ambitious. TOP uses the time line as its major diagnostic tool to determine the area of experience that is disjointed. As therapy proceeds and conflicts are resolved, a balanced temporal perspective should result.

A good example might be one of our Type-A personalities who experiences life as racing by. I also noted that this individual seemed to find little time for the simple pleasures associated with family life and frantically pursued a future *over*laden with goals. TOP, with this individual, would address all the temporal zones in concert. The past must be explored as the source of both anxiety and the value system that had produced this scheme of overactivity. The present is often a painful zone involving the potentially dangerous psychosomatic disorders associated with this personality type, along with damaged interpersonal relations. The starting point with such an individual usually involves a deep immersion in his day-to-day affairs. It is important to establish rapport in terms of the patient's preoccupation with *busy-ness*. Shifting to the question of "purpose" usually gets an initial acknowledgment that "I need to reorder my priorities." Achieving substantive change in work and life habits, however, requires that therapeutic work extend back and forward into the congested future.

Exploration of the past requires all the skills of a trained psychodynamic therapist for a well-paced, semidirected probing of the patient's historical roots. The period can last from three months to a year, depending on the individual. Unlike the traditional approach to psychotherapy, however, there has to be an occasional shift to the other temporal zones. This driven personality type will rightfully become impatient if the focus of inquiry is too rooted in history. I have had many such cases referred to me. In most instances the impatient personality was instantly relieved to find someone who could work with what appeared to be myriad emergent situations in the present and near future. Eventually the process takes a new direction as the individual develops a capacity to adopt a large-scale perspective with the flow of time becoming the central theme. The major change sought will involve some experimentation with changing the intimidating flow of temporal experience. The alliance of client and therapist becomes dedicated to saving the person from a life that is racing by without deep satisfaction.

The first order of business is to teach this individual how to slow his experiential clock. This task is conceptually simple, but difficult to achieve. In order to gain a sense of mastery over temporal flow, one must construct a situation in which there are no goals allowed. Thus, games and many other activities that are called restful are not relevant to this task. To break into the Type-A person's tendency to pressure himself and others, it is often necessary to find a novel context in which the usual goals associated with achievement, efficiency and success are absent. This step requires considerable creativity on the part of the therapist in terms of both selection and persuasion. I have found the Outward Bound program to be dramatic for some individuals. Though it is directed toward achieving survival skills, the daily routine is fairly repetitive and often involves transporting equipment, preparing food and exploring oneself in the context of a situation in which control is largely in the hands of an experienced trainer.

However, one needn't go to such extremes to recapture time in one's life. I have sometimes suggested that someone go to the beach (off-season) and spend a few days learning to let time pass in a more friendly way. For other individuals, a hotel room in a nearby city or even in one's own city can provide a perfect context to break the excessive momentum of one's temporal flow. A hidden treasure to which most of us have some access is small children. Spending an extended period of time with a child can produce a dramatic pathway to timelessness. If one can allow the child to control the flow of activities and their duration, then outer reality, schedules and purposes can recede and seem less important. Spending a day on and off the floor arranging and rearranging blocks and other toys, coloring or inventing spontaneous games can be very powerful. When I think of all the time-slowing activities, I prefer steering people toward children because our agitated Type A's have often neglected the dependent people in their lives. Learning to take walks or have extended dialogue with elderly relatives or friends can have the same powerful effects. It is essential to underscore that this is not a behavioral solution. The individual will usually not easily accept the prescription of "slowing it down." In fact, the initial complaint will be that it is too difficult to move at this pace. One man with whom I worked told me that the fishing outings I had suggested he undertake with his daughter were not working at first. He said it wasn't until *she* took charge of the outboard motor that they could settle down and fish in one spot long enough to catch any fish. Resistance to change has to be overcome in TOP as in any other far-reaching approach to treatment. The key to successfully moving the person forward lies in the strength of relationship that has been forged in the exploration of the patient's life. In order to achieve substantive change, the therapist has to actively manage the direction of the therapeutic plan in terms of the temporal blueprint that is developed. I have not found too many overactive individuals who can permanently achieve more balance without long-term intermittent prodding and reinforcement.

The future of this type of individual does create an illusion of successful future extension. Unlike some telepressed individuals, they have "marks" on their time lines that give the appearance of plans. The typical problem, however, is that the future is narrowly defined in terms of present business plans, so that the future is usually not very distant. In addition, this "near-future extension" is often crowded and unrealistic. This overconcentration of goals makes the temporal experience of this person disjointed because time moving too quickly means time not personally controlled. It is precisely this sense of no control that causes the feeling of "inauthenticity" that Heidegger expounded in his philosophical work. The experience of desynchronization with objective time creates the general feeling that there is no clear purpose to life.

At this point there is intersection with the large pool of individuals who cannot effectively extend into the future. In the first case, the images of life beyond the present are stereotyped in terms of career and money. In the broader cases of telepression, the future is more fully blocked, with content that is often just as stereotyped, but in a less predictable way. In either case, the problem centers on the question of whether an individual feels his life is meaningfully propelled by a viable constellation of values. When one lives without a clear value structure, it is both difficult to direct life in the long run and difficult to experience the sense of meaningfulness that comes from following a prescribed course. It is possible to sail a boat, for example, without charts or a compass. However, the absence of a chart prevents the possibility of a journey. One is limited to "day" sailing, so that new destinations and new challenges are out of reach. Eventually the same seascape and circumstances will produce a tedium not unlike the absence of meaning associated with a present-centered existence.

TOP starts from the definition of the individual's current life, and proceeds forward and back with a regular rhythm. The presumption is that a blocked future represents a failure to develop a "momentum" that takes a person from his past and into the future. The goal of the therapeutic process is to establish or re-establish the momentum by unblocking the future. You will recall from Chapter 2 that Megin, the young schizophrenic girl I treated, originally experienced her life in a very narrow band in the present. As her simple future was *safely* explored, she was also able to find access to her past. This synergism between past and future allowed for the thread of her existence to be re-established. She began to feel like a whole person again.

The past must be explored in order to hone the individual's sense of identity into one that projects itself forward. The concept of identity is a very useful abstraction in conceptualizing temporal balance. It was used in one of the original studies presented in Chapter 9. There was a very strong relationship between a person's sense of knowing who he is and the ability to extend into the future. The therapeutic task of "self"-exploration is not unique to TOP. Most contemporary therapeutic models strive to help the individual arrive at a viable definition of "who I am."

Screening out self-definitions that have been provided by others, such as parents and spouses, is a crucial step. It can take an extended period of time. In the process of exploring the sources of personal knowledge about the individual, we must make frequent extensions forward in order to root the emerging sense of self in the future. We also must overcome the defense (telepression) that has functioned to block imagination from working into the unknown years ahead. Many of us live as though the momentum to our lives is generated by others. There is often a sense of anguish when the realization emerges that we have to generate our own momentum by the images we have of ourselves and the future. In a sense we are discussing the burden of making choices versus the ease of just "letting life happen." It is not uncommon to hear objections to this idea of the planned future. This resistance to an identity that has a "map" is a problem on both the individual and the collective level.

I have already given examples of older adults who have learned to think about their life on a day-to-day basis. It is also pretty clear that it requires less "work" to be carried forward in life by whatever "programs" are continuing. It is certainly difficult to continually assess values, generate ideas and plan accordingly. This burden of having to "fill time" is what draws us to structures in our lives that are momentum-generating. Jobs and careers are one of the primary sources of definition in that they provide day in and day out activities and the satisfying sense that we are accomplishing something. I am certainly not questioning the inherent personal or social value of work. I am only suggesting that for many people their jobs become an abandonment of personal decision making. A comment I hear frequently, "My job makes me feel like I'm on a roller coaster ride," is quite apropos. On an amusement park ride we put ourselves in a captive position in which we have no control and let ourselves be thrown around in accordance with the physical properties of the ride we have chosen. When a job feels like an amusement park ride, it is usually associated with a feeling of great activity and emotional turmoil.

This yearning to have things happen "automatically" also shows up in the way people approach relationships. I have been surprised by how many relationships are predicated on fortuitous factors. I discussed a few cases earlier in which marital choices were based on the exigencies of the "biological clock." In these situations, individuals had decided to get married while there "was still enough time" to reap the rewards of family life. Others have approached settling into a full-time relationship with a comparable temporal rationale. For these individuals, single life is a great strain in that they find the task of filling their time especially difficult. Weekends, in particular, seem to cause anxiety. In such cases, there seems to be a definite disruption in the "élan," so that they feel no momentum in the nonwork part of life.

Yet settling into life with another person does not relieve the week-to-week burden of "what to do." On the surface, the imperative to get involved in social affairs and other activities alters, so that the consensual feeling I have heard is "now I can relax." In this way, the sense of new comfort is quite reasonable. Single living is certainly lonely for many, and part of the relief of "connecting" is the establishment of intimacy. On the other hand, the urge to ignore momentum is not a satisfactory by-product of a new relationship. This type of individual will then rely on the structure of his relationship to determine his momentum in life. As this structure evolves into increasing degrees of complexity, the identity of the individual becomes increasingly less personal, and values and goals become more and more stereotypical.

The arrival of children grounds the identity further in the family system. For many years, the parents' time will be shaped by the role of nurturing and participating in the lives of children. At this stage of life, one is well-sheltered from the task of personal temporal planning. Spare time is almost automatically filled with the myriad activities of raising children. In fact, some parents speak about the child-rearing years as if they had been on "automatic pilot." Their momentum in life was driven by child-related decisions and goals, which, as we have seen, accelerate the perceived rhythm of temporality. As we look back at all the years of car-pooling, homework, sports attendance, and the readiness to drop personal needs in response to our children's needs, the refrain that "it was all a blur" is not uncommon. The busy middle years of life that are crammed with a blend of work-related and family-related expectations tend to pass with a sometimes disconcerting rapidity.

One of the vexing human paradoxes has to do with this somewhat universal conflict about how much our life should be controlled by increasing amounts of responsibility and complexity. To be sure, humans do not thrive in either the absence or excess of these "natural" structures. As Erich Fromm (1941) put it, we yearn to "escape from freedom" only to find we yearn to be free. TOP works to address the

194

fundamental conflict by assisting the individual in achieving balance. Each stage of life can be satisfying if it reflects the ego identity of the person. Whether we are speaking about careers, family life, raising children or the pursuit of private goals, time will not become the enemy if we have not "exploited" these structures in order to forgo our responsibility to tailor our lives. The person whose momentum is derived from other people or from the context of his life is, after all, at high risk. Sudden changes in these external structures or in expectable transitions become overwhelming. As structure changes, there is the dreaded feeling that one's life is grinding to a halt. Whether the experience is a relationship ending, the loss of a job, the growing up of one's children or one's own aging, the failure to achieve a sense of personal identity leaves one in a state of psychological risk.

A good indicator of vulnerability can be found in the content and balance of the RTL (time line). The obvious factor is a line that lacks a balanced extension back and forward. In addition, we can look to the content of the milestones marked on the line. The greater the percentage of stereotyped content, the more likely we are dealing with a "foreclosed" identity, which derives its images of the past, present and future from external sources. As particular periods of life no longer offer solutions to how to spend time, depression, particularly, is possible. Depression is the mood which overtakes us when our personal momentum is blocked and the future seems empty. I was recently speaking to a patient who had seen me for problems with depression over an eighteen-month period. She had come back to visit after a six-month break from therapy, as a form of "checkup." She conveyed that her personal identity had solidified so much during the past six months that she was experiencing a "surge" such as she had never felt before. She said she felt that she was plunging into her current and future life with such "gusto" that she needed to develop some attenuation skills so she didn't "overwhelm" her family and friends.

TOP is by no means a finished product. At this stage it is truly a model with explicit fundamental philosophical and psychological premises. It would be counterproductive to suggest that TOP represents a totally new point of departure. On the contrary, many components associated with other systems of treatment are clearly applicable. Interviewing technique, which includes empathic and communicative abilities, is essential to any psychotherapeutic enterprise. A solid understanding of psychosocial development, interpersonal dynamics and systems theory will all expedite the treatment process. TOP does, however, point us in a somewhat revolutionary direction. The concept of psychological defense has been extended to the future and the "missing" concept of temporality has been positioned at the center of the theoretical framework. Needless to say, further research and a broader clinical application are now necessary in order to shape and refine the model.

X

LOOKING AHEAD

In many respects, life in McLuhan's electronic age has gone the way he predicted it would. There has been a shift away from what he termed the private, introspective, linear approach to time, and television has indeed created a culture of shared consciousness. However, we do not seem to be celebrating the spontaneity of a life dedicated to the "here and now." Rather, we are a culture struggling to find ways to cope with anxiety, depression and addiction. Many of these problems, as we have seen, derive from the combined dread and telepression of the future.

Most of my clients do not rejoice in the fact that they have little conscious relationship to their extended future. It is more likely that they will "draw blanks" when attempting to project themselves forward. In one respect, both our culture and its individuals are failing to grasp what could be termed a viable life's vision. There is, after all, a dialectical relationship between the explicit values of a society and the corresponding values that individuals form. In tight societies, the relationship is very close. In contemporary Western society, there is a distinct absence of explicit and effective ideals. Our cultural myths and symbols have descended into a relatively irrelevant and amorphous state. When we begin the task of constructing a value system with an individual, we confront a relative void.

The absence of cultural ideals is most evident at stages of life when change is most imminent. A large segment of our adolescent population is suffering from an anomic condition that is related to this vacuum in values. However, if our young people were grounded in a system of values that included ideals and dreams, they would simply not have the "time" or inclination to lose themselves in chemicals. Life for this vulnerable age group is not being experienced as meaningful because they are not being energized by the strength of future images. Ironically, the older population is struggling in a similar way. They, like their teenage counterparts, are finding few options in how they live out their lives beyond family and work.

There are indications that diverse elements in Western society are responding to the vacuum in our system of beliefs and myths. There has been a sharp rise in membership in religious fundamentalist sects, and cults seem to have an increased appeal. Without going into the specifics of fundamentalism, there is one relevant characteristic for our present discussion. In addition to mobilizing deep feelings about faith, most of these new sects offer and prescribe a plan for life. Through the creation of closely knit social units, the new splinter religions are giving their constituents simplistic solutions to the problem of what constitutes ideal behavior. They emphasize literal translations of religious doctrine, so that individuals will have unambiguous notions of how to plan and live their lives. These closed systems contain a distinct emphasis on trading freedom for the security of taking predetermined paths.

Ironically, I have recently worked with several individuals who have had strong connections to several different "charismatic" religions. They chose to work with me because they had heard that I could help them with their secular problems while being sympathetic to their religious views. From a temporal perspective, they showed greater balance in that strong explicit values were instrumental in allowing them to extend into the future. In this sense, they were similar to the subjects in our study who had been identified as the "identity foreclosures." They had stopped striving to personally resolve the problem of identity and had adopted a system that gave them a renewed sense of purpose.

Over the course of their working with me, a few of these individuals came to feel that their religious reference group was not serving them well. They began to find the literal flavor of their sect too childlike and searched for less closed systems. Two of these individuals worked with me a shorter period of time. One found my lack of a common faith to be such a disadvantage that he found it necessary to seek help within his religion. The other worked with me to the point where she claimed to get a better understanding of her immersion in fundamentalism and concluded TOP feeling a solidification with her faith.

Despite my relative success in working with individuals associated with dogmatic religion, I am concerned about the rise of such movements. The "believers" who seek out secular clinicians like me are not those I am concerned about. They are searching to integrate their spiritual beliefs and the associated dogma with a more tempered non-authoritarian orientation. I worry about the movements in small towns all over the United States where dogma, social intolerance and a frightening kind of parochialism are taking hold. The scandals of the famous television evangelists during the late 1980s revealed how far into American life these new movements had forged. The economics of these religious empires were an indication of how many Americans were yearning for concrete solutions to the dilemma of creating a vision of their lives. The power of these television preachers is underscored by the popularity they command even in the face of what ought to be devastating disgrace. It would appear, based on recent news, that most of them will return to their television pulpits and continue to "shepherd their flock in a moral direction."

We should not be deluded into thinking that it is only the "Bible belt" that manifests this yearning for an "easy" value structure. Yuppies have been targeted for their devotion to a system of economic values. During the 1970s cultlike organizations like EST seemed to mimic the founding of new religious orders. Huge numbers of zealous Americans subjected themselves to the somewhat humiliating submission to the authority of would-be charismatic "trainers." These leaders, I have been told, operated with all the flair and flamboyance of their television evangelical counterparts in trying to help their constituents "get it." Fortunately, these secular evangelical movements have dissipated. However, the yearning to "get it" is as powerful now as it has ever been in human history.

When traditional sources of leadership and values are not effective, there is a historical tendency for individuals to search out alternative solutions, which are unfortunately sometimes fanatical. The great Spanish philosopher José Ortega y Gasset (1932) wrote of the danger when there is a philosophical vacuum in the social order. Others, such as Ignazio Silone (*The God That Failed*, Crossman and Silone, 1950) and Eric Hoffer (*The True Believer*, 1951), more recently addressed the tendency of societies to seek out totalitarian solutions when there are no other apparent solutions to social ills. While I am not making a case that we are about to witness anything like the rebirth of fascism, there is nevertheless a disquieting awareness that we are living in a period of underlying upheaval in the absence of strong moral leadership. I was surprised to find that even retired Senator Barry Goldwater (1988), known as an arch conservative, was disturbed about the direction of our political leadership. Commenting on the presidential campaign of 1988, he said, "As an American citizen, I'm damned concerned about where we're going." He was noting that this campaign, more than others, seemed to be devoid of substance. The candidates seemed, like much of the culture, to lack vision and a sense of ideals.

When I first decided to pursue clinical psychology in the 1960s, there was a great deal of excitement about the potential of this relatively new applied field. Many of the best students from premedical, physics and philosophy backgrounds were attracted to psychology as a discipline that could address the complexities of modern society. That excitement seems to have waned. One branch of the field became infatuated with the experimental models of the physical sciences and dedicated itself to the elaboration of probability models, more commonly known as statistics. The majority of clinical psychologists in recent years have gravitated toward working with a narrow range of human problems through the applications of neobehavioral techniques. Though there is still a substantially large group of practicing psychologists who identify with the psychoanalytic movement, they seem to have adopted Freud's "scientific ethos" and shied away from the problems of values and morality. The smaller "third force" in psychology, which was more attuned to the issues of identity, values and futurity, has drifted into a methodology that is largely organized around maximizing comfort. In a recent conversation with Rollo May, the eminent existential theorist, he indicated that he felt that "self psychology" had not lived up to its promise. He was emphatic in suggesting that the field needed to address itself to the problems of values and meaning.

As I already touched on in Chapter 3, temporally oriented psycho-therapy is quite taxing for the clinician. The anxieties associated with the future projections of the client stir comparable apprehension in the therapist. When the forlorn client expresses exasperation at his failure to generate future images, the therapist, too, feels the burden of shaping one's destiny. It is out of what Maurice Friedman calls the "healing dialogue" that the fragile character of life's meanings is consistently revealed as the client reaches out for the therapist's provision of com-fort. It is a far safer activity to discuss day-to-day life or search for memories of what has *certainly* happened. It is more complex to probe for what has not yet occurred and for a value structure that acts as life's catalyst. Finally, the psychotherapy of the future brings client and therapist into constant contact with the realization of finiteness. Those of us who had some psychoanalytic training were trained to look for indications that the client's conflicts were mobilizing unresolved conflicts in the analyst. Other, more mainstream practitioners are not really prepared to see the relationship between the course they set with their patients and their own personal level of safety. The future is an uncharted sea for all of us.

Temporally oriented psychotherapy, then, is intended to be more than another methodology for doing psychotherapy. Considering the collective problems with futurity that I have outlined, it is clear that we need to deal with the underlying sources of the problem in a more extensive way. Many individuals in the United States, and probably other parts of the industrialized world, do not have the tools to deal with the task of developing a viable identity and creating a balanced life plan that incorporates the temporal flow of life. At the risk of sounding pessimistic, I must say that it appears that our children are having trouble "getting in" to their lives and our older people are struggling to figure out how "to complete" their lives. In the middle, people are struggling to make sense of life in a period of history when the sense of purpose and the corresponding future do not easily flow.

I do not want to paint an overly negative picture of our culture nor do I intend to suggest that scientifically trained psychologists can to-tally resolve the complex and far-reaching dilemmas I have outlined. Nevertheless, "timely" ideas that are introduced at the right point and place can have a dramatic effect on the way we think and feel about the business of living our lives. A good example is the book written by Dr. Benjamin Spock at a time when young parents were searching for help in the rearing of infants and young children. While I do not agree with much of the content of "Dr. Spock," it is clear that this seemingly benign parenting book has had a dramatic effect on how a whole generation of children were reared. Drawing on an eclectic foundation of medical, psychological and sociological knowledge, Spock provided a prescription for countless young parents who were not given these tools by other generations.

My own goal is to address a similar vacuum that seems to be present in our contemporary context. Parents need help understanding how they provide or destroy the tools their children need to deal with time, values and the future. From the first moments a child spends in the crib, he begins to learn about the passage of time. Comfort with the flow of time, as I have discussed, begins with how and why we make children wait for the things they need and care about. The social, economic and physical environments in which we live have dramatically altered our sense of the future in modern life. Children begin to address the task of creating their vision of the time-related life cycle at a very early age. Families and educators need to be willing to see that the drug epidemic is directly related to how our young people feel about the present and their hopes for the future. However, it is not only children who need help addressing their emerging identity and its connection to the future. The blurred vision I have been outlining affects people at every stage of life. It is my hope, then, that psychology can adjust to confront the issues of values and futurity.

I am frequently asked what my "prescription" for filling the so-called vacuum would be. This is a reasonable question, as I have been suggesting that our cultural telepression can and should be addressed in a broad psychotherapeutic enterprise. I recently asked a young man in his early thirties to complete an RTL. He had been in therapy for about six months clearing up emotional residue from a failed marriage. After struggling with the task for a while, he looked up at me and said, "Give me some examples of goals." It should be painfully clear by now that there is no simple solution to the complex business of "marking time" throughout the life cycle. However, solutions do become possible when we can understand the terms of our current predicament. For all the reasons we have explored throughout this book, our society and way of life have drifted into a present-centered, day-to-day existence in which the future feels alien and sometimes accidental.

My "prescription," then, is really fourfold. First, our leaders in the social sciences, health sciences and the clergy need to converge on the difficult task of exploring and refurbishing our myths, celebrations and ideals. At the very least, at the family level, children need to experience the fertile power of consistency and tradition. They, more than adults, yearn to be included in the rites of passage (for example, weddings and funerals) from which they are usually excluded. It is the immersion in family-based culture that facilitates the development of values and eventually the identity that is so deeply connected to the achievement of balanced temporal perspective.

Second, as I have indicated, TOP is as much an attitude toward the nature of psychotherapy as it is a specific technique. Contemporary approaches to treating the vast spectrum of human psychological disorders have largely ignored temporality. Despite the urging of some of our foremost philosophers and thinkers, the area of "lived time" remains somewhat esoteric in the professional establishment. The temporal approach to addressing psychopathology is complex and offers neither simple causal explanations nor techniques. If psychology and psychiatry are going to meet the challenge of our burgeoning mental health problems, they are going to have to raise the tolerance for complexity. Almost any doctoral student quickly becomes aware that "neat" behavioral solutions do not effectively address the whole person as he is immersed in the stream of life. Our love affair with inductive statistics and parsimony need serious reconsideration.

Third, we cannot speak of an openness toward the future without being cognizant that there are real and powerful barriers in the world. Poverty, political oppression and a fragile environment each have the potential to signal the individual to pull down the curtain to the future. To be sure, it is difficult to establish goals and feel positive about their chances for realization when there are overwhelming odds. It is precisely during these periods, however, when some individuals are able to mobilize established value systems that engender a sense of optimism and meaning. When Aleksandr Solzhenitsyn or Victor Frankl describe their survival in Russian and Nazi work camps, we realize that these extraordinary men were able to maintain their balance under the worst possible circumstances. Neither one simply lived one day at a time. Rather, they reflected on their predicament and were able to generate future images.

At this point in our civilization we seem to be lacking mythical or real heroes. We live in a skeptical age and tend to distrust legend and fantasy. The heroes we do have are not really appropriate to the role but are created out of necessity. For example, some are talented but immature athletes, who often respond to their unsolicited status by disappointing their followers. We have recently seen scandal detract from the status of our leaders in the business, political and religious sectors. It is difficult in our culture to know what to be when one "grows up" or "grows old." The lack of inspirational real or fictional heroes is a pervasive problem with no simple solution. However, I am confident that if we collectively address this vacuum, we will be co-incidentally exploring the foundation of our culture and personal values. With an enlightened perspective, we will find there is no shortage of historical or contemporary "real" heroes.

Finally, any solution to the problems I have been discussing must ultimately begin with the individual. Those who take the risks and are willing to be reflective can discover meaning in life. Though the "unexamined life may not be worth living," the quest for productive self-awareness is not an easy matter. The achievement of an identity is not a guarantee of permanent balance, as identities must be redefined over the course of one's life. However, even an incomplete value system provides a basis for venturing forward in one's life. Paradoxically, when we make *commitments* to these values, we become energized and have the vitality to gradually refine our identities.

The threshold to the future is not easy to cross. Many individuals, as we have seen, have found a way not to project themselves forward in a meaningful way. Yet we cannot take refuge in the "here and now," and it is insufficient to live one's life in the remote past. The future, as Minkowski exclaimed, is the domain of "hope and possibility." We have been persuaded recently that most of us need to spend more time "smelling the roses." This is sound advice, as we all need access to these "timeless" moments uncluttered by the strain of goals. On the other hand, as an older man with whom I worked said as he dealt with his own future, "I hope that while so many are out smelling the flowers, someone is taking the time to plant some."

BIBLIOGRAPHY

Allen, M. G. "Twin studies of affective illness" in *Archives of General Psychiatry*, 33, 1976.

Allport, G. W. *Becoming*. New Haven: Yale University Press, 1955.

American Psychiatric Association. *Depression*. Washington, D.C.: 1988 (pamphlet).

American Psychiatric Association. *Substance Abuse*. Washington, D.C.: 1988b (pamphlet).

Barchos, J. D., Akil, H., Elliot, G. R., Holman, B., and Watson, J. J. "Behavioral Neurochemistry: Neuroregulators and Behavioral States" in *Science*, 200, 1978.

Barry, H., III. "Cultural Variations in Alcohol Abuse" in *Culture and Psychopathology*, edited by I. Al-Issa. Baltimore: University Park Press, 1982.

Baudelaire, C. P. *The Flowers of Evil*. Edited by May Thiel and Jackson Mathews. New York: New Directions, 1958.

Beck, A. T. *Cognitive Therapy and the Emotional Disorders*. New York: International University Press, 1976.

Becker, E. *The Denial of Death*. New York: Free Press, 1973.

Bergson, H. *Creative Evolution*. Translated by A. Mitchell. London: Macmillan, 1971.

Bibring, E. *Mourning and Melancholia*. Baltimore: The Johns Hopkins University Press, 1961.

Binswanger, L. "The Existential Analysis School of Thought" in *Existence*, edited by R. May, New York: Simon & Schuster, 1958.

Bleuler, E. *Dementia Praecox or the Group of Schizophrenias*. Translated by J. Zinkin. New York: International University Press, 1950.

Blum, R. *Society and Drugs*, vol. 1. San Francisco: Jossey-Bass, 1969.

Boorstin, D. J. *The Discoverers*. New York: Random House, 1983.

Brown, B. "Depression Roundup," *Behavior Today*, 5, 1974.

Brown, N. O. *Life Against Death*. Middletown, Conn.: Wesleyan University Press, 1959.

———. *Love's Body*. New York: Vintage Books, 1966.

Bugenthal, J., Jr. *The Search for Authenticity*. New York: Holt, Rinehart & Winston, 1965.

Buzell, R. J. "Drug Abuse: Methadone Becomes the Solution and the Problem" in *Science*, 179, 1973.

Callahan, D. *Setting Limits: Medical Goals in an Aging Society*. New York: Simon & Schuster, 1988.

Cancro, R. "Overview of Affective Disorders," in *Comprehensive Textbook of Psychiatry*, edited by H. I. Kaplan and B. J. Sadock. Baltimore: Williams & Wilkins, 1985.

Coleman, J. C., Butcher, J. N., and Carson, R. C. *Abnormal Psychology and Modern Life*. Glenview, Ill.: Scott, Foresman, 1984.

Cooper, D. *The Death of the Family*. New York: Pelican, 1972.

Cottle, T. J. "The Location of Experience: A Manifest Time Orientation" in *Acta Psychologica*, 28, 1968.

———. "The Duration Inventory: Subjective Experience of Temporal Zones" in *Acta Psychologica*, 29, 1969.

———. "Temporal Correlates of the Achievement Value and Manifest Anxiety" in *Journal of Consulting and Clinical Psychology*, 33, 1969.

Cottle, T. J., and Klineberg, S. L. *The Present of Things Future: Explorations of Time in Human Experience*. New York: Macmillan, 1974.

Crossman, R., and Silone, I. *The God That Failed*. New York: Harper and Brothers, 1950.

Douvan, E., and Adelson, J. *The Adolescent Experience*. New York: Wiley and Sons, 1966.

Erikson, E. H. *Childhood and Society*. New York: Norton, 1963.

———. "Identity and the Life Cycle" in *Psychological Issues*, 1, 1959.

———. *Identity, Youth and Crisis*. New York: W. W. Norton, 1968.

———. *Life History and the Historical Moment*. New York: Norton, 1975.

Fenichel, O. *The Psychoanalytic Theory of Neurosis*. New York: Norton, 1945.

Fossler, R. J., Rappaport, H., and Gilden, D. "Future Time, Death Anxiety and Life Purpose Among Older Adults." Submitted for publication, 1989.

Fowler, R. C., Rich, C. L., and Young, D. San Diego suicide study: "Substance Abuse in Young Cases." *Archives of General Psychiatry*, 43, 1986.

Framo, J. "Symptoms from a Family Transactional Viewpoint" in *Progress in Group and Family Therapy*, edited by C. Sager and H. Kaplan. New York: Bruner/Mazell, 1972.

Frank, J. *Persuasion and Healing*. Baltimore: The Johns Hopkins University Press, 1961.

Frankl, V. E. *The Doctor and the Soul: An Introduction to Logo Therapy*. New York: Knopf, 1955.

———. *Man's Search for Meaning*. Boston: Beacon Press, 1960.

Fraser, J. T. *Of Time, Passion and Knowledge*. New York: George Braziller, 1975.

———. *Time, the Familiar Stranger*. Amherst: University of Massachusetts Press, 1987.

Freud, S. *New Introductory Lectures on Psycho-Analysis*. New York: Norton, 1933.

———. "Mourning and Melancholia" in *Collected Papers*, vol. 4. London: Hogarth, 1956.

———. *A General Introduction to Psychoanalysis* (1924). New York: Washington Square Press, 1964.

Friedman, M. *The Healing Dialogue in Psychotherapy*. New York: Aronson, 1985.

Friedman, M., and Rosenman, R. H. *Type A Behavior and Your Heart*. New York: Knopf, 1974.

Fromm, E. *Escape from Freedom*. New York: Holt, Rinehart & Winston, 1941.

Gallatin, J. *Abnormal Psychology: Concepts, Issues, Trends*. New York: Macmillan, 1982.

Ginsberg, A. *Howl and Other Poems*. New York: City Lights Publishing, 1956.

Goldwater, B. "Newsmakers," *The Philadelphia Inquirer*, page 3A, October 16, 1988.

Goodman, P. *Growing Up Absurd: Problems of Youth in the Organized System*. New York: Random House, 1960.

Goodman, P. "Today's Youth." *Chicago Tribune*, September 14, 1969.

Guerra, F. *The Pre-Colombian Mind*. New York: Seminar Press, 1971.

Hartocollis, P. "Time as a Dimension of Affects," *Journal of the American Psychoanalytical Association*, 20, 1972.

Hawking, S. *A Brief History of Time*. New York: Bantam, 1988.

Heidegger, M. *Being and Time*. Translated by J. Cacquarrie and E. Robinson. New York: Harper and Row, 1962.

Hesse, H. *Steppenwolf*. New York: Bantam Books, 1969.

Hoffer, E. *The True Believer*. New York: Harper & Row, 1951.

Hoffman, A. "LSD Discoverer Disputes 'Chance' Factor in Finding." *Psychiatric News*, 6, 1971.

Hook, S. "The Uses of Death," *New York Review of Books*, April 28, 1988.

Horn, J. L. "Human Ability Systems," in *Life Span Development and Behavior*, vol. 1, edited by P. B. Baltes. New York: Academic Press, 1978.

Horney, K. *The Neurotic Personality of Our Time*. New York: W. W. Norton, 1937.

James, W. *The Principles of Psychology*. New York: Holt, 1980.

Jarvik, M. E. "The Psychopharmocological Revolution," *Psychology Today*, 1, 1967.

Jones, E. *The Life and Work of Sigmund Freud*, vol. 1. New York: Boni Books, 1953.

Jung, C. G. *Analytical Psychology*. New York: Moffat, Yard, 1916.

Kaplan, J. R. "Ludwig Binswanger's Existential Analysis," *Existential Psychiatry*, 6, 1967.

Kaufman, W. A. *Nietzsche: Philosopher, Psychologist, Anti-Christ*. Princeton: Princeton University Press, 1950.

Kelly, G. A. *The Psychology of Personal Constructs*. New York: W. W. Norton, 1955.

Keniston, K. *The Uncommitted*. New York: Harcourt, Brace and World, 1965.

Kerouac, J. *On the Road*. New York: Viking Press, 1957.

Kierkegaard, S. *The Sickness unto Death*. Translated by Walter Lowrie. New York: Doubleday, 1954.

Kilpatrick, William. *Identity and Intimacy*. New York: Delta, 1975.

Klein, M. "A Contribution to the Theory of Anxiety and Guilt." *International Journal of Psychoanalysis*, 29, 1948.

Kübler-Ross, E. *On Death and Dying*. New York: Macmillan, 1969.

———. *Questions and Answers on Death and Dying*. New York: Macmillan, 1974.

Lachman, J. L., Lachman, R., and Thronesberry, C. "Metamemory Through the Adult Life Span," *Developmental Psychology*, 15, 1979.

Laing, R. D. *Anti-Psychiatry*. New York: Penguin, 1972.

Lasch, C. *The Culture of Narcissism*. New York: Norton, 1978.

Levinson, D. J. *The Season's of a Man's Life*. New York: Knopf, 1978.

London, P. *The Modes and Morals of Psychotherapy*. New York: Holt, Rinehart & Winston, 1964.

Mahler, M., Pine, F., and Bergman, A. *The Psychological Birth of the Human Infant: Symbiosis and Individuation*. New York: Basic Books, 1975.

Marcia, J. E. "Development and Validation of Ego Identity Status," *Journal of Personality and Social Psychology*, 3, 1966.

————. "Identity Six Years After: A Follow-Up Study," in *Journal of Youth and Adolescence*, 5, 1975.

Marcuse, H. *One-Dimensional Man*. Boston: Beacon Press, 1970.

Masters, W. H., and Johnson, V. E. *Human Sexual Response*. Boston: Little, Brown, 1966.

May, R., Angel, E., and Ellenberger, H. F. *Existence*. New York: Simon & Schuster, 1958.

McLuhan, M. *Understanding Media: The Extensions of Man*. New York: McGraw-Hill, 1965.

Melges, F. T. *Time and the Inner Future*. New York: Wiley, 1982.

Metcalf, F. V. "Indian Alcohol Abuse and Alcoholism: Etiology, Ethnology, and Rehabilitation." Paper delivered at the annual meeting of the Western Psychological Association, San Diego, California, April, 1979.

Miller, L. M. *American Spirit: Prescription for a New Corporate Culture*. New York: Morrow, 1984.

Mills, C. W. "Letter to the New Left." *New Left Review*, 5, 1960.

Minkowski, E. "Findings in a Case of Schizophrenia Depression," translated by B. Blies. In *Existence*, edited by R. May, E. Angel, and H. F. Ellenberger. New York: Simon & Schuster, 1958.

————. *Lived Time*. (N. Metzel, trans.) Evanston, Ill.: Northwestern University Press, 1970. (Original publication, 1933).

Morrison, J. "Adult Psychiatric Disorders in Parents of Hyperactive Children," *American Journal of Psychiatry*, 137, 1980.

Murphy, G. E., Armstrong, J. W., Jr., Hermele, S. L., Fisher, J. R., and Clendenin, W. W. "Suicide and Alcoholism," *Archives of General Psychiatry*, 36, 1979.

Needham, J. T. "Time and knowledge in China and the West," in *The Voices of Time*, edited by J. T. Frazer. New York: George Braziller, 1966.

O'Leary, K. D. "Pills or Skills for Hyperactive Children," *Journal of Applied Behavior Analysis*, 13, 1980.

Ortega y Gasset, J., Jr. *The Revolt of the Masses*. New York: W. W. Norton, 1932.

Overton, W. F. "World Views and Their Influence on Psychological Theory and Research: Kuhn-Lakatos-Landan." In *Advances in Child Development and Behavior*, vol. 18, edited by H. W. Reese. New York: Academic Press, 1984.

Packard, V. *A Nation of Strangers*. New York: D. McKay, 1972.

Page, J. *Psychopathology: The Science of Understanding Deviance*. Chicago: Aldine, 1975.

Perls, F. S. *Gestalt Therapy Verbatim*. Moab, Utah: Real People Press, 1969.

Piaget, J. *The Construction of Reality in the Child*. Translated by M. Cook. New York: International University Press, 1952.

Project Dawn Drug Enforcement Agency. *Drug Abuse Warning Network: Project Dawn*, 1980.

Rank, O. *The Trauma of Birth*. New York: Harcourt, Brace, 1929.

Rappaport, H., Enrich, K., and Wilson, A. "Ego Identity and Temporality: Psychoanalytic and Existential Perspectives," *Journal of Humanistic Psychology*, 22, 1982.

————. "Relation Between Ego Identity and Temporal Perspective," *Journal of Personality and Social Psychology*, 48, 1985.

Rappaport, H., and Rappaport, M. "The Integration of Scientific and Traditional Healing," *American Psychologist*, 36, 1981.

Register Report. "Aging in the United States." June, 1988.

Rifkin, J. *Time Wars*. New York: Henry Holt and Co., 1987.

Rochlin, G. "How Younger Children View Death and Themselves" in *Explaining Death to Children*, edited by E. Grollman. New York: Beacon Press, 1967.

Rogers, C. *On Becoming a Person*. Boston: Houghton Mifflin, 1961.

Rose, K. J. *The Body in Time*. New York: John Wiley, 1988.

Ross, A. O., and Pelham, W. E. "Child Psychopathology" in *Annual Review of Psychology*, 32, 1981.

Roszak, T. *The Making of a Counterculture*. New York: Pantheon, 1969.

Rychlak, J. F. "Manifest Anxiety as Reflecting Commitment to the Psychological Present at the Expense of Cognitive Futurity," *Journal of Consulting and Clinical Psychology*, 38, 1972.

Sartre, J. P. *Being and Nothingness*. Translated by Hazel Barnes. New York: Philosophical Library, 1956.

Saterfield, J. H. "The Hyperactive Child Syndrome: A Precursor of Adult Psychopathology?" in *Psychopathic Behavior: Approaches to Research*, edited by R. Hare and D. Schelling. Chichester, England: Wiley, 1978.

Seligman, M. E. P. *Helplessness*. San Francisco: Freeman, 1975.

Slater, P. *The Pursuit of Loneliness*. Boston: Beacon Press, 1970.

Southern, T., and Bryan, P. *Dr. Strangelove* (screenplay). New York: Bantam Books, 1964.

Spinoza, B. *The Chief Works*. Edited by R. H. Elives. New York: Dover, 1951.

Spitz, R. A. "Anaclitic Depression" in *Psychoanalytic Study of the Child*, vol. 2. New York: International Universities Press, 1946.

Spock, B. *Baby and Child Care*. New York: Pocket Books, 1970.

Stoudemire, A., Frank, R., Hedemark, N., Kamlet, M., and Blazer, D. "The Economic Burden of Depression." *General Hospital Psychiatry*, 8, 1986.

Time. "Alcoholism: New Victims, New Treatment." *103*, April 22, 1974.

———. "Native American Tragedy: The Young Men of Wind River," October 21, 1985.

Toffler, A. *Future Shock*. New York: W. W. Norton, 1970.

United State Department of Health and Human Services, National Institute on Drug Abuse. *Highlights of the 1985 National Household Survey on Drug Abuse*. NIDA Capsules. Rockville, Md.: Press Office of the National Institute on Drug Abuse, 1986.

United States Department of Health, Education and Welfare (1978), *Vital Statistics of the United States*. Hyattsville, Md.: National Center for Health Statistics.

Weisskopf, M. "Scientist: Greenhouse Effect at Work," *Philadelphia Inquirer*, page 1, June 25, 1988.

Wessman, A. E., and Ricks, D. E. *Mood and Personality*. New York: Holt, Rinehart & Winston, 1966.

Whorf, B. L. *Language, Thought and Reality*. Cambridge, Mass.: M.I.T. Press, 1956.

Wyrick, R. A., and Wyrick, L. C. "Time Experience During Depression," *Archives of General Psychiatry*, 34, 1977.

Yalom, I. D. *Existential Psychotherapy*. New York: Basic Books, 1980.

INDEX

McCarthy, Eugene, 162
McCarthy era, 161
machismo, 97
McLuhan, Marshall, 167–69, 197
Mad, 162
Mahler, Margaret, 34
manic-depressive syndromes (cyclical mood disorders), 24, 57, 110, 118
manic states, 19–20
Man in the Grey Flannel Suit, The (Wilson), 97
manipulation, 37, 108
Marcia, James, 152
Marcuse, Herbert, 162
marijuana, 72, 73
marriage:
  biological clock and, 104, 193–94
  therapy and, 184
Marx, Karl, 168
Master, W. H., 126
materialism, 103, 104
May, Rollo, 184
  on need for values in self psychology, 200
  on past determined by future, 61–62, 67
MBA programs, 171
media, McLuhan's theories of, 167–169, 197
Megin, (schizophrenic patient), 15–17, 192
Melges, Frederick:
  future-oriented psychotherapy of, 185–86, 187
  on Hopi Indian time sense, 173
  on mechanical time, 21
  on nurturing, 37
memory:
  in childhood, 33–35, 39, 40
  as creative act, 61
  emotions and, 40–41
  in later adult years, 125–26
mescaline, 73
midlife crises, 170
milestones, 46, 47, 154
Miller, Arthur, 97
Miller, Lawrence, 97
Mills, C. Wright, 162
ministers, time pressures felt by, 100–101

Minkowski, Eugene, 204
  on depression and temporal imbalance, 60, 61, 137, 143–44
  "élan vitale" theory of, 60, 61, 66, 145
  on future anxiety, 64, 184
  on linearity of time, 26, 145–46
money, 103, 104, 130, 172
moods:
  beliefs and, 56
  biochemistry and, 58
  Hippocrates's theory of, 117
mortality, *see* death
mourning, 47, 54–55
"Mourning and Melancholia" (Freud), 54
music, rhythms of, 24

narcissism, rise of, 170–71, 172
NASA, 157
Nation of Strangers, A (Packard), 176
Native Americans, *see* American Indians
nature-nurture question, 31
neurotic depression, 57
neurotic symptoms, 22
neurotransmitters, 57, 58, 59
newborns, 36, 37, 108
  see also infants
Newton, Isaac, 21, 167
New Year's Eve, 11–13, 14, 15, 18, 23
Nietzsche, Friedrich, 63, 111
Nightline, 158
night terrors, 41
1920s, 160
1950s, 159–61, 165
1960s, 69, 103, 124, 161–66
1970s, 69, 103, 170–72
Nixon administration, 166
nonscientific cultures, temporal orientation of, 36, 173–74
North, Oliver, 176
nuclear arms, 161, 165
nursery rhymes, 43–44
nursing mothers, 37–38, 117
nurturing, 36–38, 40, 110
  depression and, 88, 89
  Type-A personality and, 107, 108

object relations theories, 34, 36, 55
oil price increase, 166
One-Dimensional Man (Marcuse),
162
opium, 72–73
oral fixation theory, 84–85, 86–87,
88, 107
in alcoholism treatment, 85, 87–
88
organizers, personal, 114
Ortega y Gasset, José, 200
Outward Bound, 190
Overton, W. F., 32

Packard, Vance, 176
Page, James, 81
passivity, 107
past, 21
depression and, 19, 23, 29, 52, 55,
60–63, 80, 82–83, 91, 92, 144,
195
determined by future, 61, 62, 67
emotions and, 40–41
mourning for, 47, 54–55
orientation toward, 18, 19, 23, 29,
52, 60–63, 80, 82–83, 91, 92,
155, 195
in psychotherapeutic approaches,
18, 62, 63
synergism between future and,
192
see also memory
peek-a-boo games, 43
Perls, Fritz, 165
personality, 49
personal organizers, 114
personal uniqueness fantasy, 44, 45,
112–13
perspective, 21
Persuasion and Healing (Frank), 51
Physician's Desk Reference, 58
Piaget, Jean, childhood studies of,
31, 32, 39, 43
political ideology, 162, 163
power politics, 108
prayer, 43, 51, 179
present, 21, 23, 30, 39, 153
addictive personality oriented in,
83, 87, 91, 92
"disadvantaged children and, 47

older adults' orientation in, 127,
138
in McLuhan's theories, 167–69
yuppie orientation in, 101, 172,
188
professors, mandatory retirement of,
130
progress, Western concept of, 172,
173
projective techniques, 148
Protestant ethic, 169
Proust, Marcel, 149
psychiatry, psychotherapy, 58, 183,
203
alcoholism as seen by, 85–86
awareness of mortality and, 135
depression as seen by, 54–59
Laing on, 164
older adults and, 122, 139
past orientation of, 62, 64, 66, 85–
86
temporal orientation ignored by,
144–45, 184, 201
see also Temporally Oriented Psychotherapy
psychology, 58, 183, 203
behavioral school of, 56–57
branches of, 200
of child development, 31–49, 84–
85, 107
determinism in, 61
limitations of experimental research in, 25–26, 147
need for awareness of values in,
67–70
other fields of inquiry ignored by,
61
past orientation of, 64, 66
temporal orientation ignored by,
144–45, 184, 186, 201
values in, 67, 68, 69
psychosomatic disorders, 94, 116,
117
psychotic depression, 57

Raiders of the Lost Ark, 45
Rank, Otto, 35
Rapaport, David, 86
Rappaport Time Line (RTL), 14, 27–
30, 135, 148–56

218

ABOUT THE AUTHOR

Herbert Rappaport is currently on the psychology faculty at Temple University in Philadelphia, Pennsylvania, where he was the director of clinical training from 1980 to 1985. He is also engaged in private practice and has served as a consultant to the mental health system and industry in several states. He received his Ph.D. from the State University of New York at Buffalo in 1969 and spent two years as a Fulbright-Hayes scholar at the University of Dar es Salaam in Tanzania, East Africa.